Language on Display

Russian Language and Society Series

Series Editor: Lara Ryazanova-Clarke, University of Edinburgh
This series of academic monographs and edited volumes consists of important scholarly accounts of interrelationships between Russian language and society, and aims to foster an opinion-shaping 'linguistic turn' in the international scholarly debate within Russian Studies, and to develop new sociolinguistic and linguo-cultural perspectives on Russian. The series embraces a broad scope of approaches including those advanced in sociolinguistics, rhetoric, critical linguistics, (critical) discourse analysis, linguistic anthropology, politics of language, language policy and related and interdisciplinary areas.

Series Editor
Dr Lara Ryazanova-Clarke is Senior Lecturer in Russian, and the Academic Director of the Princess Dashkova Russian Centre, at the University of Edinburgh.

Editorial Board
Professor David Andrews (Georgetown University)
Professor Lenore Grenoble (University of Chicago)
Professor John Joseph (University of Edinburgh)
Professor Vladimir Plungian (Institute of Russian Language/Institute of Linguistics, Russian Academy of Sciences)
Professor Patrick Seriot (Université de Lausanne)
Dr Alexei Yurchak (University of California, Berkeley)

Titles available in the series:
The Russian Language Outside the Nation, ed. Lara Ryazanova-Clarke
Discourses of Regulation and Resistance: Censoring Translation in the Stalin and Khrushchev Era Soviet Union, Samantha Sherry
French and Russian in Imperial Russia: Language Use among the Russian Elite, ed. Derek Offord, Lara Ryazanova-Clarke, Vladislav Rjéoutski and Gesine Argent
French and Russian in Imperial Russia: Language Attitudes and Identity, ed. Derek Offord, Lara Ryazanova-Clarke, Vladislav Rjéoutski and Gesine Argent
Russian Speakers in Post-Soviet Latvia, Ammon Cheskin
Public Debate in Russia: Matters of (Dis)order, Nikolai Vakhtin and Boris Firsov
Language on Display: Writers, Fiction and Linguistic Culture in Post-Soviet Russia, Ingunn Lunde

Visit the Russian Language and Society website at
http://www.euppublishing.com/series/rlas

Language on Display
Writers, Fiction and Linguistic Culture in Post-Soviet Russia

Ingunn Lunde

University Press

Edinburgh University Press is one of the leading university presses in the UK. We publish academic books and journals in our selected subject areas across the humanities and social sciences, combining cutting-edge scholarship with high editorial and production values to produce academic works of lasting importance. For more information visit our website: edinburghuniversitypress.com

© Ingunn Lunde, 2018

Edinburgh University Press Ltd
The Tun – Holyrood Road, 12(2f) Jackson's Entry, Edinburgh EH8 8PJ

Typeset in 11/13 Monotype Ehrhardt by
Servis Filmsetting Ltd, Stockport, Cheshire

A CIP record for this book is available from the British Library

ISBN 978 1 4744 2156 0 (hardback)
ISBN 978 1 4744 2157 7 (webready PDF)
ISBN 978 1 4744 2158 4 (epub)
ISBN 978 1 4744 5229 8 (paperback)

The right of Ingunn Lunde to be identified as the author of this work has been asserted in accordance with the Copyright, Designs and Patents Act 1988, and the Copyright and Related Rights Regulations 2003 (SI No. 2498).

Contents

Acknowledgements vii
Note on Transliteration and Translations ix

Introduction: Sociolinguistic Change and the Response of Literature — 1

Part I Post-Soviet Language Culture

1. Newspeak, Counterspeak and Linguistic Memory — 17
2. Challenging the Standard — 29

Part II Language, Writers and Fiction

3. Languages and Styles of Post-Soviet Russian Prose — 45
4. The Literary Norm — 59

Part III Writers on Language: Telling and Showing

5. *Pisateli o iazyke*: Writers' Reflections on Language — 69
6. *Abanamat*: Reactions to the Ban on Profanity in Art — 84

Part IV Language on Display

7. Confronting Linguistic Legacies: Evgenii Popov and Vladimir Sorokin — 107

8. Language, Time and Linguistic Dystopia: Tat'iana Tolstaia and Evgenii Vodolazkin   137

9. Language Ideologies and Society: Valerii Votrin and Mikhail Gigolashvili   167

    Conclusion: Towards a Theory of Performative Metalanguage   195

References   204
Index   219

Acknowledgements

Most of the research for this book was undertaken within the framework of two international research groups supported by the Research Council of Norway and based at the University of Bergen in the years 2005–14, 'Landslide of the Norm: Linguistic Liberalisation and Literary Development in Russia in the 1920s and 1990s' and 'The Future of Russian: Language Culture in the Era of New Technology'. I am deeply indebted to the inspiring exchange of thoughts and ideas that took place in the many venues where project participants met during these years, from conferences in St Petersburg, Passau, Berlin, Edinburgh and Bergen to informal dinners, hiking adventures, Bavarian pubs and cultural outings. Special thanks to the core members and network participants of the two groups, Aleksandrs Berdicevskis, Brita Lotsberg Bryn, Michael S. Gorham, Karin Grelz, Gasan Gusejnov, the late Daniela Hristova, Ilya Kukulin, Roman Leibov, Elena Markasova, Kåre Johan Mjør, Martin Paulsen, Tine Roesen, Ellen Rutten, Lara Ryazanova-Clarke, Irina Sandomirskaja, Henrike Schmidt, Sali Tagliamonte, Dirk Uffelmann, Daniel Weiss, Susanna Witt, Alexei Yurchak, Ludmila Zubova and Vera Zvereva.

A fellowship at the Wissenschaftskolleg zu Berlin (Institute for Advanced Study) 2014–15 provided perfect conditions for the writing part. I am most grateful to the staff of the Wissenschaftskolleg for their professional and caring attitude; in particular, I would like to thank Kathrin Biegger, Daniel Schönpflug, Thorsten Wilhelmy, and, above all, Sonja Grund and her colleagues in the library. The 2014–15 class of fellows and partners was a constant source of scholarly inspiration and creativity. Too numerous to list in a preface, let me at least extend my thanks to Barbara Gromes, Monika and Onur Güntürkün, Barbara Hahn, Jannie Hofmeyr, Yogi Jäger, Hilde Janssens, Andrea Kern, Brandon

Kilbourne, Aden Kumler, Shigehisa Kuriyama, Philip Manow, Simone Reber, Meredith Reiches, Sebastian Rödl, Martin Sack, Hans Thomalla and William Marx. I would also like to thank Jannis Androutsopoulos, Susanne Strätling and Heike Winkel for providing opportunities to present and discuss my work with colleagues in Hamburg and Berlin during my stay at the Wissenschaftskolleg.

I thank Lara Ryazanova-Clarke for including the book in Edinburgh University Press's series 'Russian Language and Society', and Joannah Duncan, Richard Strachan and Laura Williamson of EUP for their excellent handling of the publication process. My thanks also to the anonymous reviewers of EUP for their helpful remarks. I am indebted to Alexei Evstratov, Fabian Heffermehl, Jan Plamper, Marina Scharlaj and Klavdia Smola for their useful input on specific points, and to Peter Alberg Jensen, Johan Tønnesson and Georg Witte for stimulating discussions at critical stages of the project. I am extremely grateful to Stehn Mortensen and Martin Paulsen for their careful reading of the whole manuscript in its near-final form. The Department of Foreign Languages at the University of Bergen generously provided me with a grant for English-language editing, which was expertly carried out by Ursula Phillips.

I thank the following publishers and journals for their permission to incorporate material that appeared in: 'Language culture in post-Soviet Russia: The response of literature', in Ingunn Lunde and Tine Roesen (eds), *Landslide of the Norm: Language Culture in Post-Soviet Russia* (Slavica Bergensia 6), Bergen: Department of Foreign Languages, 2006, pp. 64–79; '*Pisateli o iazyke*: Contemporary Russian writers on the language question', *Russian Language Journal* 58, 2008, pp. 3–18; 'Performative metalanguage: Norm negotiation through verbal action', in Ingunn Lunde and Martin Paulsen (eds), *From Poets to Padonki: Linguistic Authority and Norm Negotiation in Modern Russian Culture* (Slavica Bergensia 9), Bergen: Department of Foreign Languages, 2009, pp. 110–28; 'Footnotes of a graphomaniac: The language question in Evgenii Popov's *True Story of "The Green Musicians"*', *The Russian Review* 68 (1), 2009, pp. 70–88; '"A stroll through the keywords of my memory": Digitally mediated commemorations of the Soviet linguistic heritage', in Ellen Rutten, Vera Zvereva and Julie Fedor (eds), *Memory, Conflict and New Media: Web Wars in Post-Socialist States*, London/New York: Routledge, 2013, pp. 101–11; '"Abanamat": Reactions from the cultural field to the 2014 Russian anti-obscenity law', *Zeitschrift für slavische Philologie* 73 (1), 2017, pp. 1–29.

Note on Transliteration and Translations

I have used the Library of Congress system of transliteration for Russian words and names. This goes even for proper names that are more widely known in alternative spellings, such as Ulitskaia (Ulitskaya), Vysotskii (Vysotsky), with the exception of names of people who use(d) alternative spellings themselves (Brodsky, Oushakine). All translations from Russian into English are my own, unless otherwise specified.

INTRODUCTION

Sociolinguistic Change and the Response of Literature

This book explores the response of writers and of fiction to the current language situation in Russia. In a period of linguistic liberalisation, instability and change, followed by sundry attempts to regulate and legislate language usage, post-Soviet Russia may be characterised by the language question permeating all spheres of social, cultural and political life. Taking as my point of departure the debates on language change in post-perestroika Russian culture, I examine the interpretations these debates receive within the realm of literature. 'Literature' refers here to both 'writers of fiction' and 'fictional writing'. In other words, my framework includes not only explicit reflections on language by writers of fiction in the contexts of the language debate, language legislation or linguistic codification (for example, in interviews or roundtable discussions), but also implicit responses that may be elicited from their literary works. In combining these two perspectives, I aim to shed light simultaneously on two significant issues: first, the role of writers in the broader social and political context of language culture in contemporary Russia and, second, the various ways in which the linguistic and aesthetic practices of literary art can engage with questions related to the negotiation of linguistic norms.

Both issues have a prehistory in Russian culture, since social commitment, as well as moral and philosophical authority, traditionally accompany the task of being 'a great Russian writer', on the one hand, while literary texts have long played a norm-maintaining role in education, on the other. Whereas the continuity of this tradition was seriously challenged by the break-up of the Soviet Union, radically changing the conditions for both writers and their literary texts, there are signs of its re-emergence in a new, refashioned form in the post-Soviet era. To be sure, literature and its creators do not set the entire agenda for linguistic development and norm negotiation in contemporary Russia; I hope to show, however, that writers and the linguistic practices of literary art offer original, creative, sometimes idiosyncratic but always engaging contributions, to the broader discussion of language culture and society.

SOCIOLINGUISTIC CHANGE

It is often argued that language change and language debates are particularly intense in periods of radical political and social transformation. In both professional and lay talk about language, connections are frequently made between political development and language development, between cultural trends and ideas about language usage. Clearly, any analysis of the complex interrelationships between these processes requires the use of tools and theories developed in a variety of disciplines.

To capture the nature of language change and the debates surrounding it in the post-Soviet era, it is useful to introduce the concept of *sociolinguistic change*. Sociolinguistic change seeks to bring together the study of linguistic and social change, seeing these as 'mutually constitutive processes' (Androutsopoulos 2014: 5). This implies the study of changes in language and in society, but also the study of changes in the relationship between language and society. Moreover, the concept of sociolinguistic change allows us to consider the interrelationships between linguistic change and social change, not within a simplistic paradigm of cause and effect, but within a framework that includes the complex interaction between the institutions, groups and people that engage in linguistic norm negotiation. Norm negotiation, discussed in more detail below, is a term that captures some of the ways in which we interact with (conflicting) linguistic norms in a linguistic society. Finally, sociolinguistic change provides a conceptual framework for studying linguistic practices and metalinguistic reflections within a broad understanding of language culture. As Nikolas Coupland explains,

> the concept of sociolinguistic change [. . .] urges us to ask broader questions, where the interest is less in discovering structural change in language systems and more in discovering changing relationships between language and society and their instantiation at the level of practice. Sociolinguistic change research carries the specific presupposition that whatever we identify as language change happens in the context of social change, and that these dimensions need to be handled integratively. (Coupland 2014: 70)

Following Coupland (2014: 74), we can distinguish five interlinked dimensions of sociolinguistic change: discursive practices, language ideologies, social norms, cultural reflexivity and media(tisa)tion. Change in *discursive practices* includes developments in particular speech styles and their distribution, use and interaction with other modes of communication (visual, audio). *Language ideologies* amount to ideas about language and language practices that define, for instance, the borderlines between different spheres of usage, the status of different varieties and similar issues. Language ideologies are closely linked to *social norms*, and provide guiding principles on the level of linguistic practice. *Cultural reflexivity* spells out the ideologies and attitudes; this dimension introduces the metalevel and includes all kinds of 'talk about talk' – reflections on language change, social change and their interconnections. Metalinguistic activity tells us how (socio)linguistic change is acknowledged and negotiated in society. It provides us with evaluative discourses about language ideologies and language practices, thus responding both to top-down linguistic policies and to a variety of observable linguistic practices. Finally, *mediatisation*[1] is 'a social change which creates new affordances for language use' (Coupland 2014: 78), particularly relevant with regard to the interrelationship between new technology and language development. New technology has provided language users with new platforms and genres of interacting socially with and through language, in addition to stimulating the use of multimodal means of communication.

The concept of sociolinguistic change is significantly broader than the much more frequently studied 'language change'. For the purposes of this book, it is essential that it includes, first, the changing relationship between social change and language change, and, second, the metalinguistic dimension.

It is important to point out that reflexivity and practice need not always be two separate ways of engaging with language. In other words, linguistic practices may well have a metalinguistic dimension. In this book I propose to analyse a particular linguistic and artistic practice with reference to this reflexive dimension: contemporary Russian prose writing. By combining literary analysis with sociolinguistic questions in interpretive readings of a selection of post-Soviet Russian prose works, I aim to shed light on the ways in which fictional texts can comment on linguistic issues. In order to achieve this, it is essential that the reflexive dimension of prose writing be analysed within the framework of broader questions about sociolinguistic change. What is the role of writers with regard to 'the language question' in Russian society? What kind of issues related to language and language change are of concern to contemporary Russian prose writers? Which particular topics in the language debates do they respond to? How do writers, and their texts, relate to official language planning? What is the (changing) relationship between the language of literature and the standard language? In what ways can fictional texts contribute to the language debates? These and related questions will guide our way through the two kinds of material analysed in this book: statements of writers and their literary works. This combined approach allows us to map the 'voices' of writers and of fiction, to compare them with other voices in the language debates, and thus to bring instances of individual agency into dialogue with institutional policies. Finally, it enables us to widen the perspective of language debate research, through investigating the role of writers and of fiction as part of broader processes of sociolinguistic change.

What have been the main public discourses in Russia about language in the 1990s and 2000s? Let us turn to the chief linguistic developments and concerns of the post-Soviet era.

VERNACULARISATION

Many aspects of late and post-Soviet sociolinguistic change can be described in terms of 'vernacularisation' in Coupland's sense, reflected 'in the aspiration to allow previously "blocked" linguistic features, styles and genres to "pass the filter" into domains that have been the preserves of standardness [. . .]' (Coupland 2014: 87). With perestroika, glasnost and the subsequent break-up of the Soviet Union, shifting linguistic ideologies contributed to questioning the authority of the standard language. As a result, a strong tendency of norm relaxation could be observed – that is, the use and acceptance of non-standard linguistic elements such as swear words or slang – in official speech culture, in the mass media and other written genres, including literature, and, with the advent of new media technology, in digital genres.

In the late 1980s, the shift in linguistic ideologies was closely linked to transformations in the political and social domains, which again had an impact on the nature of sociolinguistic change. Gorbachev's politics of glasnost made it possible to discuss things formerly forbidden, to do so in language that had hitherto been considered unsuitable for the public sphere and to question the meaning of ideologically charged words. Boundaries between different spheres of speech, firmly consolidated by official regulation during the Soviet period, were seriously challenged, while the abolition of censorship in virtually all areas of official language usage led to a stylistic and lexical diversity unheard of before. In public speaking a transition took place from a linguistic culture dominated by prepared texts and adherence to strict norms overseen by state control to a culture open to spontaneous speech and verbal unpredictability. The new linguistic trends became even more apparent after the dismantling of the Soviet Union in 1991, which also led to a massive influx of words from English, the language of globalisation.

Due to the ideologisation of language culture in the Soviet era, language had not been discussed in public to the same extent as in the debates that arose in the late 1980s and 1990s. Parallel to the developments that became central topics in the language debates – loanwords, non-standard varieties, norms and regulations – the attitude towards language as something that could and ought to be discussed also changed. Moreover, in the time that has passed since the late perestroika years, the debates themselves have developed. During perestroika and the early post-Soviet years, the new linguistic situation was largely welcomed as reflecting society's recently won freedoms, and elicited a general celebration of verbal diversity and spontaneous speech. Changes in the language culture were hailed as signs of 'democratisation' and 'liberalisation'. However, as the rigorous probing of the limits of acceptable language escalated, calls for the articulation of new norms, or the adherence to old ones, gradually became more vociferous. Towards the end of the 1990s, issues of language legislation and regulation began to dominate the discussions of language culture, with purist tendencies coming to the fore. At the same time, questions of language culture and language cultivation tended to be linked to broader issues of national identity, cultural legacy or ethical standards (Ryazanova-Clarke 2006a; Gorham 2014: 98–132). The 2000s have seen a number of state-initiated language programmes and legislative proposals targeted at language regulation, the most recent of which have also entered the realms of literature and art.

RESEARCH ON POST-SOVIET LANGUAGE CULTURE

The processes of language change, shifting linguistic ideologies, and the interrelationship between language and politics have been studied quite extensively since the late perestroika and early post-Soviet years, both in Russia and abroad. Early assessments of the 1990s tended to focus on the language of the media and public speaking, highlighting the contested issues of foreign loanwords and non-standard elements (e.g. Dulichenko 1994; Kostomarov 1994; Zybatow 1995, 2000; Zemskaia 1996; Shaposhnikov 1998; Kupina 1999a; Becker 2001; Fleischmann 2007). Lara Ryazanova-Clarke and Terence Wade's *The Russian Language Today* (1999) provided the first systematic, English-language textbook, while the series *Russkii iazyk segodnia* edited by Leonid Krysin (2000–12) covers a broad range of issues related to linguistic and sociolinguistic change. Non-standard varieties of Russian have become an extensive field of research and lexicographical publishing activity (e.g. Elistratov 1995; Grachev 1997; Khimik 2000; Plutser-Sarno 2000, 2001, 2005), while general sociolinguistic studies of contemporary Russian are scarcer (e.g. Krysin 2004; Mechkovskaia 2005), although in certain areas, for instance on the status of Russian within the former Soviet countries, research is active (Pavlenko 2008; Bak et al. 2010).[2] The published results of a research group based at the University of Bergen represent an attempt to restructure the research field by integrating (socio)linguistic, literary, cultural and anthropological research on contemporary Russian language culture, and by situating the negotiation of linguistic norms in Russia historically (Lunde and Roesen 2006; Lunde and Paulsen 2009a; Gorham et al. 2014). Michael Gorham's recent *After Newspeak: Language Culture and Politics in Russia from Gorbachev to Putin* (2014) provides an up-to-date and highly readable cultural history of the politics of Russian language culture from the late perestroika time up to the present day, while popular books by leading Russian linguists such as Maksim Krongauz (2007, 2013) and Irina Levontina (2010, 2015) offer the informed insider's invaluable view and analysis of current developments in language and linguistic culture.

With this book I should like to broaden the perspective on the language debates by including 'voices' that are usually not taken into account, namely the voices of writers of fiction. This undertaking is based on the assumption that in order to fully assess the processes of sociolinguistic change in post-Soviet Russia, we need to reorient ourselves towards a greater integration of cultural and literary practices. Such practices are often focal areas for metalinguistic activity in less explicit forms, such as verbal play, creative word formation, or original representations of language and linguistic situations. Indeed, John Lucy (1993: 21) writes that 'verbal art is a form of creative metalinguistic play with the power to affect social reality', while Deborah Cameron (2004: 313) speaks of the 'ludic dimension of metalanguage'.

Several such cultural practices in Russia have been the subject of research in recent years (e.g. Norman 2006; Graham and Mesropova 2008; Graham 2009; Babenko 2010), but few scholars, if any, have seen the rich potential of this material in the context of metalinguistic practices, and even fewer have sought to relate such findings to the current changes in linguistic culture. For example, Liudmila Zubova, a great authority on the language of contemporary Russian poetry (2000, 2010), offers a fascinating exploration into how contemporary Russian poets provide statements about language in their poetic practice. However, such statements are not related to today's discussions about language in Russian society, or discussed from a theoretical perspective. Instead, Zubova focuses on the interpretation of individual poems, demonstrating how the poetic statements about language are decisive for a proper understanding of the text. Similarly, Marina Shumarina's book (2011), which explores metalinguistic reflection in fictional texts, covers a lot of material and offers preliminary categorisations of metalinguistic markers, but pays little attention to non-explicit metalinguistic commentary (in her terminology, 'zero reflexives'), and she does not relate her findings to the discussions about language that have taken place in Russia over the last decades.

In what ways, then, can writers contribute to the public debate about language?

THE RESPONSE OF LITERATURE

The debate on the Russian language has been taking place in a number of different forms and forums. Conferences and round tables on the state of the Russian language are organised regularly by institutions such as the Academy of Sciences, universities or other academic establishments, often supported financially by one of the state's language cultivation programmes. The most substantial among such programmes is the 'Russkii iazyk' federal target programme, launched in 2002 and recently prolonged for another four-year period, 2016–20. The state also sponsors radio programmes devoted to the language question, such as the popular *Govorim po-russki* (*Let's speak Russian*) broadcast on Ekho Moskvy since 1998. Another major state initiative in language cultivation is the internet site Gramota.ru, established in 2000 and featuring, among other things, an information service that by May 2016 had received and answered more than 288,000 questions. A presidential decree by Vladimir Putin declared 2007 as the 'Year of the Russian Language', with numerous events in Russia and abroad promoting the study of Russian as well as its status as an international means of communication. The written mass media also provide much space for linguistic discussion, featuring columns or article series devoted to language, with contributions from linguists, philologists, teachers, journalists, critics and writers. Finally, the internet has become in recent years a popular platform for linguistic norm negotiation, both in explicit terms, in blogs, forums and social media communities devoted to the language question, and in more implicit ways, in the multifaceted, and often playful, linguistic practices of online communication.

'Linguistic practice' as a form of indirect metalinguistic statement brings us to the question of the different ways in which statements about language are made, or speakers engage in metalinguistic activities. Here, it is useful to introduce in more detail the concept of *norm negotiation* (Andersen 1989, 2009; Lunde and Paulsen 2009b). Norm negotiation may be explicit, taking the form of linguistic debates and discussions, and implicit, taking the form of individual linguistic practices. Henning Andersen understands implicit norm negotiation in concrete terms as the choices speakers make all the time between various linguistic possibilities, choices that in every case give preference to one of several conflicting norms in a linguistic society.

We can also think of intermediate forms between the straightforward explicit and the various implicit forms of metalinguistic statements or views. A dictionary editor, for example, may express his or her view on the status of non-standard linguistic elements by including or not including particular words and by providing them with a stylistic marker or leaving them unmarked. Daniel Müller's (2013) study of non-standard lexical items in authoritative dictionaries, for example, shows that different editions of the authoritative *Tolkovyi slovar' russkogo iazyka* (*Interpretive Dictionary of Russian*) by Sergei Ozhegov signal a movement from non-acceptance to acceptance of certain such words. The word *kaif* ('high', 'thrill') was thus not included in the 1994 edition of the dictionary, was included in the 1999 edition with the stylistic marker *prostorechnoe* ('sub-standard') and only with the marker *razgovornoe* ('colloquial') in the 2008 edition.

In an attempt to achieve a broader, yet more specific understanding of implicit norm negotiation, I have suggested the term *performative metalanguage* (Lunde 2009) to describe statements about language communicated through a concrete linguistic practice, an exposition or representation of language, for example, in literary fiction. The term's specificity lies in the notion of performance. Performative metalanguage contains an element of creativity, display, and often playfulness. Its broadness lies, as we will see later in this book, in the various forms it may take, and in the interpretive implications it may have. It is a term that is shaped to a certain extent by my material, and I will therefore develop the concept in more detail in a concluding chapter, following my readings of six works of Russian prose fiction in Part IV of this book.

What is the role of literature, and of writers, in today's discussions about language? In order to shed light on this question, I will examine both 'writers' and 'literature' – that is, analyse statements and actions by writers related to the language question, as well as their artistic and linguistic practices in their fictional writing. This approach requires a complex analysis of explicit and implicit (or performative) forms of metalinguistic engagement, using tools from sociolinguistics as well as literary and cultural analysis. In the readings in Part IV, we will see examples of how contemporary Russian literature responds to institutional initiatives in the realm of language regulation, to the contested issues of non-standard linguistic elements, to questions of linguistic legacies and to shifting language ideologies. The response of literature, taken together with the positions writers adopt when engaging as citizens in discussions about language, forms part of what Coupland (2014) terms the 'cultural reflexivity' dimension of sociolinguistic change.

There are many ways to engage in metalinguistic discussion or even active language cultivation as a writer. Aleksandr Solzhenitsyn, for example, consistently used new (or very archaic) words or word forms in his writings and even authored a *Russkii slovar' iazykovogo rasshireniia* (*Russian Dictionary of Linguistic Expansion*, 1990, with new editions 1995 and 2000). Other writers participate in surveys about language culture, write newspaper columns on linguistic issues, or experiment with language in their texts. Indeed, the language of the 'new' literature was one of the things that upset people with regard to the language question during late perestroika and the 1990s. In the words of Iurii Karaulov (1989: 15), linguist and director of the Russian Language Institute 1982–96, people's anxiety about the 'state of the Russian language' stemmed from three main sources: the mass media, the language of fiction and public speaking. It is remarkable that the language of fiction is singled out as one of three main issues that aroused the concern of people with regard to developments in language and language culture. It reminds us of the traditional norm-maintaining role of literature. Meanwhile, research into the reception of Russian literature of the 1990s confirms that the language of literature was one of the main and most contested topics among literary critics (Paulsen 2009).

Since the 1990s, the range of topics to which contemporary Russian writers respond in their artistic practices has broadened from a relatively narrow focus on foreign (mostly Anglo-American) loans and non-standard varieties to more complex issues of vernacularisation, standard language ideology, language legislation, linguistic cultivation, and the right to define the conditions for language usage, within and outside the realm of verbal art.

In approaching this rich material, there is nevertheless a need for restriction. The writers chosen for scrutiny in Part IV of this book are all prose writers, a necessary limitation not only for reasons of space, but also in order for the book to have a clear focus and for the works to be able to be compared. Evgenii Popov, Vladimir Sorokin, Tat'iana Tolstaia and

Evgenii Vodolazkin are prose writers who are widely read and discussed. Valerii Votrin and Mikhail Gigolashvili are somewhat less well known but still considered to be important representatives of contemporary Russian literature. The decisive criterion for being included in this book is that the selected works can be read as responses to the language question. Even if I explore both explicit and implicit responses to the post-Soviet language debates, I have chosen works where language is, beyond doubt, a central issue. Furthermore, I have tried to pick a selection of literary works that address central topics in the post-Soviet language debates, such as the question of the Soviet linguistic legacy (Popov and Sorokin), the past and future of Russian (Tolstaia and Vodolazkin), linguistic variation (all authors, in particular Popov, Vodolazkin and Gigolashvili), as well as language policy and linguistic ideologies (Votrin and Gigolashvili). I also wish to include works from the first post-Soviet decade (Popov, Tolstaia) and more recent texts (Sorokin, Vodolazkin, Votrin, Gigolashvili).

CHAPTER OVERVIEW

The book's focus on linguistic debates implies that we will look less at isolated instances of concrete linguistic change and more at the ways in which such change is acknowledged and negotiated in society, in particular in the realm of literature – understood as meaning both 'writers' and 'fiction'.

Having outlined in this Introduction the major linguistic issues subject to contestation and debate, the chapters of Part I explore more closely several central topics of the post-Soviet language question. Issues surrounding language ideologies are highlighted in Chapter 1, 'Newspeak, Counterspeak and Linguistic Memory', which focuses on the ways in which the role and function of Soviet-style language have been transformed in the post-Soviet era. Through scrutinising how linguists today handle the Soviet linguistic legacy in dictionaries and handbooks, I identify a general emphasis on 'counterspeak' (e.g. word play, anecdotes, alternative interpretations of acronyms) and show how this trend is mirrored in lay reflections on Soviet language culture in a number of online forums. After a brief exposition of the history and status of the standard language in Russia, I look at the various ways in which the standard language has been challenged in the post-Soviet era (Chapter 2, 'Challenging the Standard'). The case of the internet slang *iazyk padonkov*, a 'fashion' of the mid-2000s, serves to illustrate the potential of a linguistic practice not only to inspire explicit language discussions, but also to comment implicitly on language issues, that is, acquire a metalinguistic dimension. The chapter is rounded off by a brief analysis of the radical *grammar nazi* movement, a post-*padonki* reaction to linguistic liberties and orthographic errors.

Part II focuses on the historical transformations of literary institutions, the profession of the writer and the status of literary texts. Chapter 3, 'Languages and Styles of Post-Soviet Russian Prose', offers a general overview of post-Soviet literature focusing on its predominant languages and styles, ranging from the literature of *Vergangenheitsbewältigung* to the literature of glamour. Assessing the plethora of styles and aesthetics in contemporary Russian prose fiction, I argue that the end of the Soviet era has led to a general linguistic reorientation of post-Soviet writers and discuss its implications. Against this background, in Chapter 4, 'The Literary Norm', I discuss the new and changing conditions for linguistic norms in literary fiction of the post-Soviet era. In particular, I look at how the interrelationship between the language of literature (*iazyk literatury*) and the standard language (*literaturnyi iazyk*) has been challenged by several processes of sociolinguistic change, including initiatives in language policy.

Parts III and IV discuss the responses of writers and of literature to the language question in a number of case studies and close readings. Chapter 5, '*Pisateli o iazyke*: Writers' Reflections on Language', analyses explicit responses by writers participating in surveys, interviews, roundtable discussions or conferences dedicated to the language situation. Such statements on the language situation illustrate the linguistic attitudes of individual writers towards some of the central topics in the language debates, while conveying the writers' own assessments of their status as opinionmakers in this area. Chapter 6, 'Reactions to the Ban on Profanity in Art', explores the reactions of people working in the cultural field to the 2014 Russian ban on the use of verbal obscenity in film, literature and public performances, reactions that have not only taken the form of commentaries and statements in interviews or the social media, but have also provoked protest actions featuring linguistic and artistic practices (readings, performances), thus responding and commenting in ways bordering on the implicit and performative. This provides a transition to Part IV, which moves into the realm of literary fiction.

Part IV presents critical, interpretive readings of a number of contemporary Russian writers who address the language question in their artistic practice. Writers studied in this part include Evgenii Popov, Vladimir Sorokin, Tat'iana Tolstaia, Evgenii Vodolazkin, Valerii Votrin and Mikhail Gigolashvili, while topics range across norms and norm-breaking, non-standard varieties, language policy and linguistic ideologies, the historical dimensions of language and linguistic memory, as well as representations of linguistic dystopia. The analyses provide insight into the highly original views on contested linguistic issues offered by individual writers, but also into the ways in which such issues may be expressed in the context of verbal art itself.

Chapter 7 sets out to investigate how the implications and broader dimensions of the Soviet linguistic legacy are represented in two post-Soviet prose texts, Evgenii Popov's novel *Podlinnaia istoriia 'zelenykh muzykantov'* (*The True Story of 'The Green Musicians'*, 1999) and Vladimir Sorokin's short story 'Monoklon' (2010). Popov's 'novel in footnotes' comments on a text from the 1970s (reproduced in the novel), using humour and satire to expose the emptiness of clichés and make links to the present-day language debates. Sorokin, in turn, invokes the historical memory of Sovietspeak through fragments, slogans, words and concepts, creating in his text a 'simultaneity of the non-simultaneous' by juxtaposing elements from two very different parts of the Soviet past and showing the need to tackle this past (or these pasts) in present-day Russian society.

In Chapter 8 I explore how prose writers create fictional representations of a past, or a future, where language emerges as an essential theme. I offer close readings of two works, one portraying a fictional future for Russian – Tat'iana Tolstaia's 2000 novel *Kys'* (*The Slynx*), and one diving into the language's past – Evgenii Vodolazkin's *Lavr* (*Laurus*, 2012). The analysis shows how both authors challenge the standard language by stretching its potential and including a wealth of elements taken from non-standard varieties and older forms. Whereas Tolstaia's novel depicts a brutal, destructive world of linguistic dystopia with, or so it would seem, no real past and no future, Vodolazkin's text presents a smoothly created linguistic amalgam characterised by flexibility and multifunctionality. I discuss the linguistic attitudes implied in the two approaches and their relevance to the post-Soviet language debates.

Chapter 9 offers readings of two recent novels, Valerii Votrin's *Logoped* (*The Speech Therapist*, 2012) and Mikhail Gigolashvili's *Zakhvat Moskovii: natsional-lingvisticheskii roman* (*The Occupation of Muscovy: A National-Linguistic Novel*, 2012). Votrin represents a linguistic dystopia governed by strict orthoepic norms. The story is told through the portrayal of two persons, a speech therapist representing the authorities, and a journalist, expelled for his oppositional views. Gigolashvili's novel tells about a young German student of Russian and his encounter with the grammar nazi movement, a group of self-appointed language mavens who monitor, expose and ridicule linguistic liberties and orthographic errors in highly aggressive ways. Both novels can be read as responses to language legislation and language cultivation, highly topical issues in present-day Russian language culture.

The book's Conclusion discusses the findings of Parts III and IV and their implications for a general theory of what I propose to call *performative metalanguage*. Arguing that literary works may contain a metalinguistic dimension and intention, I maintain that a theory of performative metalanguage helps us understand this particular form of linguistic commentary, mapping out ways in which we can identify and assess such reflection.

NOTES

1. Mediation refers to 'the cultural, material, or semiotic conditions of any communicative action' (Androutsopoulos 2014: 10); mediatisation 'points to societal changes in contemporary high modern societies and the role of media and mediated communication in these transformations' (Lundby 2009: 1, cited in Androutsopoulos 2014: 10). See Androutsopoulos (2014: 9–12) for a discussion of the two terms.
2. See also the Edinburgh research unit 'Russian in Context', available at <http://www.ed.ac.uk/schools-departments/literatures-languages-cultures/delc/russian/postgraduate-study/russian-in-context> (last accessed 22 June 2017).

PART I

Post-Soviet Language Culture

CHAPTER I

Newspeak, Counterspeak and Linguistic Memory

The question of linguistic legacies – of both recent and more distant origin – is a central one in the present-day linguistic debates. When it comes to the handling of the Soviet linguistic heritage, in particular, one of its challenges – for today's scholars and language users alike – is that it is not always recognised as something 'inherited', that is, as something that stems from a particular linguistic register with specific historical and sociopolitical connotations. While certain slogans and phrases can easily be recognised as 'Soviet', even by younger generations of Russians, it takes a special effort of linguistic reflection – or even a philologist – to pin down the Soviet element in much of present-day Russian political and everyday talk, or to draw up a broader picture of 'the Soviet language'. In Gasan Guseinov's terms, Soviet sociopolitical language culture may be viewed as a *linguistic experience*, or even *competence*, accumulated, developed and refined during some seventy years of Soviet rule. Accordingly, in his comprehensive dictionary of Soviet sociopolitical language, Guseinov (2003) treats the Soviet linguistic legacy from the point of view of its implications for the post-Soviet era. This is an important and necessary perspective, and one that can help us understand the role played by elements of Soviet language culture in today's linguistic and metalinguistic practices.

Soviet language culture is not only talked about; elements of this language are alive and thriving in various contemporary genres: in bureaucratic, official speech, in political speech, in sayings, in formulaic expressions, but also in linguistic humour, in satirical language, and the like. This is clearly a competence in flux, a linguistic practice which, one would expect, is decreasing among the average population, or at least changing in nature and depth. The various forms and degrees of this competence are partly the consequence of different generations, and of shifting political cultures – with their accompanying shifts in attitude towards the Soviet linguistic legacy.

This chapter focuses on the implications of the deideologisation of language after the dismantling of the Soviet Union. I will look at the transformed role of Soviet language culture in post-Soviet Russian society by way of two case studies that represent two different contexts of metalinguistic reflection, one professional, one lay: the first case study scrutinises how Russian linguists represent the Soviet linguistic legacy in post-Soviet dictionaries and monographs; the other investigates how Soviet language culture is discussed in a selection of online forums.

PHILOLOGY'S RESPONSE TO SOVIETSPEAK

After the fall of the Soviet Union, the role and function of typical Soviet-style language – sometimes known by the Orwellian term 'newspeak'[1] – were transformed in several respects. A considerable part of the lexicon has been 'de-sovieticised' in one way or another: certain words have become marginal, or even historicisms, because what they denote is no longer of any relevance to post-Soviet reality; words have been deideologised, and may have changed their connotation from positive to negative, or vice versa, or become altogether neutralised; and words may have changed their meanings. Certain elements of Soviet-style newspeak have been retained in a particular type of bureaucratic style, partly in the provincial press, and within certain political groups (Kukulin 2015). The greater part, however, of what is considered typical of Soviet political language has disappeared from post-Soviet political speech culture, above all the predictable and ritualistic elements. Since the 1990s, political language has been characterised by spontaneity, unpredictability, and a polemical and rhetorical style, as well as by a high degree of stylistic and lexical heterogeneity (Weiss 2000; Gorham 2014).

Meanwhile, elements of Soviet language culture are used and re-used today in a quite different context: in slang, ironic word play and linguistic humour. Linguistic clichés are inverted, played upon and re-contextualised in an ironic manner which often verges on the absurd. This particular response to the Soviet linguistic legacy was especially frequent in the mass media, literature and informal speech of the 1990s and early 2000s, while the 2010s have seen a new revival of many elements derived from Soviet language culture, in particular in patriotic discourses (Iampol'skii 2014; Ryazanova-Clarke 2015).

Within this context of re-functionalisation and re-contextualisation, Soviet language culture has also become the subject of intensive study

– both documentary and critical. In the decade between the mid-1990s and the mid-2000s there appeared a number of important publications which dealt, in various ways, with Soviet language culture (Kupina 1995, 1999b; Mokienko and Nikitina 1998; Sarnov 2002; Kheveshi 2002; Guseinov 2003, 2004; Pikhurova 2006).[2] What is covered by the term 'Soviet language' in these books? As it turns out, a great many different things. The notion includes, of course, the official genres – political slogans, characteristic phraseology, concepts and terms – but also a considerable amount of everyday Soviet terminology, engendered by the social and political reality, such as *dostat'* ('get hold of') or *stoiat' za* ('line up for') instead of *kupit'* ('buy'); *sidet'* ('sit') instead of *sidet' v tiur'me* ('be in prison'), and so on. Furthermore, several of the books include personal names, toponyms, names of institutions, enterprises, products and pets, and not least many slang expressions, which demonstrate the unofficial double or parallel life of Soviet language culture, both during the Soviet period and afterwards.

The sources from which these studies take their cues are not only political speeches, handbooks or newspaper editorials, but also literature, anecdotes, listeners' responses to *Radio Svoboda* (*Radio Liberty*), *chastushki* (a folk genre of short, often humoristic and ironic, verses), and a variety of other genres. In this respect almost all the publications mentioned above employ a very broad notion of 'Soviet language', and the unofficial double life of this language is more often than not a main, if not the main, focus.

These various kinds of countercultural reaction to official newspeak include puns, *anekdoty* ('jokes') and similar phenomena – in short, the popular tradition of *protivoiaz* ('counterspeak', Sarnov 2002), what Nataliia Kupina (1999b) calls *iazykovoe soprotivlenie* ('linguistic resistance'), and both Gasan Guseinov (2003) and Anna Wierzbicka (Vezhbitska 1993) term *iazyk samooborony* ('the language of self-defence').[3]

In Mokienko and Nikitina's dictionary, it becomes clear that this very broad conception of *sovetizmy* is quite intentional, as they explain in the foreword:

> Словарь языка Совдепии, с одной стороны, должен всесторонне представить советскую эпоху в лексическом отображении, а с другой – раскрыть особенности «двойной жизни» советизмов при Советах, показать их постсоветскую судьбу, функционирование в новом качестве, с изменившимися коннотациями, всевозможными структурно-семантическими трансформациями, переходом в разряд жаргонной лексики и.т.п. (Mokienko and Nikitina 1998: 5–6)[4]

If we take a closer look at the publications in question, we can see that 'counterspeak' is perceived in several different ways. At one end of the spectrum, we find Nataliia Kupina's detailed examination of counter-cultural responses to official verbal ideology, or 'totalitarian language', where the latter is defined (Kupina 1995) in quite narrow terms on the basis of Dmitrii Ushakov's four-volume dictionary published in 1935–40. 'Linguistic resistance', as portrayed in Kupina's 1999 monograph, includes examples of prison-camp poetry, anecdotes, but first and foremost the work of a range of first-class writers such as Platonov, Zamiatin and Zoshchenko. In examining Soviet linguistic counterculture, Kupina criticises the deideologising tendencies of the 1990s for not paying due respect to the deideologising resistance which already took place in Soviet times.

I believe that the philologists' focus on the 'double life' of Soviet linguistic practices captures something essential about this language culture, and it is quite impressive that scholarly books are able to document successfully such an elusive phenomenon. However, Soviet language culture, as argued above, is also a particular linguistic experience, and this aspect is probably even harder to document than Sovietspeak's double life. The book that comes closest to achieving this is Benedikt Sarnov's *Nash sovetskii novoiaz* (*Our Soviet Newspeak*, 2002), written in a genre oscillating between the dictionary and the personal memoir. Lexical items are loosely arranged here according to the following general structure: the item itself is usually listed as an element of official newspeak, such as *doska pocheta* ('roll of honour'), *strana sploshnoi gramotnosti* ('a country of universal literacy'), or *kommunisty, vpered!* ('Communists, forward!'). Then its official meaning is illustrated by a definition from an authoritative dictionary or simply by an explanation. There frequently follows a further definition or explanation taken from, for example, Mokienko and Nikitina's dictionary of Soviet language, which brings in other, alternative meanings of the word or phrase. After this short introduction, we get Sarnov's personal, and very subjective, response to the term in question. It consists of a number of linguistic reactions in the form of anecdotes, short verses, *chastushki*, or the author's own reminiscences. In short, Sarnov is engaging here in 'humanising' Soviet reality, and Soviet political discourse, through language. These responses are usually humoristic and illustrate the great capacities of humour and irony to confront pathetic and ritualistic linguistic practices.

All the stylistic and generic differences between Kupina's and Sarnov's books notwithstanding, their depiction of totalitarian language and the various creative cultural responses that it generated is conceived according to a binary model which has been highly influential in Russian studies, and which – even if criticised from time to time – still seems to inform major works on the topic that concerns us here. This model operates with an understanding of 'official newspeak', on the one hand, and a wide range of 'counterspeak expressions', on the other. While 'pure newspeak' may perhaps exist in certain genres, for example in the editorial of a newspaper such as *Pravda*, I believe it is difficult to account adequately for all the forms of cultural responses to this particular discourse in terms of binary oppositions.

A useful corrective to this interpretation is Alexei Yurchak (2006). Yurchak shows how the cultural and linguistic practices of late socialism were not 'divided into spheres or codes that are fixed and bounded', but took the form of 'processes that are never completely known in advance and that are actively produced and reinterpreted' (Yurchak 2006: 18). The main characteristic of the many forms of cultural practices described by Yurchak is their notorious ambiguity. The humoristic genres, such as, for example, *steb*, refuse to accept 'any boundary between seriousness and humor, support and opposition, sense and nonsense', rejecting the very dichotomy between these sentiments, and 'always balancing in multiple zones in-between' (Yurchak 2006: 243, 252).

While it is certainly difficult for a dictionary to reflect pragmatically this linguistic situation (perhaps it is a little easier for a monograph), an excellent genre, as we shall see later in this book, is literature, with its room for ambiguities, irony and multiple perspectives. Apart from literature, or art in general, people's memories can also highlight elements of this particular linguistic experience, and this is what we will look at next.

COMMEMORATING SOVIET LANGUAGE CULTURE

Most people do not publish their linguistic experiences as a personal memoir. But new technology, and the internet in particular, has created a new, broad venue for digitally mediated commemorations of the Soviet past, including its linguistic legacy (Rutten et al. 2013). From time to time, the concept of a 'Soviet language' pops up in forums and blogs, and people are invited to share their associations and memories of typical Soviet linguistic expressions. In the remainder of this chapter, I examine one such source, an online discussion following a radio broadcast by the BBC on *sovetizmy* in 2005,[5] focusing in particular on two questions: first, what distinguishes these kinds of linguistic commemorative reflection from the academic collections discussed above; and second, what do they add to our understanding of the post-Soviet linguistic situation?

In addition to the obviously broader picture provided by the sheer mass of people taking part in online commemorative practices, two aspects lend themselves to particular attention: first, personal reminiscences (including reflections, assessments and associations arising in connection with concrete examples of Soviet language culture); and second, reflections on the process of commemoration. By highlighting these factors, I suggest some ways in which these online commemorations and thematisations of Soviet language culture may add to both historical and contemporary understandings of this phenomenon. This knowledge, in turn, will provide useful background to my examination of literature's response to the question of linguistic legacies in Chapter 7.

Let us start by asking whether the particular focus of the philological publications on the 'countercultural response' to Soviet language culture is also reflected in online commemorative practices. What is understood by 'Sovietism' in this material? The answer emerges from the scope of the examples provided. *Sovetizmy* are clearly not thought to comprise only the official genres, ideological slogans and political styles, but also the other side of the coin, the satirical, ironical twist, word play, linguistic humour, and everyday lexicon from the Soviet period. This becomes clear in the way people introduce all kinds of Sovietisms without explicitly distinguishing between the 'official' and 'unofficial'. Obviously, they all belong to the same, broad linguistic stockpile of expressions 'made in the USSR'. The examples below, provided by two different users, are listed without any introductory context or motivation: individual voices of the past simply add up to a collective response to the question 'What is a *sovetizm*?':

Объявление в газетном киоске: «Правды» – нет. «Россия» – продана. Остался «Труд» за 3 копейки. [...] Огромными буквами на доме № 101 по проспекту Мира висел плакат: «СТАЛЬ – РОДИНЕ!» [...][6]

«Ты начальник – я дурак. Я начальник – ты дурак».
«Начальник делает вид, что платит мне зарплату – я делаю вид, что работаю».
«Пусть лошадь думает, у неё голова большая».
«Закон как столб – не перепрыгнешь, но обойти можно».
«Закон как дышло, куда повернёшь туда и вышло».
«Партия честь и совесть советского народа».
«Партия наш рулевой».
«Россия родина слонов».
«Советское – значит отличное».

«Был бы человек, а дело на него найдётся». (В смысле, посадить в тюрьму можно любого.)
«Хочешь жни, а хочешь куй – всёравно получишь» ... (В смысле, в Союзе вообще работать не стоит.)[7]

We see here that official slogans stand side by side with ironic distortions, humoristic or sarcastic sayings, or an anecdote – without any further commentary on the mixture of genres. This demonstrates the degree to which the official and alternative linguistic practices of Soviet language culture were intertwined and interdependent. If there is a contextualisation, it tends to be linked to someone's personal experience with Sovietisms. Let us look at an example:

> Вспоминаю лозунг у здания парткома села Богатое тогда Куйбышевской области. Был самый расцвет хрущевщины и поэтому нам внушали: «Будет мясо и сметана, колбаса сортов любых, если всюду сеять станут кукурузу и бобы!» А в продуктовом магазине села и в помине не было ни сахара, ни колбасы, вообще никаких продуктов питания, только консервы с килькой и водка. А буханку хлеба, если успеешь купить, называли «шлакоблоком», до того она была черна, спекшаяся, сыра и тяжела. В местной столовой дежурным блюдом была только отварная вермишель – холодная и склизкая. Через несколько месяцев такого питания я заработал «желтуху».[8]

The example nicely brings out the wide gap between ideological language and real life in Soviet times. It provides a context, a couple of concrete examples, and some reflections and thoughts, all of which add up to a personal experience. It does not make any attempt at generalisation – but we, as readers, are free to do so, holding up our own experience or knowledge alongside the examples and comments provided. With the possible exception of Sarnov's book, this opposition between official language culture and real life is not particularly prominent in the philological literature on the subject, but very much present in the online material.

Not unexpectedly, many users recall funny and absurd constellations of official slogans and the surrounding realities:

> Вспоминается огромная фотография Л.И. Брежнева с вытянутой рукой и надписью «Правильной дорогой идёте, товарищи!» В общем ничего особенного, если бы в направлении

куда указывала рука Леонида Ильича не находилась известная всем местная пивная ...⁹

В нашем военном городке было два лозунга. Один стоял метров 300 от другого.1-Наша цель – коммунизм, 2-Каждую бомбу – точно в цель.¹⁰

These and similar examples evoke personal reminiscences, mostly relating to one person, and one concrete memory (as opposed to attempts to generalise, inherent in the genres of dictionary and monograph). The format means that these personal memories can be supplemented by all sorts of commentaries, sometimes in a laconic manner, sometimes with more passion: «Народ и партия – едины!» Эта неоновая надпись на ГОРКОМе не гасла даже когда в округе не было электричества.¹¹ Видел во Владикавказе лозунг в неоне – Победа коммунизма неизбежна. (фатально как-то это, как сама смерть).¹²

Comments like this add a personal tinge of reflection, association, assessment or emotion. They provide glimpses into a private linguistic history, examples of individual encounters between the official language culture and a personal linguistic, cultural and social horizon.

As we will see from the readings of literature's response to the language question later in this book, the problem of sensibility towards linguistic phenomena, including linguistic ideologies, is a crucial topic, and part of the post-Soviet process of linguistic deideologisation. This makes it particularly interesting to look at explicit or implicit reflections on the process of commemoration in the current material. Such comments are often given in passing: От саксофона до ножа один шаг!¹³ Тлетворное влияние запада! Партия сказала: надо! Комсомол ответил: есть! В то время, когда вся страна... Судьбоносное время. Боюсь глубоко уйти в воспоминания. ;)))).¹⁴ In this example, we can see how the flow of memory results in a flow of language: it proceeds from one example to another, before adding a couple of comments and finally a spontaneous reaction to the very process of commemoration.

Я – бывший киевлянин. Как и всё население СССР, был погружён в «советизмы». *Даже коллекционировал чувства, испытываемые советскими людьми, судя по газетам*: 1. Горячего одобрения. 2. Огромной благодарности. 3. Безграничной преданности. 4. Законной гордости. 5. Всесторонней поддержки. 6. Большого подъёма. 7. Беззаветной самоотверженности. 8. Искренней признательности. 9. Монолитной сплочённости. 10. Небывалого энтузиазма. 11. Безраздельной монолитности. 12. Полной сопричастности. 13. Невиданного героизма. 14. Всемерной ответственности. 15. Глубокого удовлетворения. 16. Твёрдой уверенности в завтрашнем дне. 17. Гражданского единства. 18. Полновластного хозяина своей страны. 19. Пролетарского интернационализма. 20. Величия дела, которому служишь. 21. Революционного обновления. 22. Преисполненного долга. 23. Глубокой скорби. Дарю, т.к. коллекция давно не пополняется. (My italics)[15]

The structure of this comment is reminiscent of the popular tradition of cataloguing official terms or phrases and embedding them in new genres or contexts, a widespread practice of language play in Soviet times. A famous example is Vladimir Vysotskii's song 'Pis'mo rabochikh tambovskogo zavoda' ('A Letter from Workers in a Tambov Factory'). The highlighted phrase, in turn, pinpoints the same opposition between ideological language and real life that we saw above, simply combining without commentary the seemingly incompatible. Human emotions are reduced to abstract, ideologised notions, while the emptiness of such phrases is reinforced by the high degree of elatives and analogous linguistic forms in the expressions themselves (*goriachii, ogromnyi, bezgranichnyi, vsestoronnii, nebyvalyi*).

Вообще-то интересно прогуляться по ключевым словам памяти,[16] reflects one user of the forum. Again and again we come across 'keywords', signal words, slogans, which immediately surface in the minds of the respondents as soon as they are asked to think about Sovietisms. In a similar vein, a word or phrase posted by another commentator triggers a response: a similar slogan, a new context, a different interpretation. Such keywords activate the flux of commemorative language at work in these settings.

REFLECTING ON LINGUISTIC LEGACIES

As we try to understand the phenomenon of Soviet language culture, its historical role and its contemporary incarnations, taking a combined look at the handling of this linguistic legacy in post-Soviet philology, on the one hand, and the online commemoration of it, on the other, is quite illustrative. The parallel listings of official and satirical Sovietisms in the online forum show that the emphasis on the 'double life' and countercultural aspects of Sovietspeak, which is prominent in philological writings on the Soviet linguistic legacy, not only reveals the particular interests of philologists, but is a feature firmly grounded in the general perceptions of the Russian-speaking community of the post-Soviet era. The online material, however, provides a broader scope and many additional instances of spontaneous responses to suggestions, memories and associations, which convey a more nuanced picture on the level of detail. The general tone of voice of the online comments oscillates between nostalgia and derision, horror, sarcasm and irony, as users relish reminiscences of absurd, appalling or simply comic expressions.

The two aspects I have focused on in particular – personal reminiscences and reflections on the process of commemoration – are, I believe, the ones that are specific to, or at least more typical of, online discussions, when compared with the professional philological contributions. We are dealing with personal, often spontaneous assessments of the question of the Soviet linguistic legacy, which testify to the individual's reaction to the profound disparity between abstract ideological language and everyday human life. We see the ways in which keywords and associations arise and trigger new associations, how memories add to memories, while we witness typical turns and ways of thinking about language cultures as such – as many discussions on Soviet language culture become a discussion or even argument about today's linguistic situation: Почему вместе с исчезновением советской эпохи дали дуба такие слова, как «тысячелетие» (ныне миллениум), «бег трусцой» (джоггинг), «очаровательный, шикарный» (гламурный), «поход по магазинам» (не рискну произнести)? Мне лично больше всего жаль «бифштекс»![17]

The study of online commemorations of Soviet language culture highlights the articulation of personal human linguistic experience, which also features occasionally in books such as Sarnov's *Nash sovetskii novoiaz* (2002).

In literary fiction, room for this kind of reflexivity is wide open, and indeed, post-Soviet literature provides ample evidence of the various ways in which artistic and aesthetic practices engage with the linguistic legacy of Soviet language culture. These range from Sots Art's display of the emptiness of ideologised language to a great variety of accounts that thematise people's personal encounters with the historical dimensions of language – in individual words, concepts, slogans, historicisms, or specific linguistic registers.

NOTES

1. For a recent examination of how the Russian term for the Orwellian 'newspeak', *novoiaz*, has been used and understood, see Krongauz (2016a).

2. Before *perestroika*, Soviet newspeak was, except for a few seminal Russian works of the 1920s, studied mainly in the West.
3. See Sandomirskaja (2015) for a fascinating study of the 'Aesopian' language culture in a broader context, emphasising its notorious ambiguity and complexity.
4. 'The Dictionary of *Sovdepiia* should provide, on the one hand, a comprehensive representation of the Soviet epoch as reflected in its vocabulary, and, on the other, lay bare the particularities of the "double life" of Sovietisms in Soviet times, show their post-Soviet destiny, their functioning in a new capacity, with their shifting connotations, all sorts of structural and semantic transformations, and transition to the realm of jargon, and similar.'
5. Confining myself to a source from 2005 renders the material suitable for a brief comparison with the philological contributions of 1995–2005 treated above.
6. 'Announcement in a newspaper kiosk: No "Pravda" ['truth'], "Rossiia" ['Russia'] has been sold out. All that's left is "Trud" ['Work'] for 3 kopeks. [. . .] House no. 101 on Mir Avenue had a poster on it with gigantic letters saying: "STEEL FOR THE HOMELAND!"' All quotations are taken from the BBC Russian Service forum on *Sovetskii iazyk* broadcast on 11 October 2005 ('Sovetskii iazyk' 2005). The punctuation and orthography of the source have been retained, with the exception of signs for inches, which have been replaced by quotation marks, and hyphens, which have been replaced by en dashes.
7. '"If you're the boss, I'm the fool. If I'm the boss, you're the fool."/"The boss pretends to pay me, I pretend to work."/"Let the horse think – it's got a big head." [I don't like to think too much. Let others think if they want to.]/"The law is like a pillar – you can't jump over it, but you can bypass it."/"One law for the rich, and another for the poor."/"The Party is the honour and conscience of the Soviet people."/"The Party is our helmsman."/"Russia is the homeland of elephants."/"Soviet – that means: excellent."/"As long as you provide someone, we'll find a case on him." [In the sense that anyone can be imprisoned.]/"You may reap or forge – you'll get f*** all." [In the sense that in the Soviet Union it doesn't make sense to work at all.]'
8. 'I remember a slogan in front of the *partkom* building in the village of Bogatoe in what was then the Kuibyshevskaia oblast. This was at the height of the Khrushchev era and therefore everywhere we heard: "There will be meat and sour cream, sausages of all sorts, if maize and beans are sown everywhere!" But in the village grocery store there was no trace of sugar, no sausages, no food at all, only canned sprats and vodka. A loaf of bread, if you were lucky to get one, was called *shlakoblok* ["cinder block"] – that's how black, clotted, raw and heavy it was. The local canteen had just boiled noodles – cold and slimy. After a few months of this sort of food, I got jaundice.'
9. 'I remember a huge photo of Leonid Brezhnev with an outstretched arm and the inscription "You are on the right path, comrades!" Nothing special about that, if the hand of Leonid Brezhnev hadn't been pointing at a well-known local pub . . .'
10. 'In our garrison town, there were two slogans. One stood about 300 metres from the other. 1-Our goal (target) is communism, 2-Every bomb – right on target.' This example turns up in a couple of variants in other forums, which may indicate that it is, perhaps, an urban legend or anecdote (which does not mean that such a situation could or did not arise, of course).
11. '"People and Party are one!" This neon sign on the *Gorkom* building did not turn off even when the area had no electricity.'

12. 'I saw a slogan in neon in Vladikavkaz – The victory of communism is inevitable. (Sounds fatalistic in a way, like death itself.)'
13. The saying stems from Soviet propaganda against jazz.
14. 'From the saxophone to the knife is only one step! The pernicious influence of the West! The party said: We must! The Komsomol said: We will! At a time when the whole country . . . A crucial time. I'm afraid to delve deep into my memories. ;))))'
15. 'I'm a former resident of Kiev. Like the rest of the USSR's population, I was immersed in "Sovietisms". *I even collected the feelings experienced by Soviet people as described by the newspapers*: 1. Fierce approval. 2. Immense gratitude. 3. Boundless devotion. 4. Legitimate pride. 5. Universal support. 6. Major surge. 7. Unwavering self-sacrifice. 8. Sincere gratitude. 9. Monolithic unity. 10. Unprecedented enthusiasm. 11. Unbreakable unity. 12. Complete engagement. 13. Unprecedented heroism. 14. Utmost responsibility. 15. Profound satisfaction. 16. Unflinching confidence in the future. 17. Civil unity. 18. Sole master of his country. 19. Proletarian internationalism. 20. The majesty of the cause you are serving. 21. Revolutionary renewal. 22. Filled with a sense of duty. 23. Profound sorrow. I offer it here, as the collection hasn't been added to for years' (my italics).
16. 'It's actually quite interesting to stroll through the keywords of my memory.'
17. 'Why, with the disappearance of the Soviet era, did we see some words die out, such as *tysiacheletie* (now *millennium*), *beg trustsoi* (now *dzhogging*), *ocharovatel'nyi*, *shikarnyi* (now *glamurnyi*), *pokhod po magazinam* (I dare not utter this one)? Personally, I miss "bifshteks" the most!'

CHAPTER 2

Challenging the Standard

A STANDARD LANGUAGE MODEL

The standard language is a variety of language whose norms are defined by dictionaries and grammars and whose rules and usages are taught in schools. It is a variety which is functionally differentiated, allowing it to operate across wide areas of social interaction, and which is accepted and used by a given community of speakers. This narrative definition incorporates the central elements that constitute a given language's historical standardisation process and its subsequent maintenance, as these are understood according to the subdiscipline of sociolinguistics known as modern standardology: it involves (1) the *selection* (among several varieties) of a norm that is elevated to the status of a standard; (2) the *codification* of the norm, its rules and usages; (3) the *elaboration* of the norm to make it able to fulfil a wide range of functions; and (4) the *acceptance* and active use by the community of the selected norm. The model I summarise here is that of Einar Haugen (1966), and we can note how its use of terminology reflects the presence of several actors in the establishment – and partly also maintenance – of a standard language: politicians, linguists, language users. It is not particularly explicit, however, about the roles of these various actors in standard language development. Haugen's focus, shared by many other models of the standard language, is on linguistic properties.

Meanwhile, the rise of standard languages is closely connected to the rise of the modern nation states, as demonstrated in the case of France by Pierre Bourdieu in his influential study *Language and Symbolic Power* (1991). Bourdieu shows how the formation of a standard language is the result of power struggles, or, put differently, how political struggles have a linguistic dimension, where political unification is shaped by, and shapes, linguistic unification. The essential insight of Bourdieu is the awareness of a network of correspondences between language, power and authority, endowing certain groups in society with the power and legitimacy of defining, regulating and controlling the use of certain varieties of language. Here the official language, or standard variety, sits at the top of the hierarchical system, linked to prestige, education and vital areas of official language usage.

We can note in both of these complementary approaches to standard language development that this variety is conceived of as something abstract, constructed, planned and cultivated. Recent research in standardology has become increasingly aware of the implications of the ideological nature of the standard language, starting with Lesley and James Milroy's radical conception of it as an 'idea in the mind rather than a reality – a set of abstract norms to which actual usage may conform to a greater or lesser extent' (Milroy and Milroy 1985: 22–3; see also Milroy 2001). One of the lessons to be drawn from the conception of the standard language as an 'idea' is that it is always only partially realised. Every instance of standard language usage will, in principle, be unique, and differ from the idea, or 'ideal', of a standard language. In continuation of this perspective, many sociolinguists now prefer the term 'standardisation' – understood as a process – to the term 'standard language' – understood as a distinct variety (Coupland 2014: 80).

A related, but different idea of flexibility and dynamism is also central to Monika Wingender's (2003, 2013) standard language model, inspired by modern standardology, but developed within the empirical framework of the various Slavic standard languages. Wingender's model insists on the graduality of a set of standard language markers and their dynamic correlations. The model consists of four components – the linguistic, functional, social and situative – which are linked by non-hierarchical correlations. The *linguistic component* includes elements such as 'the heterogeneity of the linguistic basis', 'influence of other languages', 'influence of other varieties', 'standardisation' and 'codification'; the *functional component* relates to the 'extension of the functional spheres', 'vitality' and 'official attitudes'; the *social component* embraces 'user attitudes', 'tradition and history' and 'symbolic value'; while the *situative component* has to do with the degree of 'autonomy' and 'sociolinguistic embeddedness'. Wingender explains that any given standard language is dependent on these four components, the elements of which may, however, be present to a stronger or lesser degree. Most important, the model conceives of the standard language as being dependent upon the dynamic interrelationship between elements within and across the four areas (or components):

Ein Idiom, das über eine unzureichend ausgebaute sprachliche Komponente verfügt, kann die ihm zugeordneten Funktionen nicht erfüllen. Ist die funktionale Komponente nicht ausgebaut, wird das Idiom weder sprachpolitisch gestützt, noch wird es verwendet. Ist die soziale Ebene nicht ausgebaut, wird das Idiom von der Sprachgemeinschaft nicht getragen, so dass die Akzeptanzprobleme zu Sprachaufgabe führen. Ist die situative Ebene nicht ausgebaut, ist das Idiom wegen fehlender Autonomie und soziolinguistischer Einbettung bedroht. Verfügt ein Idiom nur über eine sprachliche Basis, wird es weder von den Schöpfern noch den Verwendern gestützt und auch nicht verwendet, ist also ein bloßes Artefakt. (Wingender 2013: 27–8)[1]

In addition to the important notions of dynamism and graduality, we can observe in Wingender's model a shift in attention from the creator element (*Schöpferseite*) towards the interrelationships between this element and the user element (*Verwenderseite*), thus somewhat balancing the strong focus on the political power structures (creator element) that informs classic accounts of standard language development. One of the reasons for this is probably the similar shift in focus from the establishment and history of the standard languages toward their maintenance and existence in – for Wingender's approach – the Slavic-language countries today.

Wingender's dynamic model of a standard language is useful in our context, because it helps us to understand and describe how the various components, and the interrelationships between them, change and affect the Russian standard language in the post-Soviet period. Moreover, it gives us an idea of what is at stake when certain central elements of the standard language are challenged – as we can see in the post-Soviet Russian language situation – and thus contributes to our understanding of the particular nature of the debates about the standard language. It fits well with the notion of *sociolinguistic change* outlined earlier, allowing us to study processes of destandardisation with a view to comprehending broader issues of linguistic and social change, and their interdependencies.

The established Russian term for the standard language is *literaturyi iazyk* ('literary language'),[2] and in order to understand the particular connotations of this notion, we need to take a brief excursion into the history of the Russian standard language.

LITERATURNYI IAZYK – THE STANDARD LANGUAGE IN RUSSIA

From the earliest time of written culture in medieval Rus', the idea of written languages was linked to conceptions of style and text type, Church Slavonic being mainly confined to the sacred genres of hagiography, homiletics and hymnography, while Rusian – the East Slavic vernacular – was used for legal and administrative texts. Not entirely without overlaps, as seen, for example, in historiographical works. We may choose to see the different forms of premodern Rus(s)ian writing as different *languages*, *varieties*, *functional styles* or *registers*,[3] the main point for the present context being that until Peter the Great's reforms in the early eighteenth century, there was no codified standard language of Russian that could serve the wide range of functions required for such an idiom. Peter the Great's reform programme implied a radical secularisation of society, as he took control of the church and introduced a new, secular alphabet, the *grazhdanskii shrift* ('civil type').

More than actively reforming the language itself, Peter the Great's reforms created an entirely new language situation. Russians travelled to the West and people from Western Europe came to Russia, not only bringing with them many new words, but also considerably increasing the usage of foreign languages in Russian society (Offord et al. 2015a, 2015b). In this process Church Slavonic lost its privileged position as the main language of written genres. Furthermore, the changes enabled the phenomenon of 'literature' in the modern sense to emerge, which in turn led to the search for a plurifunctional language that could serve the needs of the new literary genres. The new linguistic situation naturally brought about an increase in metalinguistic reflection, and 'the language question' became an important ingredient in the cultural debates of the late eighteenth and early nineteenth centuries (Gasparov 1984; Uspenskij 1984).

Several factors influenced the subsequent development of a standard language in Russia, a development that involved political initiatives, engagement by scientists and writers, debates on language and national identity and more, but one pragmatic factor was Peter's translation programme of western, mainly scientific, literature.[4] Peter's translation ideal was that of a 'simple language' as opposed to the language of the church, and the question of the role of Church Slavonic elements was to dominate linguistic and cultural debates well into the nineteenth century.

Writer and scientist Mikhail Lomonosov (1711–65), the author of the first (Russian) grammar of Russian (1755), attempted to solve this question by devising a tripartite theory of styles and prescribing the number of Slavonicisms to be used in various genres. Although propagating a classicist three-style system in a time when classicist ideals were fading, Lomonosov's conception of the relationship between genre and style, with the high style – including many Church Slavonic words – reserved for the genres of ode and tragedy, had a great effect on the understanding of the 'language of literature'. Meanwhile, the Petrinian 'simple language' and 'write as you speak' ideals were confronted by the problem that educated society usually spoke French. The opposition Church Slavonic vs Russian was thus compounded by the opposition between French (or other foreign languages) and Russian, while the mantra 'write as you speak' was rather turned around to become 'speak (Russian) as you write', as the emerging spoken standard language oriented itself largely towards the example of written texts (Koreneva 2011: 2029). In this process the linguistic norm came to be, to a large degree, associated with the 'language of literature'. Most important, the status of literature rose to extreme heights during the nineteenth century, as translated literature was superseded by original Russian masterpieces in poetry (the Golden Age) and later prose (Realism), and Russian literature became world literature.

We should not forget, however, that throughout the nineteenth century, loanwords from the West continued to enter the Russian language. The fact that, between 1803 and 1880, twenty-two dictionaries of foreign words were published in Russia (Koreneva 2011: 2033) testifies to their topicality.

We should also note the continuous interest and involvement of the rulers in questions related to language – Peter the Great's reforms had wide-ranging consequences for linguistic and literary development, Catherine the Great initiated purist campaigns, Paul I tried to establish a canon of Russian political vocabulary, Nicholas I was involved in a new Polish orthography. This did not change with the new regime after the Bolshevik revolution. Both Lenin and Stalin wrote articles on Russian language and linguistics, and Stalin's reference to contemporary language as being basically the same as 'the language of Pushkin' contributed to the legitimisation of the model role of classic, nineteenth-century literature in questions of language and style, and gave rise to the mythology of Pushkin as the founder of the modern Russian standard language:

Со времени смерти Пушкина прошло свыше ста лет. [. . .] Однако если взять, например, русский язык, то он за этот большой промежуток времени не претерпел какой-либо ломки и современный русский язык по своей структуре мало чем отличается от языка Пушкина. (Stalin 1950: 18–19)[5]

The responses to Stalin's dictum by authoritative linguists and literary scholars of the time further confirmed both the close link between the language of literature and the standard language, and Pushkin's particular status in the history of the Russian *literaturnyi iazyk*:

Конечно, не только художественная литература участвует в выработке литературного языка, но именно ей принадлежит первое место в этом процессе. (Tomashevskii 1951: 177)[6]

Роль Пушкина в истории литературного языка известна: Пушкин – создатель русского литературного языка и родоначальник новой русской литературы. [. . .] Язык Пушкина, за ничтожными исключениями, остается литературной нормой доныне. (Tomashevskii 1951: 185)[7]

Even if we disregard the ideological constraints that form the context of such remarks, it is clear that the close connection between the standard language and the language of literature, as well as the role of literature in establishing and maintaining the standard language, have remained a strong tradition in Russia.

Over the last hundred years, Russian linguistics has seen three waves of sociolinguistic research which have impacted on the understanding of the standard language: first, in the initial post-revolutionary decade, with works such as Afanasii Selishchev's *Iazyk revoliutsionnoi epokhi* (*The Language of the Revolutionary Epoch*, 1928); in the 1960s, culminating in the four-volume *Russkii iazyk i sovetskoe obshchestvo* (*Russian Language and Soviet Society*, 1968) under the editorship of Mikhail Panov; and then in the post-Soviet period, with a wealth of publications, suffice it to name here only the book series *Russkii iazyk segodnia* (*The Russian Language Today*, 2000–12) edited by Leonid Krysin, of which five volumes have so far been published. In modern Russian sociolinguistics, the understanding of the standard language has acquired a greater social dimension (Paulsen 2009: 76), with questions related to speaker competence and social variables coming to the fore, together with a heightened interest in linguistic variation in both written and spoken genres.

Throughout the Soviet period there was a strong emphasis on the study and maintenance of the standard language not only from a theoretical point of view. Linguists were also actively involved in creating and upholding a programme of language cultivation that affected broad sections of society. Dmitrii Ushakov's four-volume *Tolkovyi slovar' russkogo iazyka* (*Interpretive Dictionary of the Russian Language*, 1935–40) had laid the foundations for a lexicography with a strong normative stance, prescribing correct usage and supplying words and expressions with stylistic and often ideologically charged markers. Textbooks, manuals and popular journals provided guidance for correct usage, while newspaper columns, telephone hotlines and, starting from the 1960s, radio shows offered 'linguistic first aid', responding to questions from the public (Gorham 2014: 25–47). Within this highly ideologised language culture, the standard language stood at the absolute pinnacle of the hierarchy, associated with education, prestige and the highest cultural capital.

In the Introduction we saw how, in the first post-Soviet decade, the hegemony of the standard language was challenged by a massive influx of foreign loanwords and a general celebration of stylistic and lexical diversity, spurring a lively debate that focused on 'the state of the Russian language' generally, and expressed concern about the standard language, in particular. In the remainder of this chapter, I shall take a closer look at a more recent, and more specific, example from among the many ways in which the standard language has been challenged, namely the internet slang known as *iazyk padonkov*, a particular form of jargon that reached its peak of popularity in the years 2004–6. We will also look at a couple of reactions to the anarchistic *padonki* style.

FROM PADONKI TO GRAMMAR NAZIS: LINGUISTIC FASHIONS OF THE 2000s–2010s

The *iazyk padonkov* ('scumbag language'), one of the most conspicuous linguistic phenomena on the Russian internet, originated in the early 2000s on the platform Fuck.ru. The padonki slang is based on the phonetic approximation of standard orthography to spoken Russian, in the manner of афтар (*aftar* '[blog post] author') instead of автор (*avtor*), кросафчег/кросавчег (*krosafcheg/krosavcheg*) instead of красавчик (*krasavchik* 'good-looker'), превед (*preved*) instead of привет (*privet* 'hi!'),[8] as well as a number of fixed expressions that signal a positive or negative response to, for example, a blog posting, such as афтар выпей йаду! (*aftar vypei iadu!* 'author, drink poison!'), афтар пеши исчо (*aftar peshi ischo* 'author, write more'), and the like. This deliberate distortion of the standard orthographic norm quickly acquired its own linguistic term, *errative*, coined by Gasan Guseinov (2005) and has been described and studied in some detail by linguists, cultural historians and padonki users themselves (Sokolovskii 2008; Zvereva 2009; Hristova 2011; Krongauz 2013; Berdicevskis and Zvereva 2014; Kukulin 2016).[9]

Is it possible to trace a particular linguistic attitude in the padonki slang? One should keep in mind that, at the peak of its popularity, there were tens of thousands of users of this 'language', some devoted 'padonki' themselves, others occasional users who employed the most perspicuous elements of it. Padonki elements also entered the world of offline mass media and advertising (Kukulin 2016: 233). If asked, members of the various groups of users would certainly express quite different views on the character and function of *iazyk padonkov* and on its relationship to the standard language. Now, in the post-padonki era, we see that elements of the padonki style and attitude have entered a broad range of online genres and fused with other online slangs and styles.[10] In other words, the style is less marked and perceived rather as part of a general online style of writing and interacting.

Nevertheless, it is possible to identify certain typical characteristics of a classic padonki-style linguistic practice. These usually involve linguistic play and creativity, displaying a certain *laissez-faire* approach, sometimes bordering on a more challenging attitude.[11] Using the padonki style is not just a question of exchanging written standards for spoken ones. 'Hypercorrect' examples such as кросафчег do it 'the other way round', demonstrating the systematic yet playful will to break the norms of standard orthography. Moreover, the padonki style displays not only orthographic distortion, but also ample use of verbal profanity, alternative semantisation, creative word formation, and other linguistic and stylistic devices. In other words, the padonki manner challenges the norms of the standard language on a number of levels. This becomes clearer when we look at the reactions to it.

The linguistic practice of *iazyk padonkov* activated a metalinguistic discourse and led to reactions. This is not surprising. Cross-culturally, orthography – the main target of the padonki style – is considered a core element in literacy with a strong social meaning (Sebba 2007: 12), while *gramotnost'* – the ability to read and write correctly – has traditionally enjoyed high prestige in Russian culture. Moreover, orthography, as Mark Sebba points out, is a microcosm of language itself, 'where the issues of history, identity, ethnicity, culture and politics which pervade language are also prominent' (Sebba 2007: 167). When orthography is attacked, much is at stake. Reactions came in the form of critical comments or pro-et-contra discussions[12] and in concrete counter-actions. An example of the latter is a counter-action of 2005–6 called я умею говорить по-русски ('I can speak Russian'), flagging banners on websites and blogs with slogans such as Хочу читать тексты на правильном русском языке ('I wish to read texts in proper Russian'); Афтар – стань Автором! ('*Aftar* – become an Author'); Пишу по-русски ('I write Russian'); «Афтарам» просьба не беспокоить ('*Aftars* are requested not to disturb'). Even more interesting are internal discussions among the users of *iazyk padonkov* about the norms implied by this – more often than not – conscious norm-breaking, in other words, the 'wrong' and 'right' forms of *iazyk padonkov* are being debated (Zvereva 2009). This indicates that the sense of linguistic norms is (still) very strong; it is taken most seriously by the norm-police and by norm-breakers. This is understandable in view of the long Russian tradition of linguistic cultivation sketched above, a centralised linguistic policy, the high status of normative and authoritative dictionaries and grammars, and the promotion of the one and only correct standard language in schools.

Curiously, we can note that even the famous internet Манифезд антиграматнасти ('Manifesto of antiliteracy'), written in padonki-style orthography, displays many features reminiscent of that very same culture; here, the opponents of the 'antiliteracy' of the padonki are accused of not being literate or cultured and are ridiculed: проста у них харошие спилчекиры! ('they just have good spellcheckers!'); furthermore, there is a reference to the 'mighty Russian language' (в магучим нашым изыке), which recalls Turgenev's famous phrase великий и могучий русский язык ('great and mighty Russian language'), probably the most frequently occurring quotation in the Russian language debate, cited regularly by the voices that call for measures and regulations; and finally there is a quotation from Pushkin, the number one authority on the modern Russian standard language: Биз грамотичискай ашипки я русскай речи ни люблю!, писал наш лудший паэт Аликсандыр Сиргеич Пушкин ('I don't love Russian speech without grammatical mistakes!, wrote our best poet, Aleksandr Sergeich Pushkin') ('Manifezd antigramatnasti' 1999).

The 'Manifesto of antiliteracy' also reflects, of course, an ironical attitude, not untypical of the 'higher levels' of padonki practice,[13] where the mass phenomenon becomes an art form – ORFO-art in Nadezhda Shapovalova's (2008) term. In this sense it may become something of a functional style, which can be turned on and off as the speaker moves in and out of virtual reality: «падонство» – не бандитская организация и не тоталитарный культ, а игра в некую реальность, наигравшись в которую, человек возвращается к обычной жизни (Shyshkin 2006).[14]

Moreover, as apologists of the padonki style have repeatedly observed, in order to distort the norms of the standard language not only 'correctly', but also with elegance and wit, one has to know the rules and then break them in a conscious and sophisticated way:

«Аффтары» не просто безграмотны – они безграмотны намеренно и подчеркнуто. [...] Намеренное искажение слова

> – тоже элемент творчества, попытка преобразить слово, довести до абсурда, придать ему новое звучание, новый эмоциональный оттенок и новый смысл – или антисмысл. Даже нецензурные выражения у «падонков» искажаются настолько, что предстают в комическом виде, теряя часть негативного заряда. (Shyshkin 2006)[15]

We see that the norm-breaking of the padonki style is at the same time norm-preserving, or, at least, is eager to preserve its own particular norms. The strong metalinguistic awareness of this particular slang is expressed both explicitly, in discussions among padonki users (Zvereva 2009), and implicitly, in the strong element of play in padonki usage. Linguistic play is an essential component of metalinguistic awareness and a device of which we can expect to find ample evidence in the writers of fiction analysed later in this book. Meanwhile, let us look at a very different reaction to the broader tendency of norm-breaking in online and offline Russian language usage, a social network group of self-imposed language mavens called the grammar nazis.

Although the grammar nazis are present on several sites of the Runet (the Russian-language segment of the internet), their main online home is an open, but moderated group in VKontakte, the Russian clone of Facebook, with 103,027 members (as of June 2017). Here, members post pictures, links, quotations and statements as evidence of linguistic mistakes. The mistakes are displayed and occasionally provided with a commentary, but the comment field is closed, so that other members are limited to reacting by liking or sharing the post.[16]

The most conspicuous characteristic of the grammar nazi group is its use of Nazi symbols and concepts in its visual and verbal self-promotion. Words and phrases such as *grammar-vagen* (by analogy with 'Gaswagen') and *grammatik makht frai* ('Grammatik macht frei', by analogy with 'Arbeit macht frei') are used together with images featuring the imperial eagle (*Reichsadler*) and a swastika-like G symbol, adding to the aggressive verbal style which we can also observe in many comments.[17]

At the same time, the image of the grammar nazis as an aggressive society of people ruthlessly engaged in linguistic cultivation is constructed largely in dialogue with the satirical 'anti-encyclopedia' Lurkomor'e and similar sites. For example, even if members of the VKontakte group suggest from time to time that various mistakes should be entered on the *rasstrel'nyi grammaticheskii spisok* ('grammar death list'), it is only on Lurkomor'e that we can find a complete directory listing hundreds of classic mistakes that qualify one's name to be put on the list ('Rasstrel'nyi grammaticheskii spisok' 2013). The 'table of ranks' circulating on the Runet in various blogs and directories also contributes to making the grammar nazis appear to be a more organised and structured society than it really is. The list features titles and designations such as *Grammar iugend – mal'chik-otlichnik, devochka-otlichnitsa* ('Grammar Jugend – excellent pupil'), *Obershturmfiurer – starshii prepodavatel' filfaka universiteta* ('Obersturmführer – senior lecturer at a university's faculty of philology'), *Oberfiurer – rabotnik Instituta russkogo iazyka, so-avtor slovaria* ('Oberführer – employee at the [Academy of Sciences'] Russian Language Institute, co-author of a dictionary'), and so forth ('Grammaticheskii natsizm' 2009).

The eagerness to expose and laugh at orthographic or grammatical mistakes made by others, often voiced in quite rude if not vulgar language – that is, in a style that does not adhere at all to the norms of the standard language – makes the grammar nazis typical representatives of the global phenomenon of online hate speech. At the same time, they have certain elements in common with the popular Russian tradition of linguistic cultivation (*kul'tura rechi*). We can see this if we look at the kind of mistakes they focus on. The mistakes that upset the grammar nazis usually concern spelling and punctuation conventions, and to a lesser degree, morphological errors; they also include classic native-speaker difficulties, such as distinguishing between the semantics of *nadet'* ('put on') and *odet'* ('dress', e.g. a child), or recognising indeclinable nouns. The grammar nazis seem to be less concerned about other norms usually associated with standard language ideology. Thus, they defend the use of obscene language (*mat*) as a necessary means of 'shocking people' and attracting attention to the cause of linguistic cultivation. In a survey conducted by the group's administrator in 2013, the majority of members voted in favour of using obscene language (54.6 per cent), some were fine with it without using it themselves (29 per cent), while only 20.4 per cent were explicitly against the use of *mat* in the group ('Snachala chitaem' 2013).

The grammar nazis emerge as typical practitioners of folk or lay linguistic metadiscourse. They are ardent, radical, sometimes ruthless. But they are also playful and humorous. This can be seen in the VKontakte group, where posts not only feature gross or less gross mistakes, but frequently also mistakes that are funny.

The combination of playfulness and use of radical nazi symbolism is, of course, a highly challenging one. Still, I would argue that the grammar nazis repeat, in a paradoxical way, the norm-breaking attitude of the padonki, even if their norm-breaking is more focused on the use of symbols. They further share a degree of playfulness, as well as a love of obscene language. And, while differing drastically in their views on standard-language orthography, both movements – in their radical pro and contra attitudes – demonstrate the strong symbolic value and linguistic ideology attached to this particular aspect of Russian linguistic culture.

NOTES

1. 'A variety that has an insufficiently developed linguistic component cannot fulfil the functions assigned to it. If the functional component is not developed, the variety is neither supported by language policy, nor is it used. If the social level is not developed, the variety is not borne by the language community, and problems of acceptance will lead to the language being abandoned. If the situative level is not developed, the variety is threatened by the lack of autonomy and sociolinguistic embedding. If a variety has only a linguistic basis, it is neither supported by the creators or the users, nor is it used, and is therefore a mere artefact.'
2. There are also the terms *standardnyi iazyk* or (*iazykovoi*) *standard* ('standard language' or '[linguistic] standard'), but these are much less used in the Russian linguistic tradition (see Krysin 2013: 147, n. 2). For a history of the term *literaturnyi iazyk* in Russian linguistics, see Paulsen (2009: 67–80) and, in juxtaposition with the term 'standard language' in the western tradition, Germanova (2011).
3. See Franklin (2002: 83–9) for a discussion of the various views on the interrelationship between Church Slavonic and East Slavonic.
4. Only 4 per cent of the literature translated during the reign of Peter the Great was *belles lettres* (Koreneva 2011: 2026).
5. 'More than a hundred years have passed since the death of Pushkin. [. . .] But if we take the Russian language, for example, it did not suffer any demolition over this long period of time and the structure of the modern Russian language differs little from the language of Pushkin.' For a detailed assessment of the ideological implications of this 'master-text' of Soviet linguistics, see Dobrenko (2015a).
6. 'Obviously, literary fiction not only participates in the making of the standard language, it plays a lead role in that process.'
7. 'Pushkin's role in the history of the standard language is well known: Pushkin is the creator of the Russian standard language and the founding father of modern Russian literature [. . .] With insignificant exceptions, the language of Pushkin equals the standard norm up to our own day.'
8. In addition to being distorted versions of regular Russian words, these slang words also have particular meanings, of course, and some of them function as internet memes.
9. Kukulin (2016) traces the prehistory and development of the padonki style with particular attention to its political and ideological aspects.
10. Maksim Krongauz employs the term *olbanskii* in this broader sense of online slang(s). This development is in line with findings in diachronic studies of digital writing, where phases showing innovative deviations from the standard language are followed by more conventional, standard-oriented practices (Androutsopoulos 2014: 30).
11. One should probably also mention the purely technical motivations, at least at the

beginning of the 'padonki era', of using non-standard spelling in order to escape filters and indexation tools.
12. Such as the informal survey on the 'Liubov' i nenavist" page ('Pro iazyk "padonkov"' 2006–).
13. The author of the padonki manifesto is Aleksei Andreev – also known by his internet pseudonym Mercy Shelley (*Mersi Shelli*) – poet, prose writer and the initiator of several internet projects.
14. 'The "padonki style" is neither a gangsters' organisation nor a totalitarian cult, but playing around with a kind of reality, and after you've played for a while, you return to ordinary life.'
15. 'The "*afftory*" are not just illiterate, they are deliberately and emphatically illiterate. [. . .] The deliberate distortion of the word is also an element of art, an attempt to transform the word, reduce it to an absurdity, provide it with a new sound, a new emotional nuance and new meaning–or antimeaning. Even the "*padonki's*" uncensored expressions are distorted to such an extent that they appear in a comic form, thereby losing some of their negative charge.'
16. The group seems to have been established in 2011 and featured open commentary fields for some time.
17. For a discussion of the grammar nazi society as a platform for online verbal aggression, see Efremov and Scharlaj (2016).

PART II

Language, Writers and Fiction

CHAPTER 3

Languages and Styles of Post-Soviet Russian Prose

If not overnight, then within a relatively short time, Russian society of the late perestroika and early post-Soviet years saw a radical shift in linguistic attitudes and drastic changes in official language usage: a huge number of words became historicisms, pre-revolutionary terms returned from oblivion and foreign loanwords flooded the language; the ideological substance of slogans and concepts was questioned, topics formerly kept secret could be named by their real names and taboo areas became the subject of official speech; non-standard elements challenged the hegemony of written and spoken standard Russian.

All this made 'the state of the language' stand out as a topic of discussion for a great many people, groups and institutions, as we saw in the Introduction. The focus on the language question in turn increased the general level of metalinguistic activity in society (Vepreva 2005: 8). What about professional language users, such as the writers? People who express themselves in language not only in order to communicate, but in order to create? In what sense, and to what degree, are artistic language practices such as the writing of novels influenced by changes in the language culture of a given society? The main task of this book is to answer this question by examining the ways in which verbal art engages in the language question on the level of metalinguistic activity – or in other words, to investigate how literary texts can be read as a response to the language question. In this chapter, meanwhile, I will try to characterise the language itself of this fiction and ask in what ways it reflects, or has been affected by, the changes in the language culture. In order to do this in a meaningful way, we need to operate with a broad understanding of 'language' as it overlaps with the concepts of 'style' and 'genre', dimensions of post-Soviet literary culture that are also influenced by the predominating themes and topics of the texts themselves. Let us start, therefore, by sketching the shifts in literary culture that impacted on the themes, languages and styles of post-Soviet literature, before looking in more detail at the literary texts themselves. In view of the multifarious literary landscape of Russian prose writing of the last two to three decades, it is impossible to be exhaustive. I shall therefore limit myself to outlining a couple of influential trends, with particular attention to some important shifts in emphasis in the literary texts' language and style within the post-Soviet era as a whole.

FROM ETHICS TO AESTHETICS – AND BACK?

The sociopolitical events of the perestroika and early post-Soviet years led to significant changes affecting literature and literary institutions in Russia. First of all, the fall of censorship precipitated the return of previously banned literature. By the time the Soviet Union collapsed, Solzhenitsyn, Pasternak, Bulgakov, Akhmatova, Tsvetaeva, Mandel'shtam, Platonov and Brodsky had finally all been published in Russia. Also, as the texts of the late Soviet underground moved from shelves and drawers to printed books, conceptualist and postmodern writers such as Venedikt Erofeev (born 1938), Lev Rubinshtein (born 1947), Vladimir Sorokin (born 1955), Viktor Erofeev (born 1947) and Dmitrii Prigov (1940–2007) had a significant impact on the literary trends and debates of the 'new', contemporary, often labelled 'alternative' literature of the 1990s (e.g. Porter 1994). It was essential for this literature to liberate itself from the burden of the past. This burden did not only imply censorship. It was equally important to many writers to liberate literature from the responsibilities that had accompanied the task of being a great writer in the Russian tradition. As pinpointed by Viktor Erofeev in his much-discussed essay of 1990, 'A Wake for Soviet Literature', Russian literature needed to liberate itself from the didactic, moralistic, edificatory tasks that had made writers so much more than writers:

> В России литератор вообще часто был призван исполнять сразу несколько должностей одновременно: быть и священником, и прокурором, и социологом, и экспертом по вопросам любви и брака, и экономистом, и мистиком. Он был настолько всем, что нередко оказывался никем именно как литератор. (Erofeev 1990)[1]

Even if the literature of the turbulent, post-ideological 1990s did not play the same role as in earlier debates about social affairs, history or religion, many writers and critics were searching for a new set of values, a new 'idea'. Inspired by the West, by pre-revolutionary Russian culture or other sources, writers and intellectuals moved into new directions, or engaged in a radical demontage of old structures. Much space was given over to playful experiments with languages, styles and ideologies.

In the 2000s, many prose writers turned away from the most radical experiments with language, style and theme and placed themselves within various types of mainstream literature. One can also detect a neoconservative or neotraditionalist turn in Russian literature from the beginning of the millennium, while the most progressive movements within Russian literature today are perhaps found in poetry and drama (Dobrenko and Lipovetsky 2015: 11). In addition to the neorealist trends of recent years, there seems to be a greater degree of social, ethical or political commitment among many writers, both in their writing and in their lives. This can be seen when writers take a stance in political matters by writing open letters or newspaper articles – for example, Mikhail Shishkin (born 1961) – or engage in social or educational work – for example, Liudmila Ulitskaia (born 1943). Also, the new contexts in which reading and publishing take place contribute to a closer association of works of literature with the lives and opinions of their authors. In many cases book publications are contextualised by their authors' new media presence in blogs, social media, or on publishers' websites. Comprehensive literary sites such as Vavilon.ru, OpenSpace.ru, Colta.ru, Gorky.media, Litterratura.org and others present and discuss literature in the context of literary criticism and sociopolitical commentary, thus providing a new, transformed version of the 'thick journals' of earlier times (while many of the 'thick journals' have themselves successfully moved to digital platforms).

Russia has a long and illustrious tradition of prose writing, and it is clear that its main styles of writing did not simply disappear with the dissolution of the Soviet Union. Nevertheless, political and social change has led to dramatic shifts not only in the literary market, but also in linguistic culture and language policies, and writers of fiction have needed to reorient themselves in the new conditions and respond, in one way or another, to the changed situation. As with any watershed event like the collapse of the Soviet Union, an important issue in the 'new' or 'post-' literature is, necessarily, the relationship to 'what was before'. Thus, many works of literature can be classified according to their relationship to the Soviet past, most obviously according to their different approaches to *Vergangenheitsbewältigung* – the coming to terms with the past with regard to historical events, disasters, terror or daily life – but also in a linguistic sense. During this process, Soviet traditions continued to be 'recycled', to use Dobrenko's (2015b) formulation, for several decades:

'Literature essentially continued to rework the Soviet world and the Soviet myth, which continued to be both a point of repulsion and a magnet' (Dobrenko 2015b: 21). Yet, the relationship to 'the Soviet' as something belonging to the past has redefined the ways in which writers have dealt with this legacy, including its linguistic dimensions. As a result, in the decades following the break-up of the Soviet Union we may witness a continual process of transforming the legacies of the past.

Among the changes to which post-Soviet literature may be expected to respond is the tradition of the 'language of literature' as such, the *iazyk literatury* and its strong yet complex connections with the *literaturnyi iazyk*, or standard language. We will explore this interrelationship more closely in the next chapter. Meanwhile, the linguistic practices within and beyond the standard language in post-Soviet prose writing will be an issue than runs through many of the categories or groups of texts listed below. The following subchapters describe a selection of influential trends but are in no way exhaustive. Moreover, the 'genres' or groups of texts chosen are not 'pure styles'. In fiction (as in life), styles and languages, just like themes and ideologies, often overlap. In addition, there is always a greater or lesser tension between a predominant linguistic style or variety (including that used in everyday speech or more specific social settings) and the liberties, experiments and idiosyncrasies of the individual writer and of the individual literary text. It is often in this dynamic space that metareflections about language arise, either explicitly or implicitly.

DECONSTRUCTIONS OF LANGUAGE: POSTMODERNISM AND BEYOND

The various shades of Russian postmodernism include a number of Sots-Art writers and artists of the late Soviet underground and became much-discussed phenomena in the first post-Soviet decade.[2] Russian postmodernists relish the deconstruction of totalities, not least totalitarian language culture, playfully laying bare the absurdities of ideological talk. Clichés and slogans are deconstructed and emptied of content, or juxtaposed in paradoxical ways in order to demonstrate their emptiness.

Vladimir Sorokin may serve as an example. He published a number of novels in the 1990s (mainly written in the 1980s) that contributed in radical ways to the dismantling of grand narratives and ideological discourses. Especially in his early works, Sorokin was famous for his sudden 'turns': a narrative starts off in a classic style and proceeds up to a point, whereupon it breaks abruptly with conventions, norms and readers' expectations. In some cases the narrative turns into a depiction of extremely grotesque, brutal or violent events as in *Roman* (*Roman/ Novel*, 1994), where the protagonist kills a whole village on the night of his own wedding; in others, the device leads to some kind of verbal deconstruction, as in *Norma* (*Norm*, 1994), where the last four pages are covered only by a long aaaaaaaaaaaaaaaaa. Sorokin's norm-breaking is particularly forceful in the realm of language, where the deconstruction of ideological discourses goes hand in hand with an abundant use of obscene and vulgar vocabulary. As Mikhail Ryklin notes in an early assessment of Sorokin's *oeuvre*, исключительным «героем» этого рода литературы является дискурс, речь до субъекта и объекта, речь как перформативное действие (Ryklin 1992: 100).³ Ryklin's point is demonstrated, for example, in the short novel *Ochered'* (*The Queue*, 1985). *The Queue* consists entirely of words spoken in a Soviet queue: fragments of dialogues, jokes, conversations, which add up to a narrative whole without there being a narrative proper. When nothing is spoken, for instance at night when people are asleep (yes, Soviet queues could last for days), the pages are empty. The queue is a collective body of speech, able to move, sleep, eat and act. For all its conceptualist poetics, *The Queue* also demonstrates the creative powers of language. This is a tendency that has grown stronger with each of Sorokin's works of the late 1990s and 2000s. While Sorokin may still be radical in his destructive devices designed to strip language of its conventional, representative function, his later works display an increasingly inquisitive attitude towards the creative, even procreative forces of language (Kalinin 2013).

Extreme linguistic diversity is one way of deconstructing hegemonic ideas of linguistic norms and of the proximity of literary language to the standard language. Sorokin is certainly not alone in juxtaposing disparate strata of language. Linguistic heterogeneity is characteristic of a number of 'postmodern' writers, ranging from the group of late Soviet writers gathered around the *Metropol'* event of 1979 – an initiative which created a forum for uncensored literary texts – that included Evgenii Popov (born 1946), Viktor Erofeev, Iuz Aleshkovskii (born 1929) and others, to writers of the 1990s such as Viktor Pelevin (born 1962), Liudmila Petrushevskaia (born 1938) and Valeriia Narbikova (born 1958).

Beyond the deconstruction of language(s), Russian postmodernist techniques include the rejection of authoritative storytelling, play with irony and metacommentary, and creative myth-making; we can sense the latter clearly in Viktor Pelevin's *Pokolenie P* (*Generation P*, 1999), one of the key texts of the literary 1990s. Returning to the focus on linguistic matters, Pelevin's novel is a prime example of a text displaying a playful attitude towards the question of foreign loanwords, a recurrent theme in the language debates. In Pelevin's novel foreign loans are combined with non-standard linguistic elements such as profanity, slang and colloquial speech, creating thereby an amalgam that was much discussed in the reception of the novel (Paulsen 2009: 137–52). Critics discussed both the status of Pelevin's language with regard to predominant understandings of 'the language of literature' (was he to be considered a writer at all?) and its relationship to other varieties of language, such as colloquial Russian in general or the more specific jargon of commercial advertisement (did the language of the novel reflect this world adequately?). These discussions highlight the contested status of the literary norm – to which we shall return in the next chapter – and how devices of deconstruction and estrangement can target not only ideological language, but also the representational powers of language, on the one hand, and ideas and expectations about the literary norm, on the other.

TRANSFORMATIONS OF REALISM

Writers continue to endow us with artistic interpretations of human life in the tradition of Russian realism also after the break-up of the Soviet Union. But, as Mark Lipovetsky (2011: 177) points out, we are dealing with 'transformations of realism', of the classic epic tradition of storytelling. Some of these writers were published during Soviet times, others first appeared in print after the disintegration of the Soviet Union, while since the turn of the century, there has been a new, strong realist trend in Russian prose writing. 'Transformations of the realist tradition' imply that these trends are not identical to what existed before, and, naturally, they differ among themselves. Writers such as Vladimir Makanin (born 1937) or Mikhail Shishkin use a wide range of modernist techniques in creating their epic worlds. Liudmila Ulitskaia and Tat'iana Tolstaia (born 1951) employ a number of postmodernist devices, while Liudmila Petrushevskaia writes hyper-naturalistic stories and novels on bleak subject matter. Aleksei Slapovskii's (born 1957) works capture different social milieus in a colloquial style, and a great variety of prose works explore the genre of the historical novel, including those of Aleksei Ivanov (born 1969).

Vladimir Makanin's *Andegraund, ili geroi nashego vremeni* (*Underground, or a Hero of Our Time*, 1999) is a representative example of a psychological epic dealing with the post-Soviet condition. Но что, если в наши дни человек и впрямь учится жить без литературы? (Makanin [1999] 2010: 403).[4] The question is asked by the narrator of Makanin's book, Petrovich, a former writer of the underground who has not been able to publish during Soviet times. Neither does he publish now, he just *is* a writer: Я не пишу. Я бросил. Но машинка, старая подружка (она еще югославка), придает мне некий статус (Makanin [1999] 2010: 30).[5] The figure of Petrovich illustrates the question pinpointed by the title of Andrew Wachtel's book *Remaining Relevant after Communism: The Role of the Writer in Eastern Europe* (2006). Wachtel discusses the changing role of writers in the post-Soviet condition and in the context of the traditionally perceived high status of literature and writing in Russia and Eastern Europe. In *Underground* Makanin explores the tension between individual freedom and society's constraints as experienced by Petrovich, a representative of the underground intelligentsia. The novel opens in medias res, Petrovich is reading Heidegger in Russian translation when he is interrupted by a visit from his drunken neighbour. This combination of 'high' and 'low' is characteristic of the novel as a whole, including on the level of language and style. Makanin writes in the classic realist style, but does not hesitate to bring in slang and colloquial language. Such broadening of the linguistic registers is a general tendency that was not entirely absent, of course, from Russian literature of the Soviet era, but frequently unpublishable, since the requirements of Socialist Realism affected not only the content, but also the language and style of a literary work.

Another 'transformative' approach to the epic style is found in Mikhail Shishkin's prose, grounded in the tradition of the classic novel, but employing bold modernist devices. Shishkin's most famous book, *Venerin volos* (*Maidenhair*, 2005), has rather a complex narrative and temporal structure. The character that brings together the different stories is an interpreter who translates for asylum-seekers arriving in Switzerland from former Soviet republics. In a parallel strand, he reports on his reading of the Greek historian Xenophon, introduces his own memoirs, and writes letters to his son that are never sent. On yet another parallel level, he tells the life story of the romance singer Isabella Iur'eva, based on her own memoirs, which convey a kind of private history of the twentieth century. Let us look at a passage early in the novel, which also expresses some of Shishkin's aesthetic and linguistic philosophy in quite explicit terms:

Пусть говорящие фиктивны, но говоримое реально. Правда есть только там, где ее скрывают. Хорошо, люди не настоящие, но истории, истории-то настоящие! [. . .] Какая разница, с кем это было? Это всегда будет верняком. Люди здесь ни при чем, это истории бывают настоящие и не настоящие.

> Просто нужно рассказать настоящую историю. Все как было. И ничего не придумывать. Мы есть то, что мы говорим. Свежеструганая судьба набита никому не нужными людьми, как ковчег, все остальное – хлябь. Мы станем тем, что будет занесено в протокол. Словами. (Shishkin 2005: 25)[6]

These are the words of one of the asylum-seekers, whose stories the interpreter translates for the Swiss official who will decide their fates. We may note the strong belief in the sheer power of words that exudes from this passage – as from many other passages in Shishkin's fiction, sometimes as explicit as here, at other times more indirect or implicit. The most explicit of Shishkin's logocentric statements is probably the epigraph to the novel: Ибо словом был создан мир, и словом воскреснем (Откровение Варуха, сына Нерии. 4, XLII) (Shishkin 2005).[7] This is a form of 'verbal optimism' that stands in stark contrast to the deconstructive approaches to language that we examined above.[8]

Transformations of realist styles may also be observed in a more recent turn towards authenticity seen, for example, in the new prison literature – a revival of a classic genre in Russian writing (Schmid 2015: 75–8). Iana Iakovleva's (born 1971) *Neelektronnye pis'ma* (*Non-electronic Letters*, 2008) is one example. The turn towards authenticity includes works that border on semi-fictional and/or (semi)-autobiographical writing. A fine example is Eduard Kochergin's (born 1937) *Kreshchennye krestami* (*Christened with Crosses*, 2009), an account of the author's six-year flight from an orphanage in Siberia to his mother in Leningrad. The trek across post-war Soviet Russia is dangerous and eventful, and the young boy survives thanks to his artistic creativity and help from other people. The text is a peculiar mixture of autobiography and strong fictional and poetic qualities. The descriptions reflect the child's perspective and are precise, direct and authentic, but with great visual richness. The colourful language of the dialogues, meanwhile, abounds in the jargon of orphans, train thieves and other criminals. All these elements combine to convey a child's simple but moving experience of post-war Russia.

Finally, a great number of Russian prose works reflect various contemporary colloquial styles, such as urban vernaculars, slang, criminal jargon, and so on. Well represented among these are popular literature genres, in particular crime fiction, action thrillers, mystery novels and glamour literature, to which I devote a separate section below.

VARIETIES OF NATIONALIST DISCOURSE

Until recently, western scholars have been more attracted to, and thus paid more attention to, the experimental, aesthetically demanding, works of liberal writers, including Sorokin, Pelevin or Viktor Erofeev, than to nationalistically inclined, conservative writers, such as Valentin Rasputin (born 1937), Aleksei Prokhanov (born 1938) or Sergei Shargunov (born 1980). Putin's return to the presidency in 2012, the Crimean crisis of 2014 and the accompanying developments in Russian politics and international affairs, however, have increased the attention we pay to politically engaged literature (and art more generally), including both the oppositional, protest factions and the more nationalistically disposed, patriotic groups and individuals. The political establishment has also paid much more attention to culture, including literature and writers, over the last decade, designing cultural programmes and devising incentives to promote the creation of culture that adheres to particular, pre-defined values such as patriotism, national heritage or 'traditional spiritual and moral values'.

From the point of view of language and style, the quite different works in this realm are generally characterised by the author's or narrator's often engaged, involved voice, which has an impact on the rhetorical tone of the text. Sometimes the style is aggressive, grandiose and even pompous, sometimes it indulges in nostalgia for bygone times.

In Zakhar Prilepin's (born 1975) prose we find an original blend of Soviet-style (at times almost Socialist Realist) narrative combined with romantic imagery in the service of ideologically charged storytelling. One of his most discussed works, his 2006 novel *San'kia* is, in terms of genre, a 'combination of a road story, a coming of age romance, and an action thriller' (Oushakine 2015: 46). *San'kia* tells the story of Sasha Tishin, a young member of a nationalist party working for a new revolution in Russia, a cause for which Sasha and his allies at the violent end of the novel sacrifice their lives. Violence and brutal force are described naturalistically and in minute detail, but also given an ideological, romantic justification (Oushakine 2015: 47). Prilepin, himself a member of the National Bolshevik Party, has voiced clear requirements that literature should be obliged to engage in social and political questions.

No less ideologically radical, but more openly didactic is the prose of Sergei Shargunov, who combines his literary career with editorial and journalistic work, as well as political activism. Prilepin and Shargunov together edit the internet portal 'Free Press', a radical political platform intended to offer an alternative to mainstream media outlets.

Shargunov's prose is realistic and often explicit and straightforward on the value-oriented level, as the following brief dialogue from his novel *1993* (2013) demonstrates:

– Мы сюда пришли за русских. Если победят демократы, умрут миллионы русских, а на наше место приедут миллионы нерусских. [. . .]
– Россия без русских – это не Россия! – Он перехватил автомат левой рукой и небрежно выбросил перед собой правую: – Слава России! (Shargunov 2013: 326)[9]

The passage reflects Serguei Oushakine's point about typical characters of ideological novels: they are often 'seen functionally – as vehicles of policies, important as long as they help advance the goals of the mission' (Oushakine 2015: 56). This makes the language of even more extreme nationalist prose works, such as Aleksandr Prokhanov's novels, come close to political treatises or journalistic writing, even if written formally – as in Prokhanov's (in)famous *Gospodin Geksogen* (*Mr Hexogen*, 2002) – in a literary genre, in the case of *Mr Hexogen* an action-thriller.

A more artistically ambitious style is found in Pavel Krusanov's work. Krusanov (born 1961) is part of the Petersburg Fundamentalist movement, a conservative circle with a clear neoimperialist ideology focused on the resurrection of Russia's cultural and historical traditions. His novel *Ukus angela* (*The Bite of the Angel*, 2000), part of a trilogy that came out in the years 2000–5, tells the story of Ivan Nekitaev's rise to power in a Russian Empire which has expanded to comprise parts of China, Turkey and the Balkans, including Constantinople/Istanbul. Nekitaev is conceived in a grotesquely depicted scene of intercourse between his dying Russian father and Chinese mother. His Chinese and non-Chinese origins (his surname is a negation of China, while 'Ivan' points to Russia) allude to the Eurasian dimension of Krusanov's imperial vision (Schmid 2015: 151). Krusanov challenges the realist tradition with regard to both content and style. His 'alternative history' of Russia verges on magical realism, while he also employs postmodern devices such as playful myth-making. Krusanov's peculiar blend of styles and devices makes the nationalist and neoimperialist ideology of his books more ambiguous than in Shargunov's prose, as the disparate reactions to his books by Russian literary critics also indicate.

THE LANGUAGE AND LITERATURE OF GLAMOUR

The radical opposite of the socially and politically engaged literature of recent years is the literature of glamour. In 2007 the word *glamur* became the Russian 'word of the year' (Epstein 2007). It refers to the lifestyle of the *nouveau riche*, a new social elite characterised by expensive clothes, glossy magazines, luxurious houses, exotic travel, social intercourse with celebrities and a largely indifferent attitude to political and societal challenges. This world has also entered the realm of literature, where it has found expression in the popular genre of glamour literature (Rudova 2008b), a type of prose fiction that depicts the luxurious life of – more often than not – rich women (or wives of rich men). The most successful among the glamour writers is Oksana Robski (born 1968), whose debut novel *Casual* (2005) became a bestseller and was much discussed among Russian readers and critics. Robski quickly established her fame as the author of glamour fiction with subsequent books entitled *Pro liuboff/on* (*On Love-off/on*, 2005), *Den' schast'ia – zavtra* (*The Day of Happiness Is Tomorrow*, 2006), *Casual 2* (2007) and others before publishing – together with Kseniia Sobchak, a TV celebrity and, more recently, political activist – the handbook *Zamuzh za millionera* (*Marry a Millionaire*, 2007).

In Tatiana Mikhailova's words, glamour literature 'emphasizes surface and downplays substance' (Mikhailova 2011: 92). Let us look at how this style manifests itself in a brief passage from Robski's *Casual*:

> Потом были похороны. И снова слезы. И слезы нашей дочери. И траурное платье с черными очками. И перезвон колоколов на Ваганьковском. И прощание вдовы с умершим.
> Я целовала его. И обнимала. И говорила ему что-то. И он благоухал туалетной водой, которую я принесла по просьбе патологоанатомов вместе с костюмом и обувью. И привычный запах его парфюма перемешался с запахом специального грима и чего-то еще, и я знала, что этот терпкий запах моего горя я не забуду никогда.
> Я прощалась с ним.
> Кто-то сказал мне потом, что я ласкала его так, что казалось – он должен ожить.
> Но его похоронили.
> А я вернулась домой. (Robski 2005: 12)[10]

Glamour fiction is a type of text where the narrative is less developed, while chattering descriptions and impressions of the glamorous world and lifestyle become all the more important. Maksim Krongauz points out the frequency of positive evaluative words, mostly adjectives and adverbs, describing the shining, flawless world of glamour, for example *elitnyi*, *ekskliusivnyi* (Krongauz 2007: 21–2). Some of these words change their semantics in the process of being employed to describe the thrills of glamour, as we can see from all the new combinations of the word *elitnyi*, such as *elitnye kholodil'niki* ('elite refrigerators') or *elitnye okna* ('elite windows') (Krongauz 2007: 22). The discourse of glamour dominated Russian public debates in the years following the publication of Robski's *Casual* to such a degree that some commentators spoke of a 'new national idea' – something Russia had been searching for since the break-up of the Soviet Union (Rudova 2008a). Such comments could also be harshly critical. The culture, or cult, of glamour has been severely criticised by writers and intellectuals. Lev Rubinshtein (2009), for example, calls *glamur* an official ideology functioning as a substitute for a viable national idea. Both Rubinshtein and Krongauz criticise the culture of glamour for its evaluative stance, which is also expressed in its linguistic traits. The ideology of glamour, Rubinshtein holds, implies a legitimisation of social and moral irresponsibility. In its language and perception, glamour culture is expressed in 'talk that bypasses the ears' and 'glances that miss the thing' (Rubinshtein 2009).

Reformulating Rubinshtein's point, we could say that glamour literature features a 'polished' linguistic style describing a world that for most people has more the quality of a dream or utopia than of a real place. Its shallow content matter and lack of social responsibility makes it very different in form and style from the realistic, dark literature of the 1990s in the style of *chernukha*, from the various shades of more recent patriotic prose, but also from the variety of other popular genres such as crime fiction, which, however unrealistic and constructed in terms of plot, nevertheless reflect, more often than not, distinct subcultures and milieus and their languages in a realistic manner. For even if glamour literature seeks to represent the 'real' world of glamour, it is so shallow and stylised that even the 'real' wives of Rublevka, the Moscow district of the *nouveau riche*, have complained, accusing Robski's portrayal of their world of inauthenticity (Mikhailova 2011: 96).

This chapter has provided a glimpse into the variety of styles and languages of post-Soviet Russian prose writing. These texts can be read as reflections of contemporary language usage, and, by implication, of the post-Soviet linguistic condition. Their vocabulary and style, their way of structuring dialogue and narrative are, first of all, parts of their individual poetics; but they are also, I would argue, influenced by the language situation of the milieu they depict, including particular sociolects, linguistic norm-breaking, or the use of foreign loans, as well as by the more general trends in linguistic usage of contemporary society. Later in this book, we will move to a different level and form of reflexivity when we read post-Soviet Russian prose texts as 'responses' to the linguistic situation and the language debates in particular. We should not forget, however, the 'reflection' of the contemporary linguistic condition offered by the language of a given prose text, which together with explicit or implicit metalinguistic statements, contributes to its response to the language question.

NOTES

1. 'In Russia the writer was frequently called upon to fulfil several duties simultaneously: to be a priest, a prosecutor, a sociologist, an expert in questions of love and marriage, an economist, a mystic. He was so much everything else that he was often no one when it came to simply being a writer.'
2. Many works of the Soviet underground of the late 1960s and 1970s were later described as postmodernist when, in the 1990s, the term entered the public debate about literature and its languages. See Lipovetsky (2015: 145–6).
3. 'the sole "hero" of this type of literature is discourse, speech prior to subject and object, speech as a performative act'.
4. 'What would happen if people of our time really learnt to live without literature?'
5. 'I don't write. I've quit that. But the typewriter, my old friend (she's Yugoslav) gives me a certain status.'
6. 'Those speaking may be fictitious, but what they say is real. Truth lies only in where it is concealed. Fine, the people aren't real but the stories, oh the stories are! [. . .] What difference does it make who it happened to? It's always a sure thing. The people here are irrelevant. It's the stories that can be authentic or not. You just need to tell an authentic story. Just the way it happened. And not invent anything. We are what we say. A freshly planned destiny is packed with people no one needs, like an ark; all the rest is the floodgates of heaven. We become what is written in the transcript. The words' (Shishkin 2012: 24).
7. 'For by the word was the world created, and by the word shall we be resurrected. – Revelation of Baruch ben Neriah. 4, XLII' (Shishkin 2012).
8. For a more detailed assessment of Shishkin's philosophy of language, see Lunde (2016).
9. '– We've come here for the Russians. If the democrats win, millions of Russians will die, and in our place there will arrive millions of non-Russians. [. . .] Russia without Russians – that's not Russia! He grabbed his machine gun with his left hand and threw out his right with a casual movement: – Glory to Russia!'
10. 'Then came the funeral. More tears, and the tears of our daughter. Black dress and sunglasses. The ringing of the bells at the Vagankovskoe Cemetery. The widow's farewell. I kissed and embraced him. I whispered something to him. He smelled of his favorite cologne, which the funeral director had told me to bring along with his suit and shoes. The familiar fragrance mixed with the smell of the undertaker's

make-up and something else, and I knew that I would never forget the scent of my grief. I bade him farewell. Someone told me later that he expected him to come alive from the way I caressed him. But they buried him. And I went home' (Robski 2006: 7).

CHAPTER 4

The Literary Norm

The relationship between the norms of the standard language and the norms of the language of literature is characterised by both proximity and distance. On the one hand, authoritative, normative dictionaries and grammars often use examples from prose fiction or even poetry to illustrate language usage, while, on the other, fictional texts – prose and poetry – have long played an important norm-maintaining, exemplary role in general education. The traditional status of the language of literature with regard to the norms of the standard language is quintessentially expressed in the preface to the Academy Grammar of Russian published in 1980:

> крупные национальные писатели – это те носители литературного языка, которые знают и чувствуют его лучше других. Именно под их пером прежде всего осуществляется отбор языковых средств из общенационального языка в язык литературный, проверка этих средств на жизненность, точность и выразительность. Поэтому язык художественной литературы, ее классиков, лучших национальных прозаиков и поэтов должен быть признан важнейшим источником для изучения литературного языка. (Shvedova 1980: 13)[1]

This view of the (ideal) relationship between the language of literature and the standard language has been challenged in the post-Soviet era by several processes of sociolinguistic change. These have to do both with the marginalisation of literature in Russian society today, and with the linguistic and stylistic make-up of the wide variety of contemporary literary texts. Still, authoritative voices in public discussions about language continue to highlight the privileged role of the standard language, as well as the idea that there should be a close link between the language of literature and the norms of the standard language. This can be seen, for example, in recent trends in linguistic and cultural policies, a topic to which I will return towards the end of this chapter. We will start, however, by examining a couple of different views on the relationship between the norms of the standard language and the language of literature.

When justifying the inclusion of writers in a broad survey on attitudes towards the language situation in post-Soviet Russia, the editors of the volume *Pisateli o iazyke* (*Writers on Language*, 2004), argue for a close interrelationship between linguistic awareness and the language of literature. A high degree of linguistic awareness and reflection is seen here as a general characteristic of literary texts and interpreted precisely in terms of the traditionally perceived proximity between the language of literature and the standard language: Чем больше внимания уделяет человек тому, как он говорит, тем литературнее характер его говорения. Художественная речь в этом отношении наиболее литературна, ведь она отличается максимальной степенью творческой обработки, а следовательно – и осознанности (Bukharkin 2004: 4).[2] The quotation is difficult to translate and illustrates the double meaning of the term *literaturnyi*, referring to both 'literary language' (language as used in literature) and 'standard language'. In order to make the distinction clear, the quotation above also includes the more specific notion of *khudozhestvennaia rech'* (literally 'artistic speech'), to refer to the language of literature, a term reminiscent of dichotomous conceptions of linguistic functions in early twentieth-century literary theories. In this particular context, however, *khudozhestvennaia rech'* is conceived of not so much as a function of language, in the sense of Roman Jakobson or the formalists, but rather as an attitude towards language.

In opposition to this view, we also find the idea that, on the contrary, literature is not a place where one should adhere to established norms, but rather a venue for linguistic experimentation, necessary for the evolution of the language. Russian philologist Liudmila Zubova argues that literature is the place where the norm and the liberties of writers ought to meet, or rather, to collide:

> в языке художественных текстов всегда создается напряжение, связанное с конфликтом между общим и личным, традицией и новаторством. [. . .] Конфликт между привычным и новым, нормой и поэтическими вольностями в художественном тексте накладывается на неизбежное противоречие между

стабильностью и динамикой языка как двумя условиями его существования и функционирования. (Zubova 1998: 5)³

Russian linguist Viktor Grigor'ev, in providing an encyclopedic definition of 'the language of literature' for an authoritative handbook, suggests there should be separate linguistic norms for literature altogether. According to him, the 'norms of the standard language' can serve only as a 'point zero' for the 'qualitatively different' norms of the language of literature: Нормы литературного языка, фиксируемые в толковых словарях и грамматиках, орфографических и орфоэпических словарях и подобных пособиях, – всего лишь «нулевая точка» эстетического отсчета для качественно иных норм языка художественной литературы (Grigor'ev 1987: 524).⁴ Grigor'ev labels these latter norms 'creative norms' that define the 'attitude towards language' (Grigor'ev 1987: 526), thereby underlining, like Zubova, the creative aspect of norm negotiation in the linguistic practices of literary art. Whereas Zubova, however, insists on a creative, productive conflict between the norms of the standard language and the linguistic practices of the writer, Grigor'ev suggests a flexible notion of 'creative norms' as the distinguishing feature of the language of literature. Zubova, in turn, echoes the stance of the editors of *Writers on Language* when she highlights the great attention that poets, in particular, pay to language: поэты – самые внимательные к языку люди (Zubova 2010: 5).⁵

The quoted scholars represent two divergent views on the interrelationship between the norms of the standard language and the language of literature: one argues that literature, by definition, is so attentive towards its own linguistic usage that norm-breaking is out of the question, whereas the other holds that precisely because of its great attention to linguistic usage, literature is a laboratory for linguistic experimentation, challenging, breaking and negotiating norms in order to promote language development and linguistic flexibility.

The opposing views are not merely the result of different understandings of the nature of linguistic norms, or of the norms of the standard language. They also have to do with different evaluations of norm-breaking in literary texts: is it to be avoided or encouraged? Art critic Boris Groys explains this in clear and simple terms: the breaking of norms can certainly be seen as something exclusively 'bad'; however, he argues, 'it can also be understood as something original, new, alternative, and – accordingly – something with value in an innovative exchange' (Grois 1993: 225).

The 'double relationship' between norms and the language of literature is reflected in public discussions about the language of literature in the post-Soviet era, especially in the literary criticism of the 1990s (Paulsen 2009). As Birgit Menzel (2001: 119) points out, the aesthetic and formal aspects of literature had not been the centre of attention in Soviet and perestroika literary criticism, which had focused more on ideology and ethics. With the changing focus of literature itself – as we saw in the previous chapter – and its 'liberation' from its traditionally perceived responsibility in terms of ideology, philosophy, religion and much more, so too the attention of literary critics, and the public in general, has moved towards questions of form, language and style.

The main topics in these discussions mirror the main topics of the language debates in general: the number of foreign loanwords, the presence of non-standard elements such as slang, jargon or verbal profanity, and the fate of Sovietspeak language and phraseology. There are, however, also more complex responses. As Martin Paulsen (2009: 156) points out in his study of Russian literary critics of the 1990s, several norm-breaking writers of the time were actually hailed by some critics as protectors and reinventors of the language: in their radical exposure of Soviet-style clichés, writers such as Vladimir Sorokin and Viktor Erofeev were seen as 'liberating' Russian from the Soviet linguistic legacy, and their norm-breaking was thus viewed as a necessary, almost purifying exercise. Here we can sense traces of conflicting views on the role of the writers with regard to the norm, similar to what we identified in the opposing views of linguists on the same topic. Whereas the conflicting views of the linguists referred to above are real enough, however, the seemingly paradoxical assessments of the language of post-Soviet Russian prose may also reflect readers' and critics' different views on the nature and constitutive elements of the standard language, or more broadly, of the language of literature. To some critics, adherence to the norms in the language of literature has to do with straightforward questions of grammatical style, semantic coherence and stylistic consistency. To others, literature and its language are associated with broader questions of identity and tradition in the linguistic and cultural history of Russian, and with the classics of Russian nineteenth- and twentieth-century literature. It is probably on this latter account that the liberating forces of radical norm-breaking – directed, more often than not, against the ideologised language of the Soviet era – are seen as positive and necessary for the future of the language.

Since the early 2000s, questions related to the norms of the standard language, and, more recently, also those of the language of literature, have entered a very different field, namely that of language policies and, more specifically, language legislation.

During the first post-Soviet decade, the state showed little interest in questions of language legislation. This changed with the turn of the century, and in 2005, Russia adopted a Law on the State Language of the Russian Federation, following several years of lively debate within and outside parliament as well as various commissions.[6] Research on both the debate and the law itself has convincingly demonstrated the ideological ends behind the legislative initiative, and how ideas about language policy are closely intertwined with notions of national identity and statehood (Gorham 2006, 2014; Ryazanova-Clarke 2006b). Linguist Maksim Krongauz went as far as naming the 2005 law a 'patriotic utterance' (Krongauz 2005). Suffice it to cite one of the many typical statements of the time, emphasising the role of language in questions of national identity, and even national security. This is how Professor Liudmila Verbitskaia, then vice chancellor of St Petersburg State University, assessed the situation in an interview of 2005: Я глубоко убеждена, сохранить русский язык – это не просто сохранить язык, по существу это означает сохранить Россию. Проблемы сохранения, сбережения русского языка – это проблемы безопасности России (Verbitskaia and Kuznechevskii 2005).[7]

The 'patriotic' trend in government involvement in the cultural sphere, including linguistic matters, has grown stronger in recent years. With regard to language legislation, we can sense already in the process leading up to the 2005 law a shift of focus away from questions about minority languages and linguistic rights, fields that sociolinguists usually refer to as *status planning*, towards a greater emphasis on questions about standardisation, norms, and the nature and functional realms of Russian, questions that belong to the field of *corpus planning*. One of the most contested paragraphs in the discussions about the 2005 law concerned the norms of the standard language: 6. При использовании русского языка как государственного языка Российской Федерации не допускается использование слов и выражений, не соответствующих нормам современного русского литературного языка, за исключением иностранных слов, не имеющих общеупотребительных аналогов в русском языке ('Zakon 2005').[8]

As Lara Ryazanova-Clarke points out (2006b: 49), the text reflects a very non-linguistic, unprofessional view of language, suggesting that 'loanwords' either have 'equivalents' or not, in which case they are acceptable. Furthermore, it refers to 'the norms of the standard language' without specifying, but with a clear underlying assumption that such a concept is possible to define and refer to. While it is obvious that a text of law cannot engage in details of definition on the same level as, say, a scholarly linguistic text, the wording of the law's text seems to reflect an understanding of 'the norms of the standard language' as a fixed and defined entity. At the same time, the concept emerges as a rather abstract notion of the highest variety of the language within a hierarchy of varieties. In other words, the text of the law reflects a linguistic culture informed by a standard language ideology in the sense of the Milroys (see Chapter 2).

The vagueness surrounding the definitions of 'norm', 'standard' and – for that matter – 'state language' becomes all the more obvious if we look at the implementation of the law. Who is to decide whether a foreign word has a Russian equivalent? Who is to define if a particular instance of language usage complies with 'the norms of contemporary standard Russian'? Although linguistic expertise was used in particular cases (see Levontina 2005; Baranov 2007; Weiss 2008, 2009; Brinev 2009), the Law on the Russian Language seems to have been notoriously difficult to implement. Its role as part of the nation-building project of the Russian state from the 2000s onwards, however, is quite clear and as such, the law should be seen in the context of the many state initiatives promoting linguistic cultivation mentioned in the Introduction: the 'Russkii iazyk' federal target programme (2002–20), the internet site Gramota.ru, 'Year of the Russian Language 2007', and so forth.

In recent years, the trend has been to widen the contexts where the 'state language' of the Russian Federation is used, and where Russian, according to the law, has to 'adhere to the norms of the standard language'. These contexts, as we shall see in Chapter 6, now include essential parts of culture, such as literature, music and theatre.[9] In other words, the state seeks to define by law, at least in theory, the language of literature. This is a long way from the 'creative norms' of the language of literature as suggested by Grigor'ev, the view of literature as a laboratory for linguistic experiments proposed by Zubova, or even the literary critics' conception of norm-breaking writers as protectors of the language. These different ideas and views about what the norms of the language of literature should be can certainly be explained in terms of language ideology, genre or context. By bringing them together here, my point is to give an idea of the wide range of linguistic attitudes, policies and beliefs with which writers are confronted, and to which they may be expected to respond, in Russian society today. In the following chapters, we will explore their responses, explicit and implicit, in more detail.

NOTES

1. '[T]he great national writers are the ones who know and feel the standard language better than others. It is above all in their writing that the process of selecting elements from the national language for the standard language takes place, as well as the probing of these elements with regard to their viability, accuracy and expressivity. That is why the language of literature, of the classics, of the best national prose writers and poets must be regarded as the most important source for the study of the standard language.'
2. 'The more attention one pays to the way one speaks, the more "literary" [adhering to the standard norm] the character of one's speech will be. The language of literature is the most literary [is closest to the literary/standard language] in this sense, since it is distinguished by a maximal degree of creative elaboration, and, consequently, also by awareness.'
3. '[I]n the language of literary texts there is always a tension connected to the conflict between the general and the personal, between tradition and innovation. [. . .] The conflict between the usual and the new, between the norm and the poetic liberties of a literary text is based on the inevitable opposition between stability and dynamism in language, both conditions *sine qua non* of its existence and functioning.'
4. 'The norms of the standard language, as laid down in dictionaries and grammars, orthographic and orthoepic dictionaries and similar handbooks – these are just a "point zero" for the aesthetic response of the language of literature, which adheres to qualitatively different norms.'
5. 'Poets are the people most attentive to language.'
6. For an assessment of these debates as a reflection of the general debates on the Russian language in the 2000s, see Krongauz (2016b).
7. 'I am deeply convinced that to protect the Russian language – means not just protecting the language, but in fact protecting Russia. The question of protection and preservation of the Russian language is a question of Russia's security.'
8. 'When using Russian as the state language of the Russian Federation, it is forbidden to use words and expressions that do not comply with the norms of contemporary Russian standard language, with the exception of foreign words which do not have commonly used equivalents.'
9. An important caveat: it is not forbidden to *write* or *sell* literature that does not adhere to the norms of the standard language; what is forbidden is to perform or read this literature publicly. See Chapter 6 for details.

PART III

Writers on Language: Telling and Showing

CHAPTER 5

Pisateli o iazyke
Writers' Reflections on Language

Russian writers have long been accorded a special role in the context of the language question. Not only have the classics of Russian literature served as models in standard language education and maintenance, but there has also been a tradition of collecting and publishing statements by professional writers on linguistic matters, often entitled *Pisateli o iazyke* (Writers on language) (Dokusov 1954; Levin and Tomashevskii 1954; Bondareva and Latynina 1974; Nikolina 2000, 2012). Against the background of this historical tradition, this chapter proposes an analysis of statements by post-Soviet Russian writers on the language question. I will give an overview of the main tendencies in the writers' opinions and try to determine whether, as a group, they give special emphasis to particular aspects; here, the current debates on the linguistic situation in Russia provide the backdrop. Furthermore, I will discuss the views of the writers on their own role and status with regard to the language question, expressed explicitly through their statements, or implicitly through their way of expressing their views.

PISATELI O IAZYKE: THE FRAMEWORK FOR DISCUSSION

As professional language practitioners or 'super users' of language, writers are regularly invited to express their opinions on the language question. Let us take a quick, socioliterary glance at the character of the various forums and selection of contributors. This chapter will analyse material from the 2000s, a period when the language debates turned from celebrating or condemning linguistic democratisation and variation to suggesting and debating policies, target programmes and language legislation. It draws on four main sources: the volume *Besedy liubitelei russkogo slova: pisateli o iazyke* (*Symposia of the Lovers of the Russian Word: Writers on Language*, Bogdanov et al. 2004a); a topical section in the journal *Otechestvennye zapiski* entitled 'Pisateli o iazyke' ('Pisateli o iazyke' 2005); a section entitled 'Iazyk nash svoboden' ('Our language is free'), which includes a panel of writers responding to particular questions inspired by an article series on *Rodnaia rech'* ('The mother tongue') featured in 2006 issues of the journal *Znamia* (Amelin et al. 2006); and a round table on 'Iazyk kak glavnyi geroi' ('The language as main hero') published in *Znamia* 7–8, 2007 (Dmitriev et al. 2007).[1] All these forums are quite formal and the writers participate by way of invitation. Also, with the exception of a few lesser-known respondents from the regions participating in the *Besedy* questionnaire, the majority of the participants are well-known, established writers. Key issues in the questionnaires and writers' responses include language cultivation and language planning, the norm, the use of non-standard linguistic elements, and, first and foremost, the relationship between the standard language (*literaturnyi iazyk*) and the language of literature (*iazyk literatury*).

Symposia of the Lovers of the Russian Word: Writers on Language includes questionnaires, interviews and a round-table discussion on the contemporary Russian language. The volume is the outcome of several conferences, research projects and a festival that took place in St Petersburg in the years 2003 and 2004. The main organisers were the Russian Society of Teachers of Russian Language and Literature (ROPRIAL, the national branch of the international MAPRIAL association) with its president Liudmila Verbitskaia and St Petersburg State University (where Verbitskaia was also vice chancellor at the time). It forms part, moreover, of a research project entitled 'The Preservation and Development of the Russian Language as a Foundation for National Security in Russia' as well as the programme 'Russian Language and Contemporary Russia'.[2] The events culminated in a 'Festival of the Russian Word' and the presentation on 23 April 2004 of gold medals to three writers (Vladimir Makanin, Andrei Bitov and Oleg Chukhontsev) for their 'contribution to the development and preservation of the Russian language'. The award ceremony was preceded by a survey in the form of questionnaires, in order to 'determine the attitude of writers to the language' (Bukharkin 2004: 4). Twenty-nine responses were gathered and published in the volume, together with interviews with Bitov, Makanin and Dmitrii Granin, as well as the transcript of a round-table discussion held on 13 April 2003 in the distinguished setting of the Derzhavin Museum, in the very room where the famous *Beseda liubitelei russkogo slova* took place some two hundred years ago.[3]

In terms of its preferences concerning language culture, the framework for the *Symposia* materials is clearly conservative; one of its main organisers, Liudmila Verbitskaia, plays a prominent role in several political initiatives relating to language planning and cultivation, for example by chairing the Russkii Mir Foundation. The Russkii Mir Foundation was established in July 2007 on Putin's initiative. Its purpose is: популяризация русского языка, являющегося национальным достоянием России и важным элементом российской и мировой культуры, и поддержка программ изучения русского языка в Российской Федерации и за рубежом ('Fond Russkii mir' n.d.).[4] In the preface to the volume, the organisers nevertheless stress the representativeness of the material, secured by means of a careful selection of participants of different orientations, regions and age (Bukharkin 2004: 5).

Otechestvennye zapiski is a critical cultural, rather than literary journal, without any explicit ideological position. The section 'Pisateli o iazyke' forms part of a thematic issue on 'Society in the Mirror of Language', with contributions mainly by linguists and philologists. The section presents a questionnaire (consisting of eight questions) and nine responses to it.[5] The participants were asked to signal their views on the changes in the Russian language and language culture, with regard in particular to foreign loanwords, to the use of non-standard language and to language planning.

Znamia is generally considered to be a liberal journal, a reputation gained mainly from its remarkable change of profile and position during the late 1980s – from organ of the Soviet Union of Writers loyal to the party, specialising in literature on military matters, to one of the main outlets for opinionmakers during perestroika (Menzel 2001: 187). It was also the first journal to claim independence from the Union of Writers. During 2006, the journal featured an article series entitled *Rodnaia rech'* ('The mother tongue'), in which writers, critics and philologists (the chosen authors often belonging to more than one of these groups) were invited to write on the (state of the) Russian language, with contributions on, among other things, 'creative philology' (Mikhail Epstein), linguistic play (Mariia Zakharova) and new technologies (Gasan Guseinov), as well as more general reflections on linguistic development and language culture. In the December issue, the editors clearly felt the need to include 'those, for whom the language is not only a means of communication, but also an ingenious tool for creative work – the poets and prose writers' (Amelin et al. 2006). In addition to stating their views and position with regard to the optimistic versus pessimistic accounts of the state of the Russian language voiced in the article series, the nine writers were asked whether they thought that they could influence the state of Russian and whether they set themselves this task. These questions, along with the invitation to writers to sum up and clarify matters, clearly point to the historical institution of publishing and listening to what writers have to say about the language (situation) – that is, the 'Pisateli o iazyke' tradition outlined above.

Finally, as an extension to its thematic focus on language, *Znamia* was also the initiator, together with the Ministry of Press and Mass Media, of a round table on the language of literature held in March 2007, with the participation of poets and prose writers, critics, linguists and culturologists. The transcript was published in the seventh and eighth issues of *Znamia* 2007. Ten participants (of whom six were writers) were asked to: обсудить состояние языка современной русской литературы и его взаимодействие с жизнью, с той языковой средой, из которой он вырастает и на которую, в свою очередь, оказывает (во всяком случае, предполагается, что должен оказывать) влияние (Dmitriev et al. 2007).[6] In such statements we can clearly sense, again, the underlying expectations of writers and their dual role model as professional language users and opinionmakers in the language debates. Moreover, it is noteworthy that the round table is entitled 'Russkii literaturnyi', which is the established term for 'standard language', while the topic of discussion is clearly the language of literature. As laid out in Chapter 4, the two terms are closely interrelated in the Russian tradition, at least historically. Whether this is still perceived to be the case by the writers themselves is one of the questions we can now ask when considering their concrete statements.

STANDARD LANGUAGE, THE LANGUAGE OF LITERATURE, AND LANGUAGE POLICY

Just as with other participants in today's debates, we find a variety of voices and positions also among the writers included in these surveys, ranging from the conservative to the relatively liberal. Generally, however, when asked about the concrete situation, challenges and prospects of the Russian language in the post-Soviet era, the writers tend to have a strong belief in the language's ability to take care of itself:

> Язык – в отличие от говорящих и пишущих на нем – может все. [. . .] Если же с языком происходит что-то болезненное (я этого не исключаю), то надо сказать ему прямо. Пусть выкручивается сам. (Vladislav Otroshenko, Znamia)[7]

Нет, нет, я думаю, я уверен, что язык, сам по себе, он сам по себе могучий, живой и огромный. Язык – это океан. И испортить его невозможно. Он сам себя защищает. (Vladimir Makanin, PoIa, interview)[8]

Язык сильнее идеологий. [. . .] Язык любую пагубу переборет. (Oleg Ermakov, Znamia)[9]

Some writers express radical views on the traditional connection between the standard language and the language of literature. In fact, several writers deny that there is a link today, maintaining that Современный русский литературный язык и язык современной русской литературы – два совершенно разных языка (Maksim Amelin, Znamia).[10] For Amelin, the standard language is something fixed and even 'enslaved', an obsolete poetics of the nineteenth and early twentieth centuries, whereas the language of literature should be at the frontiers of linguistic development, constantly featuring new, bold and surprising combinations. He explains:

Первый [i.e. современный русский литературный язык] – намеренно усредненный, закрепощенный разнообразными нормами и правилами, некий выхолощенный конгломерат отживших и устоявшихся индивидуальных поэтик русских писателей XIX – начала XX века, отраженный в общеупотребительных словарях и справочниках по правописанию. [. . .] Второй – напротив, обязан быть чрезвычайно пестрым и свободным, находиться в подвижном, расплавленно-текучем состоянии; в нем одновременно сленг может соседствовать с архаикой, просторечие с заумью, смешиваясь и не мешая друг другу. Языковое творчество призвано разрушать всякую косность и проветривать застоялую затхлость ради создания новых словесных отношений, иногда довольно причудливых и всегда неслыханных. (Maksim Amelin, Znamia)[11]

Amelin's stance is reminiscent of the conceptions of the language of literature that we saw in Liudmila Zubova's and Viktor Grigor'ev's expositions in Chapter 4. Aleksei Tsvetkov goes even further, radically denying the existence of a *literaturnyi iazyk* in literature altogether: Такого языка [литературного IL], конечно же, не существует, это жандармская фикция – ни один стоящий писатель на нем не писал (Aleksei Tsvetkov, Znamia).[12] For all its radicalism, when seen from the perspective of the history of Russian language culture, this position is actually reminiscent of one particular understanding of standard language within standardology (see Chapter 2). The Milroys, we recall, see the process of standardisation as closely linked to an ideology, while the standard language – the result of this process – is considered to be not a reality, but rather an idea. The standard language as an idea or ideal implies that no variety of a given language, including the language of literature, can ever be identical to the standard language. The standard language will, however, affect all kinds of language usage in a given linguistic society (Milroy and Milroy 1985), and thus the relationship of a particular variety to the standard language is always important – as we can see quite clearly in the case of the language of literature.

We noted above a strong confidence in language's ability to take care of itself. It is therefore not surprising that the majority of writers are sceptical about political interference in language planning, censorship or other forms of controlling influence. Language is seen to be not in need of protection or preservation, as demanded by the proponents of language cultivation, but as a living organism, capable of coping with any problem. Moreover, we can sense a deep distrust among the respondents in the ability of bureaucrats and politicians to engage with issues of language cultivation. Thus, in response to the concrete question as to whether the authorities should intervene in language development through regulation and legislation, one writer argues that, Ни в коем случае. Потому что всякое вмешательство государства в развитие языка неминуемо ведет к его упрощению и обеднению. Нечего потакать двоечникам (Mikhail Uspenskii, OZ),[13] while another responds ironically: Государство обязательно должно этим заниматься, вопрос – как, в каких формах. Мероприятие бы предложил: всем чиновникам раз в неделю два часа – курсы русского языка (Aleksei Slapovskii, OZ).[14]

These remarks should also be seen in the light of discussions surrounding the Law on the Russian Language of 2005. In these debates harsh criticism was voiced both on account of ambiguities and vagueness in the wording of the bill, and on account of the linguistic practices of the politicians themselves, as demonstrated in Duma discussions (Ryazanova-Clarke 2006a).

THE NEED FOR A NORM

On the concrete question of whether the language of literature should follow the norms implicit in the codified form of standard language, writers tend to reply by reversing the question, either in negative terms: Считаю, скорее, обратное (Aleksandr Melikhov, PoIa); Скорее наоборот (Andrei Stoliarov, PoIa), or in more positive formulations: Хорошая литература есть норма (Andrei Bitov, PoIa, interview).[15] The writers appear to be slightly provoked by the question, which is not entirely surprising, given the traditional idea of literature as a model for the standard language, rather than the other way round.

Nevertheless, even if the standard language may have lost its position and close link to the language of literature, many writers express the view that some kind of norm or standard is necessary, demonstrating in this context a rather surprising and somewhat utopian belief in the role of dictionaries. Sergei Gandlevskii describes the dictionary as a kind of linguistic guidebook for the writer:

Надо, чтобы была норма – печка, от которой плясать. Словари, прежде всего, которые старались бы поспевать за языком, но вершили бы над каждым новым словом свой авторитетный стилистический суд. Разумеется, пусть там будет слово «эксклюзивный», но пусть оно будет и аттестовано соответствующим образом, чтобы человек, следящий за своей речью, знал, что слово так себе. (Sergei Gandlevskii, OZ)[16]

The first thing we notice is that even if Gandlevskii refers to the dictionaries for authoritative guidance, it is he, the writer, who pronounces the verdict on the sample word *ekskliuzivnyi* as being *tak sebe* ('without much to it'). If we take his message at face value, however, and recall the abundant use of examples in authoritative Soviet-era dictionaries taken from literary texts in order to illustrate words and their meanings, Gandlevskii's attitude – reversing, as it were, the roles of the dictionary and the literature – may seem surprising. But he is not alone in showing this trust in dictionaries. Tsvetkov expresses a similar view, calling, at the same time, for a shift in the mainstream lexicographic tradition from a prescriptive to a descriptive approach:

Хотя литературного языка не существует, в языке развитого общества существуют стилистические слои, и совершенно ясно, что часть лексики, нормально звучащей в бане или в баре, не вполне уместна на дипломатическом банкете. В отсутствие лингвистической жандармерии роль распределения слов по таким слоям [. . .] берут на себя словари. Важно при этом, чтобы [. . .] они были не прескриптивными, как до сих пор в России, а отражающими реальное словоупотребление и его коммуникативную роль. (Aleksei Tsvetkov, Znamia)[17]

It seems that, as a tool that can be consulted by the individual writer on his or her own initiative, dictionaries should replace what is, in the view of these writers, the 'norm police' or censorship institutions – the great majority of writers in my material categorically reject political interference in terms of language planning or control. Even if dictionaries are unlikely to fulfil the functions called for here, this attitude is understandable, given the long history of literary and linguistic censorship in Russia. At the same time, it is symptomatic that the writers are calling for an implied form of standard, a kind of inner censorship or restraint (as can be seen from formulations such as печка, от которой плясать; нормально; не совсем уместно[18]). Perhaps this attitude is a consequence of the many years of strict regulation and monitoring of writing activities during the Soviet period. To the majority of respondents in my material, being a writer seems to require having the necessary degree of self-control and restraint in matters of language and style.

BEYOND NORMS: PROBLEMS AND PROSPECTS OF PROFANITY

While many professional writers emphasise the right and even duty of contemporary literature to experiment with language, explore new combinations and celebrate stylistic diversity, almost all of them demand high standards and strict rules for the ways in which this should be done. Let us look at this tension between freedom and restraint more closely by zooming in on a concrete example, the use of obscene language, or *mat*, in literature.

When asked about the role of *mat* in language use in general, the majority of writers acknowledge its right to exist, allocating its use to 'extreme situations'. For one writer *mat* is necessary in real life only when she is driving, for another because she lives in a *kommunalka*. Furthermore, almost every writer in my material distinguishes, first, between the use of *mat* in everyday language and its use in literature, and, second, between the use of *mat* in the language of the author or narrator and in the speech of the characters:

[использую мат о]чень редко, только для характеристики персонажа, если нет возможности охарактеризовать его иначе. (N. V. Galkina, PoIa)[19]

Я лишь в крайнем случае могу употребить матерное слово в речи персонажа, обычно при этом ставлю точки внутри слова.

Например, *герой говорит корове*: «Ты что, п..да рогатая, наделала?» (Nina Gorlanova, OZ, my italics)[20]

In the last example, the 'extremeness' of the situation is stressed in that the addressee of the vulgar word is not a human being, but a cow.

It is clear from the responses that many writers have a great respect for *mat* as an essential part of the language. Some of them ascribe to it an almost 'sacred' status, referring to relatively widespread romantic ideas about the uniqueness of Russian swearing (see Erofeyev 2003; Gorham 2014: 81–7; Chapter 6). An original variant of profanity's 'sacred' status is provided by Mikhail Shishkin, who sees *mat* as the opposite of the dead, official language of *prikazy* – 'commands' that come from above – and describes the use of *mat* as a sort of living, personal prayer from below. Мат – живая молитва тюремной страны (Mikhail Shishkin, OZ).[21]

As a consequence of this particular conception of obscene language, and in contrast to most language cultivators, who are concerned about the standard language being swamped by vulgar expressions, writers in general worry more about the purity of *mat* itself:

следует расходовать эти перлы бережно и по делу. (Mikhail Uspenskii, OZ)[22]

Одновременно страдает и обсценная лексика – она опресняется, т. е. утрачивает действенность. Скажем, в «Войне и мире» одно, если не ошибаюсь, бранное слово, но оно под пером мастера «работает» на 100 процентов. (Sergei Gandlevskii, OZ)[23]

я бы допустил нецензурную лексику, начиная, скажем, с третьего переиздания книги. Или даже со второго, но не ранее, чем через 10 лет после первого. (Aleksandr Melikhov, PoIa)[24]

The fear of 'desalination' also has to do with the intended effect of enunciating obscene words. As Iurii Levin (1996: 108) points out, using *mat* expressions is a performative speech act: you do not just say something, you also do something.

Similar defences of *mat* are sometimes voiced by linguists as well. Anatolii Baranov of the Institute of Russian Language at the Russian Academy of Sciences argues that 'If *mat* becomes ordinary vocabulary, it will lose its expressive and figurative functions [...] We'll lose a distinctive phenomenon of the Russian language and instead we'll get the kind of ordinary swear words that exist in the European languages' (quoted in Erofeyev 2003).²⁵ In a similar vein, Russian linguist Maksim Krongauz has characterised Russian *mat* as 'national property', lamenting (not without irony, to be sure) that: Случилось самое страшное: мы теряем наше национальное достояние, наш русский мат (Krongauz 2007: 158).²⁶ As we can see, the wish to place restraints on the use of *mat* that we often encounter among the purists is expressed by writers and linguists as well – but with quite different motives.

Meanwhile, it is clear that not just any use of *mat* is embraced by the writers. An elitist conception of high- and low-style verbal obscenity is clearly felt in many responses, where the 'cultured', sophisticated use of *mat* is contrasted with 'simple swearing'. Thus Aleksei Slapovskii holds that, Разница вообще в том, что образованные и культурные люди в мат именно играют (это довольно опасные игры), а прочие на нем говорят так же естественно, как дышат (Aleksei Slapovskii, OZ).²⁷

WRITERS AS A GROUP

Is it at all possible to treat writers as a single group? It is, up to a point. Some writers, admittedly, have very subjective views on the post-Soviet linguistic condition. Consider, for example, Asar Eppel's assessment of new words in contemporary Russian: Хороши слова «бомж» и «крутой», остальные крайне омерзительны (Asar Eppel', OZ).²⁸ Also, opinions on examples of 'good language' in contemporary literature vary significantly: when the twenty-nine critics and writers of the St Petersburg round table were asked to name contemporary writers with 'good language', sixty-five names were given, of whom only five received more than four votes.²⁹

These extremely subjective views may be explained by the fact that the attitude of writers towards language and linguistic issues is a deeply serious and often very personal matter, as becomes clear from many of their statements. Some writers even identify with the Russian language; consider Andrei Dmitriev's comment, replete with pathos: Строй моего языка есть строй моей души, моя речь есть моя мысль, структура языка – это структура моей личности, вообще русский язык – основа моей идентичности (Andrei Dmitriev, OZ).³⁰ Moreover, as in the case of the general language debates, linguistic development is often seen in close connection with cultural and ethical standards: А вообще – глобально: снижение требований народа к языку означает снижение требований к морально-этическим нормам вообще. Деградация языка – деградация нации. Или еще проще: язык – совесть народа. И если он грязен, значит, совесть не чиста *(*Aleksei Slapovskii, OZ).³¹

In Maksim Amelin's statement, this attitude is taken *ad absurdum* when he links events and disasters from the beginning and end of the twentieth century – such as 'the October Revolution', 'gangland lawlessness' (*banditskii bespredel*), and the 'controversies between business units' (*spory khoziastvuiushchikh sub"ektov*) – to what he identifies as the lack of a clearly developed category of constructions using 'be' and 'have' verbs (*byt'* and *imet'*) in Russian, as opposed to the predominant crosslinguistic structures of what is called in linguistics Standard Average European (SAE) (Maksim Amelin, Znamia).

Nevertheless, and in spite of these individual and sometimes disparate tendencies, the group as a whole can be said to (1) express a high confidence in language's ability to take care of itself; (2) have serious reservations about political initiatives in language cultivation or language planning; and (3) advocate a combination of liberal and elitist views on what the language of literature should be. This stance corresponds to the classical views of the Russian intelligentsia. In addition, some of the writers challenge the traditional understanding of the Russian standard language as well as the interrelationship between the standard language and the language of literature.

WRITERS AS OPINIONMAKERS

How do writers understand their own role when it comes to the concrete task of influencing the linguistic practices of Russian language users today? Traditionally, classical Russian literature, by being read and studied in schools, has played an important role in maintaining the standard language. What writers today say about the link between the standard language and the language of literature indicates two things: (1) that the concept of standard language is still very much associated with classical, nineteenth-century literature; and (2) that the task of today's literary language is seen as an altogether different one from that of the past. The altered relationship between the standard language – as traditionally understood by Russian language users – and the language of literature has also been noted by outside observers, for instance by linguists.³² Meanwhile, several writers point to contemporary literature's role in caring for the *future* of the language:

Возможно, необходим такой институт русского языка, где работали бы не только сухие лингвисты, занимающиеся прошлым языка, [...] но и писатели, которые занимались бы его настоящим и даже будущим. (Maksim Amelin, Znamia)³³

Поэзия движется в авангарде языка. Поэт – наиболее сенситивный, чутконюхий, но и самый зыбкий агент в этом мире речи. Если сравнить язык с шахматами, то пешками будут журналисты, турами – прозаики (с их эпической обстоятельностью и неповоротливостью), политики – конями (не знаешь, куда увильнет, и от корявого косноязычия до афоризма один ход), поэт – ферзем: он может ходить, как ему вздумается, он дерзок, размашист и почти всесилен, но его гибель наиболее разительно сказывается на всем балансе сил. (Fedor Ermoshin, Znamia)³⁴

With the fall of the Soviet Union, the collapse of subsidies and privileges for (officially acknowledged) writers, the growing commercialisation of literature, the rise of popular culture, and the differentiation in tastes and reading habits, the status of the writer has changed radically. In today's modern world of mass and new media culture, it is clear that literature is but one among many verbal arenas with a potential impact on the general language culture. The writers' views are realistic on this point, yet both in their attitudes and in their style of responding to the language question, we can still sense the traditional lines of thought of the past. The writers respond to questions about the language situation with a natural authority. Let me round off this chapter by presenting a peculiar piece of further evidence of this attitude, one that also, however, signals the change that is going on with regard to the status of writers in relation to linguistic culture. It appears in a less official publication within the *pisateli o iazyke* genre, namely the private email correspondence between two poets, Aleksandr Levin and Bakhyta Kenzheev, published on Levin's website and also in the journal *Ogonek* (Kenzheev and Levin 2000).³⁵

The main topic of Levin and Kenzheev's email exchange is the influence of foreign loanwords on Russian, with Levin representing the more liberal opinion on loanwords, focusing on their usefulness, on semantic nuances that distinguish foreign loans from their Russian 'equivalents', while Kenzheev embodies the traditionalist, conservatively inclined view of Russian as being in need of cultivation and protection against the influx of western loanwords. What is noteworthy in our context is the fact that the two poets start an email correspondence about the language question with the stated aim of publishing it in a literary journal or newspaper, clearly seeing a public interest in their – the writers' – views on the language situation. At the same time, it is hard to take the ambitious Gogolian title entirely seriously: ВЫБРАННЫЕ МЕСТА ИЗ ПЕРЕПИСКИ БАХЫТА КЕНЖЕЕВА С АЛЕКСАНДРОМ ЛЕВИНЫМ *по вопросу о проникновении в современный русский язык всяких иностранных слов, к порче или же, насупротв того, к вящему процветанию оного всенепременно приводящем* ('Selected passages from a correspondance between Bakhyta Kenzheev and Aleksandr Levin on the question of the intrusion into contemporary Russian of various foreign loanwords, which is leading inevitably to its damage, or, by contrast, to its greater prosperity'). The title is, perhaps, indicative of the need they seem to feel to play down their own seriousness, giving the whole text a slightly ironic touch.

The sociological framework of the four forums that I have discussed featuring writers' opinions on linguistic matters suggests, in turn, that some sections at least of contemporary Russian society – above all the intelligentsia and academic milieus – still have certain expectations and hopes with regard to the role of writers in the language debate. In this section we have dealt with material from the period between 2000 and 2007, with special focus on the years just before and after the adoption of the Law on the Russian Language of 2005. In the next chapter, we shall see how writers – together with other artists and intellectuals – react and respond to a more recent, and also more specific, piece of language legislation, the 2014 law banning the use of *mat* in art.

NOTES

1. I also cite a few statements from a *Znamia* 2007 article under the heading 'Russkii literaturnyi': 'Rech' pro rech'' ('Russian standard language: talk on talk'') by the philologist and writer Fedor Ermoshin (Ermoshin 2007).
2. Other publications originating from these projects include three volumes on the current language situation (Bogdanov et al. 2004b, 2006b; Glazunova et al. 2008) as well as a follow-up to the *Symposia* volume which includes statements on the language situation by the clergy (Bogdanov et al. 2006a).
3. The *Beseda liubitelei russkogo slova* (The Symposium of the Lovers of the Russian Word), established in 1811, was a literary society formed by Aleksandr Shishkov and his followers to combat foreign, in particular French, influence on Russian language and literature.
4. 'the promotion of the Russian language, as Russia's national heritage and a significant aspect of Russian and world culture, and to support Russian language teaching programmes in the Russian Federation and abroad'.
5. Without providing exact figures, the editors note that more writers were invited to participate.

6. 'discuss the state of the language of contemporary Russian literature and its interaction with life, with the linguistic environment in which it emerges, and which it, in turn, influences (at any rate it is supposed that it should do so)'.
7. 'Language – in contrast to those speaking and writing it – is capable of everything. [. . .] Now, if something bad is happening to the language (I cannot exclude that), then we should be frank and let it [i.e. the language] know. Let it work its own way out of it.' Here and in other quotations from writers' statements I refer to the name of the author and the venue of his or her statement, using the following abbreviations: PoIa = Pisateli o iazyke = Bogdanov et al. (2004a); OZ = *Otechestvennye zapiski* = 'Pisateli o iazyke' (2005); Znamia = Amelin et al. (2006); Dmitriev et al. (2007); Ermoshin (2007).
8. 'No, no, I believe, I am convinced that language in itself, in itself is mighty, vital and great. Language is an ocean. And it's impossible to destroy it. It protects itself.'
9. 'Language is stronger than ideology. [. . .] Language will overcome any harm.'
10. 'The *contemporary Russian standard language* and *the language of contemporary Russian literature* are two fundamentally different languages.'
11. 'The first is a kind of emasculated mixture of outmoded and crusted individual poetics of Russian writers of the nineteenth and early twentieth century, deliberately made uniform, enslaved by various norms and rules and represented in commonly used dictionaries and handbooks of orthography. [. . .] The second, by contrast, is obliged to be exceptionally colourful and free, and to be in a dynamic state of flux; in this language, slang may coexist with archaisms, low-style colloquialisms with "transrational" language [*zaum'*], blending and not disturbing each other. Verbal art is summoned to destroy any sluggishness and to ventilate stale mustiness for the sake of the creation of new verbal connections, sometimes rather fanciful and always unprecedented.'
12. 'Such a language [the standard language] does not, of course, exist, it's a despotic fiction. Not a single real writer has ever used it.'
13. 'By no means. Because any interference by the authorities in the development of the language will inevitably lead to its simplification and impoverishment. There is no reason to give in to losers.'
14. 'The authorities should absolutely involve themselves, the question is, in what ways. I would suggest the following measure: every bureaucrat should take Russian language classes – two hours per week.'
15. 'I would rather say the opposite'; 'Rather the opposite'; 'Good literature is the norm.'
16. 'We need a norm, a starting point. Above all, dictionaries that would try to keep up with the language, but which would make their authoritative stylistic judgement on every new word. Of course, the word *ekskliuzivnyi* ['exclusive'] should be included, but it should be qualified accordingly, so that someone who takes great care of his speech, would know that it's a word without much to it.'
17. 'Even if a standard language does not exist, there do exist in the language of a developed society stylistic levels, and it is quite clear that certain words that are all right to use in the bath-house or the bar are not entirely appropriate at a diplomatic banquet. In the absence of a linguistic police, those taking upon themselves the task of distributing words according to such levels [. . .] are the dictionaries. Here it is important that [. . .] they should not be prescriptive, as up to now in Russia, but should reflect the real usage of words and their communicative role.'
18. 'a starting point'; 'all right'; 'not entirely appropriate'.

19. '[I use *mat* v]ery rarely, only in order to describe the characters, if there is no other way of describing them.'
20. 'Only as a last resort would I use a *mat* expression in the speech of a character. When doing so I usually insert dots. For instance, *the hero says to a cow*: "Hey you, you horned c...t, what have you done?"'
21. '*Mat* is the living prayer of the prison country.'
22. 'These pearls should be consumed cautiously and professionally.'
23. 'At the same time the obscene vocabulary is suffering – it becomes desalinated, that is, loses its effectiveness. For instance, in *War and Peace*, if I'm not mistaken, there is one single swearword, but from the master's pen it "works" 100 per cent.'
24. 'I would allow vulgar language starting from, say, the third edition of a book. Or even from the second, but no earlier than ten years after the first.'
25. Erofeev's essay is an excellent introduction to *mat* in Russian culture. Himself a writer, his characterisation in this text of *mat* as 'linguistic theatre, verbal performance art' is also worth noting.
26. 'A most awful thing has happened: we are losing our national property, our Russian *mat*.'
27. 'The difference is that educated and cultivated people play with *mat* (it's a rather dangerous game), while the rest speak *mat* just as naturally as they breathe.'
28. 'The words 'bum' [*bomzh*] and 'cool' [*krutoi*] are good. The rest are extremely disgusting.'
29. This non-agreement is in line with the diversity in preferences documented in reader surveys of the 1990s and 2000s relating to the greatest Russian writers (see Menzel 2005: 48).
30. 'The form of my language is the form of my soul, my speech is my thought, the structure of language is the structure of my personality; generally, the Russian language is the basis of my identity.'
31. 'In fact, globally, people's lowering of demands for the language means a lowering of demands for moral and ethical norms in general. The degradation of language is a degradation of the nation. Or to put it even more simply: the language is the conscience of the people. If it's dirty, this means that the conscience is guilty.'
32. Cf. Irina Levontina's remarks at the round table 'Russkii literaturnyi' (Dmitriev et al. 2007).
33. 'Perhaps we need such an Institute of the Russian Language, where there would work not only dry linguists, dealing with the past of the language, [. . .] but also writers, who would deal with its present and even future.'
34. 'Poetry moves at the forefront of language. The poet is the most sensitive, perceptive, but also the most unstable agent in this world of speech. If we compare language to chess, then the pawns are the journalists, the rooks are the prose writers (with their epic circumstantiality and footdragging), the knights are the politicians (you don't know where they will wriggle out, and from the rude twist of the tongue to the aphorism there is only one step), the queen is the poet: she can move at her own sweet will, she's daring, bold, nearly almighty, but her ruin will have the most dramatic impact on the whole power balance.'
35. I thank Liudmila Zubova for drawing my attention to this material.

CHAPTER 6

Abanamat
Reactions to the Ban on Profanity in Art

On 30 June 2014, Russian writers and artists organised a nationwide event to 'commemorate' profanity (*mat*). The event was called *Abanamat*,[1] and was a response to amendments to the Law on the Russian Language that took effect on 1 July 2014, banning the use of obscene language in film, theatre and public performances of music or literature. Abanamat brought together writers, actors, musicians and artists in nine Russian cities and featured readings and performances of texts, songs, films and plays that contain *mat*. The subtitle of the event solemnly stated that: отныне великий и могучий только на улицах и кухнях (Abanamat, Kazan).[2]

Six months later, amid heated debates over Andrei Zviagintsev's prize-winning film *Leviathan* (2014), prominent members of the Russian film community, including Nikita Mikhalkov and Fedor Bondarchuk, appealed to Prime Minister Dmitrii Medvedev to reconsider and possibly revise the law (Karev and Krizhevskii 2015). *Leviathan* tells a miserable story of suffering, corruption and human cruelty, and abounds in profanity. The film premiered on Russian screens on 5 February 2015, but in order to fulfil the new requirements for distribution certificates, obscene language had to be deleted.[3] Medvedev passed the open letter to Minister of Culture Vladimir Medinskii, but the reaction from the Duma's Culture Committee was negative. Committee chairman Stanislav Govorukhin rejected the appeal by advising artists to recall Turgenev's famous poem in prose:

> Во дни сомнений, во дни тягостных раздумий о судьбах моей родины, – ты один мне поддержка и опора, о великий, могучий, правдивый и свободный русский язык!.. Не будь тебя – как не впасть в отчаяние при виде всего, что совершается дома.

Но нельзя верить, чтобы такой язык не был дан великому народу! (Govorukhin 2015)[4]

These two statements – one being the announcement of the Abanamat protests against the law, the other the official rejection of the filmmakers' appeal to amend it – are but two voices in the larger debate on the role of obscene language in Russia(n) today.[5] Interestingly, the two opposing voices both cite one and the same source in support of their case, Turgenev's famous dictum about 'the great and mighty Russian language'. In Russian language culture over the last hundred years or so, this citation, and in particular the two adjectives 'great and mighty' (*velikii i moguchii*), have indeed been used in many contexts as a synonym for the Russian standard language (*russkii literaturnyi iazyk*).

It is no coincidence that those supporting the legislative attempt to regulate the use of profanity and those opposing it employ the same quotation from Turgenev. The phrase *velikii i moguchii* is often used ironically to refer to Russian obscene language. In spite of the irony, however, there is more than a hint of sincerity involved as well: the set of feelings, values and ideas expressed in this saying reverberates in many people's conception of *russkii mat*, in their romantic ideas about the uniqueness of Russian swearing and verbal obscenity (see Gorham 2014: 81–7). More specifically, among non-standard linguistic registers of Russian, obscenity has a special status, since it not only enjoys authority and legitimacy among users with liberal attitudes towards linguistic variation and non-standard registers, but is also endorsed by larger groups in society, including cultural and intellectual elites that otherwise support the hegemony of the standard language. We saw evidence of this in the writers' statements about language examined in the previous chapter.

Taking the special status of *mat* as its point of departure, this chapter explores reactions from writers, artists and cultural activists to the recent Russian ban on the use of verbal obscenity in film, literature and public performances. It starts with a section presenting and discussing the law and its general reception, before zooming in on Abanamat. This nationwide event was initiated by the editorial team of the Kazan' journal *Karl Fuks*.[6] Beginning on 30 June 2014 between 7 and 9 p.m., readings, performances and films containing *mat* were shown in public, until, at 11.59 p.m., a moment of silence was held for *mat*, before the new law took effect. I examine the discourses surrounding this event and the linguistic attitudes they display. My material consists of promo-videoclips, interviews, and the presentation and discussion of the Abanamat event in social media (Facebook and VKontakte).[7] In examining this event as a response to a concrete institutional initiative in the realm of language regulation, I focus on the following set of questions: to what conceptions of *mat* do participants in the Abanamat events and in the discussions surrounding them adhere, and how do these differ from the conception of verbal obscenity in the context of the law text? What are their reactions to the new law and how are these reactions voiced? What kind of linguistic attitudes do their reactions reveal, and how do these relate to notions of linguistic and social norms? What, in sum, was the agenda of the Abanamat event?

THE LAW AGAINST *MAT*

The so-called new law against *mat* is actually not a new law, but a set of amendments to the 2005 Law on the Russian Language, the law regulating state support for the film industry, and the Code of Administrative Offences ('Zakon 2014').[8] The original Law on the Russian Language already contained a passage forbidding использование слов и выражений, не соответствующих нормам современного русского литературного языка, за исключением иностранных слов, не имеющих общеупотребительных аналогов в русском языке ('Zakon 2005').[9] In the revised law, the phrase в том числе нецензурной брани[10] was added in brackets after 'Russian standard language'. The Law further prescribes how Russian is to be treated when used as 'the state language of the Russian Federation', and article three lists all the instances when this is the case. The most important 2014 addition to the Law on the Russian Language is thus the paragraph adding a set of new contexts where Russian has to adhere to the norms of the standard language: при публичных исполнениях произведений литературы, искусства, народного творчества посредством проведения театрально-зрелищных, культурно-просветительных, зрелищно-развлекательных мероприятий; ('Zakon 2014').[11] Another important detail is that the original Law contained a passage allowing for the use of non-normative language in contexts where this use – является неотъемлемой частью художественного замысла ('Zakon 2005').[12] This passage has now been omitted. The new law does not prohibit writing, publishing or selling books or songs that contain non-normative words. Only their public performance is forbidden. Instead, books and audio-visual material with non-normative words have to include a notice warning of their content (e.g. содержит нецензурную брань[13]).

My deliberate use of different terms for what is actually forbidden reflects the terminological variation in Russian. 'Uncensored swearing' is the technical term used in the texts of the law, whereas in the Duma discussions and accompanying documents, a range of different terms are used: *nenormativnaia leksika* (non-normative vocabulary), *netsenzurnaia leksika/bran'* (uncensored vocabulary/swearing) and *mat* (obscene language/profanity). In the discussions surrounding the Abanamat events, *mat* is by far the most commonly used term.[14] Both *netsenzurnaia* and *nenormativnaia* (*leksika*) are terms that define *mat* by exclusion: 'bad language' that would not pass censorship and/or does not adhere to the norms. They reflect the institutional view of *mat*, whereas '*mat*' (with the accompanying *maternyi iazyk, maternaia bran'* [*mat* language, *mat* swearing]) is the preferred term of 'self-description' among *mat* users.

The question of where to draw the line between forbidden words and 'only bad' but not forbidden expressions was hardly discussed, probably because this issue was considered to have been resolved in connection with the Duma's approval of a law banning *mat* from use in the mass media (2013). In this instance the Federal Service for Supervision of Communications, Information Technology and Mass Media (Roskomnadzor), with the help of linguists from the Russian Academy of Sciences' Russian Language Institute, came up with a list of four words: *khui, pizda, ebat'* and *bliad'*. These words, and their large number of derivatives, are forbidden.[15] In addition, the text of the new law refers to the use of 'independent expertise' where there is any doubt.[16] Offenders against the new law face fines of up to 2,500 rubles for individuals and up to 50,000 rubles for organisations.

With the Russian language's rich resources for inflection, word formation and phraseological creativity, the actual possibilities for forming words and phrases based on these four roots are essentially without limits (see Plutser-Sarno 2001, 2005). This does not make it any less surprising that the Duma discussions do not touch upon the difficult question of drawing lines between the forbidden and the tolerated. Several factors, such as euphemisation or word play, may influence the meaning of a phrase that formally contains a *mat* word, and, vice versa, vagueness or ellipsis may produce statements that clearly function as *mat*, but without using the actual forbidden word.[17]

The motivations for proposing the new law were formulated largely in ethical terms: the prohibition of verbal obscenity should safeguard the moral and spiritual standards of citizens, in particular of children, as summed up by one of the bill's initiators, Zugura Rakhmatullina:

Данная законодательная инициатива действительно направлена прежде всего на культивирование и защиту здоровой духовности и нравственности, на формирование культуры речи и общения в современном обществе. Кроме того, одной из первостепенных задач в настоящее время является защита подрастающего поколения от наступающей антикультуры, в том числе в сфере языка, от явлений, негативно влияющих на его нравственное и духовное самочувствие [. . .] ('Pervoe chtenie' 2013)[18]

This set of motivations fits well with the conservative values highlighted in Russia's recent initiatives in cultural policy, as outlined in the 'Framework for a State Policy of Culture' signed by Vladimir Putin in December 2014 ('Osnovy' 2014), and reflects, as we saw in Chapter 4, a general tendency towards stronger government involvement in the cultural sphere (see Kalinin 2015; Schmid 2015). In the Duma discussions there were few questions about, or reservations expressed against, the legislative proposal, the point most commonly raised being the fact that even in the Russian classics, one may find the occasional *mat* word; in other words, 'what to do about Pushkin?' To this, the proposal's main initiator, Govorukhin, resorting again to the 'moral standard' argument, replied: Вообще, я думаю, за Александра Сергеевича беспокоиться нечего, он абсолютно нравственный человек, и поэтому его книги можно издавать без всяких опасений ('Pervoe chtenie' 2013).[19]

THE ABANAMAT EVENT

The law against *mat* has been widely discussed and debated in the mass media by politicians, journalists, linguists, writers, theatre directors and other artists. Arguments in favour of the law tended to repeat the concern about moral standards, culminating in keywords such as *bezdukhovnost'* ('lack of spiritual culture') and *bespredel* ('lawlessness') (on this term and its broader context, see Borenstein 2008: 197–212; Gorham 2014: 93–7), while arguments against it focused on the dangers of censorship in art. In addition, the usual clichés about *mat* were frequently heard, as emblematically expressed in film-maker Mikhalkov's comment: Русский мат – одно из самых великих изощренных изобретений русского народа, его нельзя перевести на другие языки (Naralenkova 2014).[20]

Thus, writers, actors and artists participated in such debates, but the desire for a more appropriate and forceful form of reaction from the cultural field is evident from the way in which the Abanamat initiative clearly resonated. In the cultural journal *Karl Fuks*'s own official announcement of the event, Abanamat was defined as an открытый проект разножанровых мероприятий, посвященных протесту против цензуры и ограничений во всех формах искусства (Abanamat,

Kazan).²¹ Pavel Florovskii, one of Abanamat's prime initiators, explains the purpose of the project in more detail:

наша задача – привлечь внимание общественности, потому что в данный момент происходят вещи чуждые искусству, которые скорее всего процессы в развитии культуры и искусства в нашей стране могут притормозить [...] даже если мы не добьемся изменения этого закона, мы по крайней мере рассказали всем о его абсурности. ('"Abanamat" – vserossiiskaia aktsiia' 2014)²²

The resonance surrounding the event can be clearly felt in social media, where new discussion and information-sharing groups were established as the initiative spread from Kazan' to other Russian cities.²³ These groups were used to share information about the upcoming event; to post links to news coverage (both before and after 30 June 2014), including interviews with linguists, writers and cultural activists; to post links to songs, videos, film clips and texts that contain *mat*, ranging from Pushkin, Lermontov and Brodsky to Vysotskii and post-Soviet rock and pop music; and, last but not least, to discuss the law and argue for or against it.

Most of the participants in these groups were sceptical towards the new law, as confirmed by an informal survey conducted in one of the groups. Out of 266 respondents (78.23 per cent of the participants in the group), 10.5 per cent supported a ban on *mat* in art ('Yes, it's possible to do without it'), 64.3 per cent were against the law ('No, this gives [art] a particular flavour'), 4.5 per cent were indifferent ('It doesn't matter') and, finally, 20.17 per cent, opted for 'What the f***? I don't have a clue'. The last option is quite telling of the style of communication in these groups, where people often use humour and indirect means of argumentation to make their case, a point to which I shall return below. Before then, I will present and discuss the main lines of argument that informed the discussions surrounding the Abanamat event in social media and online mass media.

Artistic freedom, and freedom of speech

Concern for freedom of speech is clearly the chief argument against the new legislative initiative. This can also be seen in the organisation of the Abanamat events, which in many cities became part of the annual *Otkroi rot – bez tsenzury* ('Open your mouth – without censorship') programme.

Many users emphasise that the issue at stake is not *mat* per se, but broader issues of censorship and free speech:

> Вся беда не в запрете мата, а в том, что это первый шаг к цензуре. (Abanamat, Kazan)[24]

> дело и не в мате вовсе. Это акция против введения цензуры. [...] Меня не пугает, услышат ли прохожие дети нецензурное слово [...] Пугает меня, что эти дети вырастут в атмосфере лицемерия и лжи. (Abanamat, Kazan)[25]

People who are well versed in the law point to specific paragraphs of the Constitution and argue that the new law is, in fact, anti-constitutional. Thus, Gazeta.ru quotes Drugoe Kino president Sem Klebanov's comments on Facebook:

> Он противоречит сразу трем статьям Конституции: ст. 26 п. 2 – «Каждый имеет право на пользование родным языком» (надеюсь, все согласны, что запретные слова – неотъемлемая часть этого самого языка?) [...] Ст. 29 п. 5 – «Цензура запрещается» (само определение «нецензурная лексика» уже предполагает, что вся остальная лексика цензурная); Ст. 44 1. 1 – «Каждому гарантируется свобода литературного, художественного, научного, технического и других видов творчества». (Karev et al. 2014)[26]

That freedom of speech is also of concern to officials and legislators is apparent from Govorukhin's comments, both in response to questions at the first Duma hearing of the proposal and in response to the January 2015 open letter to Dmitrii Medvedev from members of the Russian film community. In Govorukhin's remarks, however, we can sense a concern about 'freedom of speech' not as being threatened, but as being a threat in itself:

> Вы спросите: а как же свобода слова? Я думаю, вы со мной согласитесь, что нравственное ограничение и есть суть свободы в обществе. Надо сказать, что эта свобода слова в последнее время сопровождается ещё и ужасающей безграмотностью. ('Pervoe chtenie' 2013)[27]

> «Если идти по предлагаемому принципу, то можно слишком далеко зайти. Сначала вернем мат в кино, в литературу, в

театры, потом разрешим карикатуры на религиозные темы»,
– рассуждает Говорухин. ('Komitet Gosdumy' 2015)[28]

The last comment makes a direct connection between allowing *mat* in film, literature and theatre and the Charlie Hebdo caricatures that provoked the terrorist attack in Paris on 7 January 2015, in which twelve people were killed. Govorukhin's comment is indicative of the broader legislative context of the ban on *mat*, the range of legislative initiatives designed to regulate language use in the public sphere, including laws banning the 'offending of religious feelings' (2013)[29] as well as prohibitions against vaguely defined notions of 'extremism' (2013). In the discourses surrounding the Abanamat event, we see attempts to convey quite another kind of broader context of *mat*, one that does not stress its dangers, but rather its indispensability, drawing close links between *mat*, art and life.

'Mat', art and life, and the (in)flexibility of linguistic and social norms

In the Abanamat discussions one can sense an urgency to demonstrate the broader significance and meaning of *mat*, the importance and even necessity of *mat* for artistic expression, its unique power in expressing emotions and, above all, 'the essence' of (any aspect of) life. Zarema Zaudinova, organiser of the Barnaul event, explains: Наше культурно-матерное мероприятие – это желание не поматериться, а показать, что мат в искусстве, в частности, в литературе – это средство выразительности, которое помогает вскрывать суть явления. И это совершенно мирная акция любителей искусства и русского языка [. . .] (Panikhida 2014).[30] We can note Zaudinova's labelling of the event (*kul'turno-maternoe meropriiatie*), combining the two adjectives 'cultural' and *maternoe* ('relating to *mat*'), and the bringing together of *mat* and 'the Russian language' in a relationship bordering on equivalency. Variations of the latter point are found quite frequently, as in these two comments on a blog post reporting on the Abanamat event: Правители приходят и уходят вместе со своими законами, а мат остается. Бороться с родным языком глупо)) (Stiazhkin 2014);[31] Не кастрировать лженауке – наш великий русский язык! (Stiazhkin 2014).[33]

A similar, all-embracing perspective on *mat* comes to the fore in the phrase 'to speak *mat*' rather than 'to use *mat*' (in one's speech). The winner of the Barnaul *Otkroi rot* competition (part of the Abanamat event in Barnaul), Aizhan Zhakipbekova, explains:

> Сейчас из культуры выпадает огромный пласт: совершенно не ясно, как сейчас будут отображать в литературе сантехников и электриков. Есть такие группы людей, которые не ругаются матом, а говорят на нем – это душа и эмоции, их порой трудно воспроизвести литературным языком. ('Abanamat: kak v Barnaule' 2014)[33]

The second champion from the Barnaul *Otkroi rot* competition, Ol'ga Vas'ko, elaborates: Если мы уберем все плохие слова и оставим только хорошие, то мы не сможем назвать примерно половину явлений. Язык это не только передача информации, это экспрессия, эмоции ('Abanamat: kak v Barnaule' 2014).[34]

Mat is seen as an essential part of art, of the Russian language, and even of life as such. Still, the distinction between art (artistic expression) and life (reality) turns out to be an important one in many comments. As one VKontakte user puts it: Запрещая мат в искусстве, мы запрещаем отражение жизни. Государство не запрещает мат в реальности, оно запрещает мат в отражении реальности (Abanamat, Kazan).[35]

Given the strong emphasis on the integral place of *mat* in life and language, it is somewhat surprising to see the frequency with which people argue that they would understand restrictions on the use of *mat* in everyday language, but that art is a special case and should be protected against prohibitions of this sort. Zaudinova seems to defend this stance:

> Мне непонятно зачем в такие строгие рамки загонять искусство. На мой взгляд, было бы логичнее запрещать мат не в искусстве, которое как раз высвечивает и гиперболизирует то, в чем мы живем, а, например, в публичных местах, общественном транспорте и т.д. (Bakulina 2014)[36]

So does Il'ia Kuznetsov, professor at the State Theatre Institute of Novosibirsk, who gave a lecture on the history of *mat* in Russian literature at the Novosibirsk Abanamat event: Проблема засилья мата в нашей речи – это не проблема искусства. Матерщина – прежде всего, явление массовой культуры, здесь с ней и надо бороться, элементарно вводя штрафы. Так что, по моему мнению, к этой проблеме государство подходит не с той стороны ('V Novosibirske' 2014).[37]

To some participants in the online discussions about Abanamat, the question about *mat* in art and *mat* in everyday language is a question of two totally different kinds of obscenity: Мы выступаем за «культурный мат». За «литературный мат», а не за ругать [sic].

Мат в искусстве это другое, это не бытовая быдлячая ругать [sic] (Stiazhkin 2014).[38]

The idea of a high-culture version of *mat* and a low-culture one emerging from these examples reminds us of similar ideas in the writers' statements on language examined in Chapter 5. It also echoes conceptions about pornography in Russian cultural history (Goldschmidt 1999: 47–78) and has to do, among other things, with the generally clear division between high and low culture in Russia. We saw above how *mat* is defined as a social dialect of 'plumbers and electricians', and Kuznetsov's statement makes a clear distinction between high and low culture with regard to the legitimate uses of *mat*. Seen from this perspective, the law against *mat* and the reactions to it illustrate, in Bourdieu's (1991) terms, the value and legitimacy of *mat*, and highlight the issue of who should have the power to define it. Many participants in the actions obviously do not defend *mat* per se, but only their own, high-culture version of it.

Among participants in and supporters of the Abanamat event, we see furthermore a clear awareness of certain linguistic and social norms regulating the use of *mat*. An example of the presence of such norms can be seen on the Facebook page of the Moscow Abanamat event, where users were invited to sign up for readings by writing a non-normative word or two in the comment field. While some users responded enthusiastically to this, others were more restrained: Запишите меня пжл, я все, что нужно, скажу на месте) (Abanamat, Moscow FB).[39]

In the media reports of the events, such self-censorship is only to be expected, given the 2013 prohibition on obscene language in the mass media. Here, we find circumscriptions from the innocent На футболке одного из участников было также написано нецензурное слово (Zubova 2014)[40] to more suggestive reports: Пришлось слушать, как запрещенное слово номер один (в алфавитном порядке) рифмуют с запрещенным словом номер два (в алфавитном порядке) (Punsh 2014).[41] Statements such as these make readers reflect actively on the words in question and on the possible beauty of their rhyming capabilities.

In a similar fashion, Altapress.ru's report on the Barnaul event features an image with two letters, *kh* and *u*, accompanied by the text Слово, которое пришло вам в голову при взгляде на эту картинку, запрещено законом Российской Федерации. Фото из архива редакции (Sokolova 2014).[42] Reporting on the Abanamat event in Moscow, Lenta.ru, in turn, published a 2:21-minute video clip blocking out all occurrences of *mat* with a beep, and giving the report the ironic and self-reflexive title 'Pip-pip-pip' ('Pip-pip-pip' 2014).[43]

This ironic, suggestive and humorous style, reflecting a set of unwritten norms of self-censorship, is frequently seen in the media, where it can be interpreted as a pragmatic way of dealing with the 2013 law banning *mat* in the mass media. In fact, the clarifications of Roskomnadzor in response to this law, foreseeing, as it were, the sort of attitude we notice in the last couple of examples quoted above, are even explicit about such norms, as they specify the kind of circumscriptions that should be tolerated, and those that should be forbidden. For example, while it is not permitted to omit some letters of a 'forbidden' word and retain, say, only the first and the last letter, a circumscription in the style of 'the word starting with the letter b' is tolerated (Zykov and Kondrat'ev 2013). Elements reminiscent of the mass media's playful-pragmatic response to the 2013 law can also be seen in the Abanamat events and surrounding discussions.

The aesthetics of (Abana)mat

A quick look at the 2014 issues of *Karl Fuks*, the cultural journal from which the idea of Abanamat emerged, gives an impression of the professional and elegant design that can also be seen in the promo video, which the journal produced together with *Bezdel'niki*, the Samara current events guide, in order to launch the Abanamat initiative. The video consists of two parts. The first is informative: it briefly presents the law, its consequences and the Abanamat event. The setting is 'classic', the camera moves slowly along book and film shelves, where Pushkin, Bulgakov and Venedikt Erofeev feature prominently. This part is accompanied by the soundtrack 'Mad World' in the version by Michael Andrews and Gary Jules used in the film *Donnie Darko* (2001). The second part presents a symbolic funeral for a selection of books containing *mat*, accompanied by the track 'Fire of the Mind' by Coil, the words of the song ('Does death come alone or with eager reinforcements?') adding to the solemn yet mocking style.

The original video of the cover version of Andrews and Jules's song features children filmed from above, forming animated figures with their bodies ('Mad World' 2001). This video obviously inspired the organisers of the Abanamat event in Tomsk, who assembled an exhibition of photographs of human beings forming *mat* words.[44] The result shown publicly is a recording of the silent (though not necessarily public) performance of the words, thus playfully challenging the conception of both 'art' and 'public performance' in the legislative amendments.

In Novosibirsk, a similar playful and ironic style can be seen on the poster announcing the event, entitled '[Khu iz?]' ('Who is?'): Tsar Nikita

Figure 6.1 Poster for the Novosibirsk Abanamat event, by Igor Sherko (reproduced with permission).

and his Forty Daughters Festival of Inner Freedom and Emancipation' (Figure 6.1).

While the reference to Pushkin's erotic poem of 1822, 'Tsar Nikita and his Forty Daughters', amusingly brings the national poet into the picture by hinting at what is usually treated as one of the poet's youthful sins,[45] the main title ХУ ИЗ?, a Cyrillic transliteration of the English 'Who is?', alludes to the most emblematic *mat* word, *khui* (ХУЙ). It is also vaguely reminiscent, however, of the standard abbreviations in Orthodox icons and texts of nomina sacra IC and XC (Iisus and Khristos), suggesting, perhaps, the quasi-sacred status *mat* enjoys in many contexts (Uspenskii 1994: 62). The programme promises readings and stagings containing *mat*, but also a 'collective act of *bezdukhovnost'* [lack of spiritual culture]'. News reports tell us that this act consisted of the declamation from the stage of the four cornerstone words of *mat* by all participants in the event ('V Novosibirske' 2014). Together with the insertion of the word *skrepa* in the subtitle of the event (*ras(skrepo)shchenie* 'emancipation'[46]), these details are clearly directed against the official rhetoric, which aims to define a new cultural policy in Russia. The *skrepa* reference, in particular, alludes to an address by President Putin to the Federal Assembly in December 2012, where he bemoaned the lack of *dukhovnye skrepy* in contemporary Russian society: Сегодня российское общество испытывает явный дефицит духовных скреп – милосердия, сочувствия, сострадания друг другу, поддержки и взаимопомощи, – дефицит того, что всегда, во все времена исторические делало нас крепче, сильнее, чем мы всегда гордились ('Poslanie Prezidenta' 2012).[47] The phrase *dukhovnye skrepy* (roughly meaning 'spiritual ties', 'spiritual values'), which is difficult not only to translate but also to understand in Russian, immediately became a meme in the Russian blogosphere, while the authorities responded with the launch of a tender to define 'the markers of spiritual ties' (*markery dukhovnykh skrep*) that was eventually won by the Institute of Sociology at the Russian Academy of Sciences (Shepelin 2013).

Actor and artist Sergei Pakhomov plays openly on the 'sacred' status of *mat* in his sarcastic comment on the law, and urges the authorities to go even further in the prosecution of 'holy language':

> Закон о мате я вообще поддерживаю. По той простой причине, что становится больше каких-то тайных, святых вещей. То есть мат в запрещенном состоянии превращается в «святой мат», язык избранных. Страх наказания за употребление матерных слов, с одной стороны, огромен, а с другой – страха никакого нет. Пока не будет первой публичной казни за мат, он все же будет в состоянии такой, знаете, полусвятости. А вот казнят человека за мат на лобном месте – он окончательно станет святым языком. (Karev et al. 2014)[48]

The sarcastic stance illustrates the total lack of trust that characterises the attitude of intellectuals, and, more generally, of the 'creative class',[49] towards the authorities and lawmakers during the third presidency of Vladimir Putin. In this sense, the particular form of the Abanamat event can also be linked to the wider context of protest culture in Russia today. In the autumn of 2011, when Putin's candidacy for a third presidential term was announced, many writers, artists, film-makers, journalists and intellectuals joined the wave of protests that followed, and, more generally, took a more active political stance than before. It has been argued that the contingent of 'creatives' among the protesters influenced, to a certain extent, the style and form of a number of protest events and gatherings,[50] such as the *Bol'shoi belyi krug* (Big White Circle) on 26 February 2012, a chain of people and vehicles that stretched along the length of Moscow's Garden Ring, holding white banners and other white items; the Occupy-inspired *Okkupai Abai* movement, a week-long occupation starting on 9 May 2012 of the space surrounding the statue of the Kazakh poet Abai Kunanbaev, featuring lectures, discussions, debates and performances; or the *Kontrol'naia progulka* (Test Walk), a writer-initiated stroll down Moscow's Chistye Prudy on 13 May 2012 in order to test whether Muscovites could walk freely around their own city.[51]

Since May 2012, the intensified crackdown on free expression and the flood of new legislative measures limiting civil rights have significantly stifled voices of dissent, including those of artists and intellectuals. Recourse to the kind of 'creative responses' that we see in the Abanamat case is also a direct consequence of distrust in the effectiveness (and even possibility) of more traditional means of protest and opposition. Thus, a potent mixture of sentiments – including concern for the freedom of art, strong emotions 'on behalf of' *mat*, and a generally playful and ironic style – informs the Abanamat events, which together contribute a clear statement to the debate about verbal prohibition. How can this stance be described in terms of linguistic attitudes?

THE ABANAMAT AGENDA

With the new laws of 2013 and 2014 banning *mat* in the mass media, film, literature and cultural performances, verbal prohibition has entered a new phase in Russia. The use of *mat* had been the object of legislative measures in post-Soviet Russia before 2013: it figures in §130 of the Criminal Code on insults (*oskorblenie*) and in the Code of Administrative Offenses' §20.20 on petty hooliganism (*melkoe khuliganstvo*). However, there is a crucial difference between using *mat* as an insult and using *mat* on stage or in a song, as part of an artistic representation. In the case of insults and petty hooliganism, the *mat* expression is intentionally directed against a particular person in order to offend him or her.[52] It is meant to be an insult, someone suffers and complains about it. This is not the case when *mat* is used in the mass media and even less so when *mat* figures in literature, film or theatre. This point is surprisingly absent from the discussions surrounding the Abanamat events, at least in explicit terms. Still, as we have seen, there is a constant urge to demonstrate that *mat* used in artistic expression is fundamentally different from the *mat* used in everyday life.

The solemn-cum-humoristic tone of some of the posters advertising Abanamat events, 30 июня – последний день свободного выражения мысли на русском языке в кино, спектаклях, литературе и музыке. Приходи попрощаться,[53] gives us an idea both of what is at stake for many people in the issue of *mat*, but also of the ironic flavour that accompanies the event. The freedom of speech issue ('freely expressed'), the all-embracing conception of *mat* ('in Russian [language]') and the pathos of the phrase ('the last day [...] come and bid farewell') combine to convey strong emotions together with an ironic touch. The Abanamat performances proper reflect a similar mixture of emotions, expressiveness and playful irony. As one news report puts it: К концу вечера акция переросла в надрывное прощание с чем-то родным и ценным. Собравшиеся провожали русский мат от души. В полночь состоялась торжественная минута молчания (Samoilova 2014).[54]

One major ambition of the Abanamat initiative was to highlight the greater significance and implications of *mat* in Russian culture, namely the dimensions of *russkii mat* that were felt to have been reduced ad absurdum by the listing and banning of four crucial words. The linguistic attitudes voiced in the various discussion forums, as well as the nature, design and performance of the events themselves, combine to underline this larger dimension to *mat*. The whole movement tries to present *mat* as something that cannot be isolated from the rest of the language and is thus integral to 'Russian culture'. Writer and journalist Andrei Konstantinov, interviewed for the Fontanka.ru channel, struggles to find words to express this point in explicit terms:

> огромный пласт шуток, огромный пласт какик-то прибауток, стихов, и так далее, – анекдотов в конце концов – замените там те самые слова, и уже будет не смешно, это будет не то, это не будет обладать той вот . . . какой-то энергетикой, которая в этом есть [. . .] Как можно запретить часть языка? ('Abanamat: reaktsii' 2014)[54]

The online discussions of the law against *mat* reveal that an elitist conception of *mat* is still quite widespread. Frequent references to Pushkin and other famous 'super users' of *mat* are only one sign of this. *Mat* is seen as integral to 'Russian culture', but many participants in the debate are not ready to embrace the use of *mat* everywhere – traditional social and linguistic norms regulating the use of *mat* clearly influence their linguistic behaviour and attitudes, while conceptions of 'high' and 'low' versions of swearing lay claim to *mat* as the legitimate language of particular social groups. Most importantly, art is seen to be a special case, and the new regulations are perceived as a gross violation of the right to define the conditions of artistic expression. Ultimately, the crux of the matter is the conflicting claims to the power to define *mat*, and it is here that we see the incompatibility between the notion of a list of four words and their derivatives, on the one hand, and 'holistic' conceptions of *mat* as an expression of the essence of life, on the other. The latter is easier to show and perform than to define and explain. In both form and content, the Abanamat events seek to bring out this larger dimension to *mat*, philosophically and aesthetically. Here, humour, irony and the creative artistic practices themselves play crucial roles. In the chapters to follow we will delve deeper into these performative ways of expressing linguistic attitudes and ideas.

NOTES

1. The word *abanamat*, obviously a deliberate distortion of the *mat* expression *ebana mat'*, can be traced back to a passage in Sergei Dovlatov's *Nashi* (*Ours*, 1983), where it is used as an extremely effective exclamation word: Дед по материнской линии отличался весьма суровым нравом. Даже на Кавказе его считали вспыльчивым человеком. Жена и дети трепетали от его взгляда.
   Если что-то раздражало деда, он хмурил брови и низким голосом восклицал:
   – АБАНАМАТ!
   Это таинственное слово буквально парализовало окружающих. Внушало им мистический ужас.
   – АБАНАМАТ! – восклицал дед.
   И в доме наступала полнейшая тишина (Dovlatov 1993: 161). 'My grandfather on my mother's side was known for his harsh temperament. Even for a native of the Caucasus he was considered unusually irascible. His wife and children trembled at his glance. If something annoyed grandfather, he frowned and shouted in a low voice: – ABANAMAT! This enigmatic word literally paralysed everyone in the vicinity. It impressed them with a mysterious terror. – ABANAMAT! – grandfather shouted. And a complete silence took hold in the house' (Dovlatov 1989: 9, missing parts added).
2. '[F]rom now on, the great and mighty [language] will only be [heard] on the streets and in the kitchen.'
3. According to media reports, other films that have had to be redubbed include Valeriia Germanika's *Da i da* (*Yes and Yes*, 2013, redubbed version released in March 2015) and Andrei Konchalovskii's *Belye nochi pochtal'ona Alekseia Triapitsyna* (*The Postman Aleksei Triapitsyn's White Nights*, 2014). Some theatres ignore the law, most prominently Teatr.doc, while others make changes to their repertoire. For a discussion among Moscow theatre directors of various strategies of how to deal with the new law, see Laletina (2014). There have been few reports in the media about concrete instances of where the law has been applied, but see 'Organizatora kontserta' (2016) for an instance where the organisers of a concert with the rock group Leningrad were fined because the lead singer, Sergei Shnurov, used *mat*. Leningrad is known for its extensive use of obscene language and celebration of alcoholism.
4. 'In days of doubt, in days of anxious thought about the destiny of my native land, you alone are my support and my strength, O great, mighty Russian language, truthful and free!.. Were it not for you, how should man not despair at the sight of what is going on at home? But it is inconceivable that such a language has not been given to a great people.'
5. For a chronological overview of obscenity's progression from 'unprintable' to 'printable' in Russian literary culture, see Kovalev (2014). There has been an upswing in research on verbal obscenity in Russian sociolinguistics and cultural studies over

the last few decades; see, among others, Levin (1996); Zorin (1996); Plutser-Sarno (2001, 2005); Goriunova (2009); Scharlaj (2014); Kovalev (2016). Readers are also referred to the thematic double issue of *Zeitschrift für slavische Philologie* dedicated to 'The Culture and Politics of Verbal Prohibition in Putin's Russia', only partly published by the time of completing this book (Gorham and Weiss 2016/17).

6. The cultural journal *Karl Fuks* was launched in March 2014 and published fifteen printed issues before it was closed down and fundamentally reorganised in December 2014, after which it reappeared as an online journal and website. The last double issue (16–17) was published online and could, until recently, be accessed together with all other 2014 issues at <http://karlfuks.ru/magazine/> (last accessed 30 June 2016).

7. I include two Facebook and seven VKontakte groups, one blog and around twenty news sites containing interviews, reports and general information on the events. The social network groups comprise (as of 11 March 2015) a total of 706 members and 287 postings (with a varying number of comments), the main bulk of which was published over a three-week period starting around 20 June 2014. Some groups were established only a few days before the event on 30 June.

8. All documents relating to the law (No. 190238-6), from its proposal on 14 December 2012 until it was signed by Vladimir Putin on 5 May 2014, can be found at <http://asozd.duma.gov.ru/main.nsf/(Spravka)?OpenAgent&RN=190238-6&02> (last accessed 26 June 2017).

9. 'the use of words and expressions that do not comply with the norms of contemporary Russian standard language, with the exception of foreign words which do not have commonly used equivalents'.

10. 'including uncensored swearing'.

11. 'in public performances of literature, art, folk art, in the form of theatre, cultural, educational and entertainment events'.

12. 'is an indispensable part of the artistic idea'.

13. 'contains uncensored swearing'.

14. For a discussion of the semantics of the term *mat*, see Ermen (1993: 8–10).

15. The four words were listed in the letter from the Academy of Sciences, whereas the mass media, where traditions of linguistic self-censorship were already strong, tended to apply the circumscriptions found in Roskomnadzor documents: 'The uncensored designation of the male sexual organ, the uncensored designation of the female sexual organ, the uncensored designation of the process of intercourse, and the uncensored designation of a woman of immoral conduct, and also all words formed from these linguistic elements' (Zykov and Kondrat'ev 2013). English equivalents would be 'cock', 'cunt', 'fuck' and 'slut'.

16. For general and specific discussions of the use of linguistic expertise in legal cases, see Levontina (2005); Baranov (2007); Weiss (2008, 2009); Brinev (2009).

17. Levin (1996) provides a very useful categorisation; see also Daniel Weiss's (2008) discussion with illustrative examples.

18. 'The present legislative proposal is, in fact, first of all aimed at the cultivation and protection of a healthy spirituality (*dukhovnost'*) and morality, at the formation of a speech and communication culture in contemporary society. In addition, one of the most important tasks today is the protection of the younger generation against attacks of anti-culture, including the linguistic sphere, of phenomena that have a harmful effect on its morality and spiritual well-being.'

19. 'I think there is no reason to worry about Aleksandr Sergeevich, since he is an

absolutely moral human being, and therefore his books may be published without any kind of anxiety.' Back in 1997, Govorukhin (also then chairman of the Duma's Culture Committee) was one of the initiators of the anti-pornography bill, and the motivations for the law put forward at the first reading are of a very similar nature (Goldschmidt 1999: 150–1).

20. 'Russian *mat* is one of the greatest and most subtle inventions of the Russian people, and impossible to translate into other languages.'
21. 'an open project of actions by different genres, devoted to protesting against censorship and limitations in all forms of art'.
22. 'our task is to attract the attention of society, because right now things are going on which are alien to art, and which would rather seem to slow down processes of development in culture and art. [. . .] even if we cannot manage to change the law, we have at least told everyone about its absurdity.'
23. The main Facebook page dedicated to the action is <http://www.facebook.com/abanamatrf >. The main VKontakte site is the Kazan Abanamat group, at <http://vk.com/abanamatrf>. Other local groups include <http://www.facebook.com/events/656398377776398>and <http://vk.com/abanavrot> (Moscow); <http://vk.com/overnah> and <http://vk.com/event73199051> (Novosibirsk); <http://vk.com/abaspb> (St Petersburg); <http://vk.com/abanamat_nch> (Naberezhnye Chelny); <http://vk.com/abanamatbarnaul> (Barnaul) (all last accessed 26 June 2017).
24. 'The whole problem is not to do with the prohibition of *mat*, but that this is the first step towards censorship.'
25. '[T]his [i.e. *Abanamat*] is not at all about *mat*. It is a measure against the introduction of censorship. [. . .] I am not worried about passing children hearing a non-censored word [. . .] I'm worried about these children growing up in an atmosphere of hypocrisy and lies.'
26. 'It [the new law] contradicts as many as three paragraphs of the Constitution: §26.2: "Everyone has the right to use his native language" (I hope everyone agrees that the forbidden words are an indispensable part of this very language?) [. . .] §29.5: "Censorship is forbidden" (the very notion of "non-censored vocabulary" presupposes that the rest of the vocabulary is censored); §44.1: "Everyone is guaranteed freedom of literary, scientific, technical and other kinds of creative production."'
27. 'You may ask, but what about freedom of speech? I think you agree that moral constraint is the essence of freedom in society. And I must say that in recent years this freedom has been accompanied by a frightening lack of culture.'
28. '"If one proceeds in accordance with this principle, one can go too far. First we reintroduce *mat* into film, literature and theatre, then we allow caricatures on religious topics," argues Govorukhin.'
29. The law is widely believed to be a reaction to Pussy Riot's punk performance in the Cathedral of Christ the Saviour in Moscow on 21 February 2012.
30. 'Our cultural-*mat* action is not motivated by a wish to use obscene language, but to show that *mat* in art, in particular in literature, is a means of expression that allows one to disclose the essence of a phenomenon. It's a totally peaceful action by those who love art and the Russian language [. . .]'
31. 'Rulers come and go with their laws, but *mat* will remain. It's stupid to fight against the native language)).'
32. 'Pseudoscience shall not castrate – our great Russian language!' (Note the Turgenevian echo.)

33. 'Now a whole layer of culture will be missing: it's totally unclear how literature is now going to represent plumbers and electricians. There are such groups of people that don't use *mat*, but speak it – it's soul and emotions, and these are sometimes difficult to render in the standard language.'
34. 'If we take out all the bad words and keep only the good ones, we will not be able to express roughly half of the phenomena that exist. Language is not just information transfer, it is expression, emotion.'
35. 'Banning *mat* in art, we ban the reflection of life. The state does not forbid *mat* in reality, it forbids *mat* in the reflection of reality.'
36. 'I don't understand why one should force art into such a strict framework. In my view, it would make more sense to prohibit *mat* not in art, which in fact highlights and exaggerates the milieu in which we live, but, for instance, in the public sphere, public transport, etc.'
37. 'The problem with the predominance of *mat* in our speech should not be a problem of art. Obscene language is, above all, a phenomenon of mass culture, and on this level one should fight it, simply by introducing fines. In my view, the state has approached the problem from the wrong end.'
38. 'We advocate "cultural *mat*". "Literary *mat*", not abuse. *Mat* in art is something different. It's not vulgar abuse.'
39. 'Sign me up, plz, I'll say everything that's necessary in situ.'
40. 'the T-shirt of one of the participants featured an uncensored word'.
41. 'One got to listen to how forbidden word number one (in alphabetical order) rhymes with forbidden word number two (in alphabetical order).'
42. 'The word that comes to your mind when you look at this picture is forbidden by Russian federal law. Photo from the newspaper archive.'
43. An even more extreme solution is seen in Ren-TV's report on the St Petersburg Abanamat event, where not only the sound of *mat* is blocked out with a beep, but so are its visual manifestations, with faces blurred in order to prevent people from lip-reading the bad words (Abanamat, Kazan; the video clip is available at <https://vk.com/wall-72670795?offset=0&z=video165739424_169277806%2Fce46eab3725f f17fe7>, last accessed 26 June 2017).
44. There are Russian forerunners of this kind of action as well. In 1991, Moscow performance artist Anatolii Osmolovskii and his group E.T.I. (Ekspropriatsiia territorii iskusstva ['Expropriation of the territory of art']) lay down in front of the Lenin Mausoleum, their bodies forming the word *khui* (see Jonson 2015: 27).
45. See Clayton and Vesselova (2012) for a recent analysis.
46. 'Emancipation' is also illustrated by the visual focal point of the poster, displaying a fence which plays the double role of being broken and serving as a canvas for the *mat* words. I thank Alexei Evstratov for drawing my attention to this particular point.
47. 'Russian society is currently experiencing a serious lack of spiritual ties – mercy, empathy, mutual compassion, support and help, – a lack of that which always, at all times in history, has made us stronger, more powerful, and of which we were always proud.'
48. 'I actually support the law on *mat*. For the simple reason that we get even more of those secret, sacred things. That is, when prohibited, *mat* becomes "holy *mat*", the language of the chosen ones. The fear of getting punished for the use of *mat* words is, on the one hand, huge, on the other hand, there is no such fear at all. Until we get the first public execution for *mat*, it will remain in a semi-holy state, you know. But as

soon as the first person is publicly executed for the use of *mat*, it will finally become a sacred language.'

49. 'Creative class' is a term coined by Richard Florida (2002) and originally applied to the US, but which has gained currency in Russia as a label designating the emerging cluster of young, urban, educated people including cultural workers, creative professionals, journalists and entrepreneurs. A frequently debated concept (e.g. Saprykin et al. 2012), the term came to prominence during the post-election protests of 2011 and 2012.

50. According to a survey by the state-funded polling organisation VTsIOM (2012), the percentage of protesters belonging to one of three groups defined as 'students', 'creative class' or 'clerical workers' rose from 30 to 50 per cent between February and June 2012. The question as to whether it is at all possible to speak of 'classes' among the protesters has been much debated among Russian sociologists. I agree with Aleksei Levinson, who holds that, while the protests included many people who were more or less comfortably off, one cannot, in terms of self-description, speak of a particular class identity among the protesters, other than a 'we' (Levinson 2012). However, this stance does not necessarily contradict the argument that the contingent of artists, writers and cultural activists influenced the forms of the protests. See, in particular, slogans and other material discussed in Gabowitsch (2013) and Arkhipova et al. (2016).

51. For an interpretation of these and similar events, see Gabowitsch (2013); Paulsen and Zvereva (2014); Zhelnina (2014). For a broader assessment of the role of art in protest movements in contemporary Russia, see Jonson (2015).

52. It is, of course, sometimes very difficult to prove whether *mat* is used with the intention of offending, since it has so many other functions and meanings (see Levin 1996; Weiss 2008).

53. '30 June is the last day when thoughts can be freely expressed in Russian in cinema, theatrical performances, literature and music. Come and bid farewell.'

54. 'Towards the end of the evening, the event transformed into a heart-rending farewell to something dear and precious. Participants' farewell to *mat* was heartfelt. At midnight, a solemn moment of silence was observed.'

55. '[A] huge part of jokes, a huge part of catch-phrases, verses, and so on – anecdotes, after all – take out those words, and it won't be funny anymore, won't be the right thing, won't have this particular . . . it's a kind of energy . . . some energy that's in there [. . .] How can you forbid something that is part of the language?'

PART IV

Language on Display

CHAPTER 7

Confronting Linguistic Legacies

Evgenii Popov and Vladimir Sorokin

A central topic in the language debates is the handling of the recent past, in particular the Soviet linguistic legacy. An important dimension to this legacy is *newspeak*, the official, mainly political, language culture of the Soviet period, prevalent in genres such as the newspaper editorial or political speech, as well as in a great variety of official documents and forms of spoken verbal interaction (Weiss 1986). As we saw in Chapter 1, the late 1990s and early years of the new millennium saw the publication of a number of books – scholarly as well as popular – on Soviet language culture. The implications and broader dimensions of the Soviet linguistic legacy are also thematised in works of fiction, in particular by authors with links to the conceptualist art movement, such as Vladimir Sorokin, Evgenii Popov, Dmitrii Prigov and Viktor Erofeev. In this chapter we shall take a closer look at two of these writers, Popov and Sorokin, and see how their prose writing confronts, in quite different ways, the linguistic legacies of the past.

EVGENII POPOV: CONCEPTUALISM AND BEYOND

Evgenii Popov is a writer with literary and linguistic feet in two worlds, the recent Soviet past – above all the 1960s and 1970s – and then late and post-Soviet Russia. Popov studied and started to write in the 1960s, but became famous through the so-called *Metropol'* affair: together with Viktor Erofeev, Andrei Bitov, Vasilii Aksenov and Fasil Iskander, Popov edited a compilation (entitled *Metropol'*) of short texts, including those by a number of officially unpublishable Russian writers, which created a literary scandal in 1979. The collection, originally prepared in only twelve typewritten copies of *samizdat*, was eventually published abroad (Aksenov et al. 1979), while Popov and Erofeev were expelled from the Union of Writers (Porter 1994: 26–30). In the early 1980s Popov continued to write, but could not be published. With the dramatic shift in the political climate during perestroika, however, he was readmitted to the Union of Writers in 1988, became a founding member of the Moscow PEN Club and has been widely published in Russia since the late 1980s.[1]

Popov's fictional world is saturated with allusions creating a complex mixture of absurdity, irony and parody. He often juxtaposes texts from different times or genres, while his combination of styles, texts and languages triggers the reader's powers of association and reflection. Various forms of metafictional commentary feature strongly in his works. He plays with and comments on established literary forms, styles and functions (such as the figures and voices of author, hero and narrator); he questions the concepts and conceptualisations of past and contemporary aesthetic movements, including those to which he himself belongs or used to belong (Engel 1996: 119); and he constantly blurs the borderlines between fiction and reality, creating parodies and paradoxes, and developing an unsettling style of narration that never comes to rest. This gives his texts an enigmatic aura, on the one hand, but reveals, on the other, a constant process of reflection on the part of the author or narrator, a process in which the reader is invited to engage.

Metafiction and metalanguage

Popov's works form part of a conspicuous trend in contemporary Russian literature of texts that comment on themselves, by authors such as Viacheslav P'etsukh, Nikolai Baitov, Dmitrii Galkovskii and Vladimir Korobov, to name just a few. What makes Popov's work particularly relevant to the perspective studied by this book is that reflections on language play a significant role throughout his writing. Among Popov's many metafictional works, the one richest in metalinguistic commentary is his novel *Podlinnaia istoriia 'Zelenykh muzykantov'* (*The True Story of 'The Green Musicians'*, 1999). In the following I shall propose a reading of this text as an interpretation of, and response to, the question of linguistic legacies in post-Soviet Russian culture.

Footnote literature

While the majority of cases presented in Part IV of this book introduce a mixture of explicit and implicit reflections on the language question, self-commenting texts naturally favour explicit commentary, either in the form of metafictional statements within the main text of, say, a novel or poem, or straightforwardly as footnotes. In *The True Story of 'The Green Musicians'*, explicit commentary is prominent to the extent that it defines the work generically, as an example of what we might call 'footnote literature': the novel consists of a short narrative (58 pp.) written, according to footnote one, in 1974, but not published until 1998, now provided with 888 footnotes (255 pp.) and an index of names (22 pp.). The short narrative describes the literary rise and fall of a certain Ivan Ivanych. Having had a story about the theft of a bicycle published in the local newspaper of his provincial hometown, he tries to build a literary career, a project that gradually degenerates, however, into a bohemian lifestyle: he drops out of college, loses his girlfriend Liudmila and ends up spending his days dozing on the sofa. Under the influence of drugs, he has a grotesque dream that suggests an ominous life-after-death scenario involving his relatives, various famous writers and the mysterious 'Green Musicians'. Following this vision, Ivan gives up his literary career, takes up his studies again, moves in with Liudmila, has a son and becomes a respectable and successful factory manager.

The commentary, which will be the main focus of our attention, is holistic in scope, digressive in organisation and humorous in style. Popov[2] comments on the language, style and facts of his story, providing an overwhelming amount of both relevant and seemingly irrelevant detail: background information, explanations of contemporary and past realia as well as of socio-historical or literary conditions, anecdotes, personal reminiscences and additional prose passages. In many cases the words for which he provides footnote references are quickly forgotten by the commentator and serve only as triggers for his personal reflections.

The primary object of the linguistic remarks is the language of the 1970s – as one might expect of a commentary that deals with a text originally dating from that period, and of an author 'with a history' from the same period (the *Metropol'* affair is mentioned several times in *The True Story of 'The Green Musicians'*). Set in the late 1990s, however, Popov's immediate frame of reference is the contemporary situation, and he is concerned in particular with the question of how the recent (Soviet) linguistic past should be handled. Along the way, his commentary includes numerous asides that explicitly address the general language question in post-Soviet Russia. The footnotes that relate to language and linguistic usage may be divided roughly into two categories, which will be treated in the next two subsections below: remarks on 'bad language' and remarks on 'good language'. The first section traces the main targets of Popov's linguistic criticism, while the second looks for linguistic elements that meet with his approval.

'Bad language' – or unreflective language use

Popov's critical remarks on language and linguistic usage relate, above all, to the use of officialese – that is, newspeak and Soviet clichés. In such remarks the point is often made by means of both form and content. For example, a comment on *kantseliarit*, the typical bureaucratic style of officialese, is written in *kantseliarit* style. Consider the syntactic structure of the following short note: «по выгону» из института (412); (412): Довольно неуклюжее словосочетание, обладающее за счет потери красоты фактографической точностью канцелярита.³ Another, related example is more complex:

> потом вдруг взял да и зачитал (232)
> (232): Советский «канцелярит», язык, на котором изъяснялись образованные «совки». Корней Чуковский, улучив момент, реализовал свою неприязнь к советской власти, обрушившись на «канцелярит», не достойный «строителя коммунизма». Однако на другом языке власть тогда разговаривать не умела, иначе это была бы совсем другая власть.⁴

The first part of the note contains some factual information, including a reference to the writer and critic Kornei Chukovskii, who invented the term *kantseliarit* (literally *kantseliaritis*, by analogy to other 'infections', such as *meningit[is]*). *Kantseliarit* was the title of the sixth chapter of Chukovskii's book *Zhivoi kak zhizn': o russkom iazyke* (*Alive as Life: On the Russian Language*, 1962). Popov's own note is written in a combination of *kantseliarit* syntax (gerunds, participles), colloquial words and expressions (*uluchiv moment, obrushivshis'*) and simply bad-style, clumsy newspeak (*realizoval svoiu nepriiazn'*), while various Soviet terms are highlighted through the use of quotation marks. The last sentence of the note comes as a compelling conclusion: against the background of the impersonal clichés of officialese, exemplified and simultaneously criticised in the foregoing sentences, its pithy, straightforward style and original, peculiar logic emphasise its quality as a personal comment and thus – according to the axiological hierarchy set up in this particular footnote – reinforce the validity of its argument, which points to the very close connection between authority itself and the language of that authority. A similar connection is highlighted in Chukovskii's book: Когда нам удастся уничтожить вконец бюрократические отношения людей, канцелярит сам собою изчезнет (Chukovskii [1962] 1990: 651).⁵

Popov's commentaries on the recent linguistic past have much in common with the philological literature of the 1990s and 2000s on Soviet newspeak (see Chapter 1). We recognise the critical stance, as well as the tendency to focus on various kinds of 'countercultural' reaction to official newspeak, including puns, jokes, slang expressions, or playful decipherings of standard abbreviations.

Soviet language culture also included a number of linguistic taboos. Footnote 61 in Popov's commentary concerns such a Soviet-era taboo, the word 'sex'. It starts with a concrete commentary on the word and then moves on to the phenomenon of 'sex' in the Soviet Union; both the word and the thing disappear, however, somewhere in the first third of the note, after which the author goes on to criticise, explicitly and implicitly, a number of Soviet institutions and power structures. Towards the end of the note Popov refers in passing to a joke and rounds off the comment by quoting a local Siberian *chastushka*:

(61) Слово «секс», которое тогда позволили опубликовать в «Литературной газете», органе существующих с дозволения КГБ советских либералов, любителей «ленинских норм», все-таки было долгие годы словом нехорошим, малосоветским. Недаром какая-то честная женщина заявила в начале конца «перестройки», что «в СССР нет секса». [...]
Играет Брежнев на гармони,
Хрущев пляшет гопака.
Погубили всю Россию
Два партийных мудака.[6]

If we look to the philological literature on newspeak for a parallel, Benedikt Sarnov's *Nash sovetskii novoiaz* (Sarnov 2002) is particularly close to Popov's commentary in terms of intonation, style and approach, in particular in the way it combines definitions and examples with a personal response to the linguistic item in question.

Popov's critical commentaries on linguistic matters relate both to language usage in general and to the language of literature in particular. But it is not the classic question about the interrelationship between the standard language and the language of literature that he is most concerned about. His criticism is aimed specifically at two targets: Socialist Realism and postmodernism. The former is condemned for its use of clichés, its grand style, formalistic structure and utopian subject matter, the latter for its lack of originality, insincerity, extensive use of quotations and formal experimentation. It should be noted that the author's criticism of Socialist Realism (which parallels his criticism of Soviet newspeak) is voiced in much clearer and more concise terms than his distaste for the postmodernist style(s). Here is the most drastic commentary on the latter: – Терпи! – сказал журналист (377). – Терпи, мужайся и пиши (378); (378) ЕТА И ЕСЬ, TOBAPISTSCHI, ПОСТМАДЕРНИЗИМ. МАДЕ ИН РАША.[7] In this highly idiosyncratic mixture of transliteration and phonetic transcription, of Latin and Cyrillic scripts, of English and Russian, Popov illustrates satirically what he sees as the Russian version of postmodernism. In the context of his comments on language, we may assume that this is not what he regards as the otherwise positive asset of linguistic diversity (see below). Rather, he sees it as an unreflective, and therefore negative, manifestation of it. Popov's mockery of postmodernism can be seen in other of his works as well: in *Nakanune nakanune* (*On the Eve of the Eve*, 1993), Popov's remake of Turgenev's novel, the narrator maintains that: Никто не знает, что такое постмодернизм, но все делают вид, что знают ... (Popov [1993] 2001: 431),[8] while later in the text we are told that it was invented by the KGB. The fact that Popov's prose is itself affiliated to a certain extent with postmodernist trends in Russian literature (take, for example, his extended use of footnotes or his play with the figure of the author) makes his stance on this matter complex, but obviously does not prevent him from criticising what he probably sees as extreme manifestations of the movement.

A further complicating factor in Popov's linguistic critique is that it is sometimes intermingled with nostalgia. A retrospective glance at a text from the 1970s naturally involves many comments on the use of words 'in those days', and these are frequently written in a nostalgic mood. Nostalgia, however, is no simple emotion, and pleasurable memories and nostalgic longings are often combined with slight derision or mere humorous asides. Even if there is a mildly nostalgic feel to Popov's commentary throughout the novel, nostalgia for past times is something he categorically denies:

> – нет у него вот этой самой печали, тоски по своему литературному прошлому, ностальгии, так сказать (798).

> (798) Как и у меня нет ровным счетом НИКАКОЙ ностальгии по тем временам, пропади они пропадом вместе с советской властью. Я согласен жить куда менее интересно, чем тогда, лишь бы ЖИЗНЬ БЫЛА, а не ее виртуальный коммунистический муляж со всеми этими «стройками», «гэбухами», «починами», «самиздатом», пьянством, бравадой, страхом и стыдом. [. . .][9]

The quotation marks in the last sentence indicate time-specific, Sovietspeak designations (*stroiki, gebukhi, pochiny, samizdat*), while the accompanying words without quotation marks are universal and timeless concepts (*p'ianstvo*, *bravada*, *strakh*, *styd*). The highlighting of Soviet terms clearly serves to remind us of their history and historicity. In this sense Popov's anti-nostalgic rhetoric reveals the deeply problematic nature of nostalgia, which, without critical reflection, always runs the risk of constructing an idyllic, ahistorical image of the past, as convincingly shown in the case of post-communist mass nostalgia by Svetlana Boym (2001).

In Popov's commentary, the meticulous attention to linguistic nuances demonstrates a hypersensitive, or 'hyper-reflective', linguistic attitude, precisely the opposite of the unreflective language use which is the object of its criticism. In other words, in his very manner of exposing linguistic negligence Popov demonstrates a high degree of linguistic awareness.

In note 798 quoted above, all the virtues and vices of the past are simply contrasted with *life*. How this life – in contrast to deceptive ideologies and dead language – should be rendered in words is a key question raised by the commentary, and brings us to the topic of linguistic diversity.

'Good language' – or linguistic diversity

The commentator's view of what constitutes 'good language' emerges from his use and discussion of non-standard varieties of Russian, including slang, dialect or regionalisms, *prostorechie* (low-style popular language) and profanity (*mat*). In these comments on linguistic diversity, we find explicit allusions to the contemporary linguistic situation. As we saw in Part I, according to Russian official language culture, 'good language' is usually associated with the standard language. While Popov occasionally joins in the complaints about the impoverishment of the standard language typical of public debates on the language situation, his views are very far from those of the hard-line norm police. Consider the following comment on the relationship between the standard language and regionalisms:

> (501) «Застрожился» – это нечто такое сибирское, емкое и отнюдь не адекватное расхожему «посерьезнел». В «областных» словарях есть много изумительных слов, которые нехудо бы ввести в русский литературный язык, с каждым годом теряющий эластичность. «Чо мшишься?» – спрашивает мужик мужика где-нибудь на Ангаре. Это означает: «Ну чего ты суетишься, нервничаешь, волнуешься, предаешься пессимизму, угрюмо смотришь в будущее и неласково на мир,

когда мир прекрасен, будущее – светлое, пессимизм не имманентен русскому менталитету, волноваться – себе вредить, нервные клетки не восстанавливаются, и вообще все на свете есть суета и томление духа».[10]

The note contains a concrete critical remark about the contemporary Russian standard language, accusing it of becoming less 'elastic' every year. The concept of 'elasticity' is noteworthy, since it implies a notion of semantic dynamism not usually invoked when discussing the problems and prospects of the standard language in Russia today. In such discussions, for example in the parliamentary debates about the recent amendments to the Law on the Russian Language (see Chapter 6), arguments about linguistic norms, correctness and purity prevail. The author's accompanying example, the simple two-word sentence *Cho mshish'sia?*, requires a 'translation' into the standard language that consists of 43 words, thereby illustrating the semantic richness and extreme 'elasticity' of the Siberian expression. Moreover, the 'translation' is rendered in a symmetrical (chiastic) formal structure and thus gives the impression of something 'perfect' in both form and content. The exhaustiveness of the translation gives it, of course, a humorous tone – of sympathy combined with gentle derision. However, the general tone of voice here is clearly sympathetic.

Compared with other Russian non-standard varieties in the post-Soviet era, dialects still enjoy a relatively low status, and have few spokespersons among Russian writers. There have been, however, at least two other people engaged in language cultivation whose attitude towards the Russian dialects are reminiscent of Popov's stance, even if they differ fundamentally in many other respects: the late prose writer Aleksandr Solzhenitsyn, and philologist and cultural historian Mikhail Epstein. Solzhenitsyn, we recall, compiled a *Russian Dictionary of Linguistic Expansion* (Solzhenitsyn 1990), endeavouring to reintroduce words that have 'undeservedly been abandoned' and to replace foreign loans with Russian 'equivalents'. His main source of inspiration was the classic nineteenth-century *Slovar' zhivogo russkogo iazyka* (*Dictionary of the Living Russian Language*) by philologist and ethnographer Vladimir Dal', with its numerous colourful dialect words. The cultural theorist and philologist Epstein, in turn, is the initiator of a word-formation project called *dar slova* (the gift of the word), active since 2000. The idea of the project is to create new words and derivatives from Russian roots in order to enrich both the lexicon and the structure of the language. Epstein is not categorically against foreign loanwords, but he argues that the influx of new loans should encourage linguistic creativity on native

Russian soil. Also for Epstein, dialect words and word forms are a great inspiration, as his enthusiastic report from a dialect research expedition of 2006 reveals (Epshtein and Genis 2007). For Solzhenitsyn, Epstein and Popov, then, dialects represent a source of renewal for the Russian standard language. Popov, however, shares neither Solzhenitsyn's generally hostile position on foreign loanwords nor Epstein's idiosyncratic, ultra-creative style. Moreover, both Solzhenitsyn and Epstein assume a more abstract attitude towards the living dialects than does Popov, who embraces not only dialectisms but also their users – the provincial topos has always played a special role in his literary fiction.

In Popov's text, non-standard linguistic varieties are generally regarded as positive, but it is essential that they be used in their genuine contexts, that is, not unreflectively. This is also the case with the particular Russian form of popular language known as *prostorechie*, as my next example demonstrates: Ан нет (31)!; (31) С чего бы вдруг опять это псевдопростонародное? Скорее всего опять кривлянье, ерничанье, пустое зубоскальство, неизвестно над чем и зачем, неосознаваемая глупость, ограниченность мышления.[11] While the low-style popular expression (*an net*) is denounced indignantly as a 'pseudofolklorism', the note is clearly also self-ironic and the stream of invective against the use of the expression highly exaggerated, of course. In another commentary on popular language, the humorous element takes over as the author explains an 'erroneous' prepositional phrase as being *prostorechie* and points to its effects, while informing us that this commentary is meant for future, explicitly named, translators of his novel:

– Так я же по спору (251)
(251) Просторечие. Правильно нужно сказать «на спор». Неумение правильно ставить предлоги – элемент детского обучающегося сознания во взрослой речи, зачастую становящейся от этого образной, живой и глубокой. (Комментарий специально для Fr. Rosemarie Tietze (Munchen), Mr. Robert Porter (Bristol) & тов. Jukka Mallinen (Helsinki), которые переведут этот «роман», отчего мы с ними наконец-то не только прославимся, но и разбогатеем).[12]

Popov's humorous attitude plays down the consequences of mixing styles – consequences such as the degeneration of the standard language frequently invoked in the language debates. As he comments in a note on the combination within one phrase of the expressions *libo* and *piannaia rozha*: (55) И здесь – интеллигентное «либо» и брутальная «пьяная рожа» сопряжены исключительно для веселья.[13]

This stance becomes especially clear in a whole series of comments on *mat*. Here *mat* is said to suggest exactly the opposite of the 'dead language' criticised elsewhere in the commentary, and stands for authenticity, intimacy and genuine emotions, even in contexts where this is not expected in the first place: (343) Переход на «ты», равно как и использование в деловой беседе нецензурной брани,[14] являлся легко опознаваемым знаком некоего благорасположения вышестоящего к нижележащему.[15]

Let us look at the most extensive commentary on *mat*, note 376:

А, а! . . . на! – сказал Иван Иваныч (376).
(376), но вовсе не употребил, как вы, конечно же, подумали, нехорошее слово на букву «х», на месте которого стоят три точки. Иван Иваныч не любил матерщину и правильно делал: и так все изматерились – народ, интеллигенты, партия, правительство . . .

Материться, очевидно, и вообще нехорошо, вредно. Поэтому я в какой-то степени благодарен КГБшникам, что они забрали у меня рассказ «Неваревализьм» и торжественно сожгли его у себя в топке по собственному постановлению, если они, конечно же, не врут. Рассказ этот имел крайне простой сюжет, но был написан исключительно нецензурным языком. Хотя – какая в этом моя вина, если народ так говорит и думает? [. . .]

А впрочем, все в этом рассказе любят друг друга, но только очень сильно ругаются, прямо ужасно!/Трудно русскому человеку без матерщины. У Пантелеймона Романова есть рассказ, как мужик-фронтовик поклялся, что, если останется в живых, прекратит материться. Он вернулся в родную деревню после империалистической бойни 1914–1917 гг. и вскоре повесился, так как не мог ни с кем в деревне разговаривать.

А у нас в экспедиции на Таймыре был один Саня, который знал, что «выражаться» при дамах нехорошо, поэтому он все время при разговоре давился, как объевшаяся кошка. Только и слышалось нечленораздельное «бныть, бныть». [. . .][16]

In view of the passion with which the use of profanity is generally condemned or promoted in the language debates, the style and voice of this passage stand out as extraordinarily restrained. Having initially stated that the story's main character Ivan Ivanych did not use the bad word (which nevertheless 'has been replaced by the three dots'), the narrator proceeds with a clear if somewhat naïve denunciation of *mat*. There then follows, however, a string of 'examples' or parables, which all highlight the natural function and, literally, vital importance of *mat* in people's speech and life. The effect of the whole passage is humorous, innocently provocative, but also potentially conciliatory: Popov demonstrates the integral place both in life and in literature of one of the most disputed linguistic phenomena in contemporary Russian – a stance we recognise from writers' reactions to the recent ban on *mat* in art (including literature) from 2014 (see Chapter 6).

The indignant tone of the notes directed at newspeak and ritualistic linguistic practices discussed above is rarely present in the comments on *mat* and other non-standard varieties. On the contrary, these varieties are ascribed the quality of authenticity. *Mat* is usually dealt with humorously, as the most natural thing in life, as the author illustrates by providing a number of stories and examples. In addition to note 376 discussed above, consider, for instance, note 391 about an opera singer who has a compulsive habit of commenting in rhymed *mat* on every instruction given by the director. Or note 213, where the use of *mat* is portrayed as a natural part of the rural idyll of Russian emigrants living in Germany.

Popov's celebration of non-standard varieties is in keeping with his typical character gallery (drop-outs, thieves, drunkards) and subject matter (provincial everyday life, trivialities bordering on the banal). One characteristic protagonist in Popov's fictional world is the aspiring and unsuccessful writer, such as Ivan Ivanovich in *The True Story of 'The Green Musicians'*: there is the cycle of stories about a hack writer called Fetisov (with several different first names), and then the narrator of the novel *Dusha patriota* (*Soul of a Patriot*, 1989), 'Evgenii Anatol'evich', who shares his name and patronymic with Popov, while the same combination appears in several other works. Many of Popov's writer-figures are clearly graphomaniacs, and the graphomanic element is likewise strong in *The True Story of 'The Green Musicians'*.

The commentator's stance – or graphomania

The tone of the commentary alternates between the didactic and nostalgic, on the one hand, and the ironic and parodic, on the other. The narrative attitude that emerges is playfully naïve, but at the same time quite sophisticated, poised between an ironic distance and seemingly genuine emotional involvement. While this combination makes the commentary ambiguous and difficult to interpret, it is crucial to its rhetorical effect. When we delve deeper and more critically into the style of the notes, we see that it is not only digressive and/or humorous, but also frequently over-explicit, clumsy and dilettantish. Consider, for instance, the colloquial mishmash and extreme digressive style of note 376, the *kantseliarit* in notes 412 and 232, and the openly emotional, aggressive or indignant tone of notes 798 and 31, all quoted above. This aspect of Popov's style has to do with the strong graphomanic element in the novel. Graphomania implies not only the obsession with writing; it is also an art form in its own right, an aesthetics of writing, where its recognised characteristics – the 'mistakes, digressions, repetitions, irrelevancies, faulty memory and refusal to check "facts", the cultivated sloppiness, the appearance of spontaneous, unrevised, even "automatic" writing' – become part of a deliberate bad writing style, or, in Richard Borden's (1999: 7) phrase, 'bad writing in quotation marks'.

Among the many rhetorical and aesthetic effects of graphomania is its ability to draw our attention to the metalevel of language, just as Popov's overtly critical or approving commentaries do. Graphomania is certainly no hidden device in *The True Story of 'The Green Musicians'*. On the contrary, the commentary repeatedly mentions and elaborates broadly on the phenomenon. The author's attitude towards the graphomanic elements in the story on which he is commenting is sympathetic, rather than critical, at least when compared with his harsh criticism of the typical 'Soviet' writer.

For our context, Popov's manner of exposing graphomania – namely by means of graphomania – is crucial. Footnote 589 offers a typical example: – Ладно, ладно. Без истерик (589), – сердито сказал Голос; (589) Почти графоманщина. Романтизм, фантастика – это собственно, и есть почти графоманщина. И наоборот.[17] Here, the definition of graphomania is itself rather graphomanic – imprecise and tautological. Moreover, Popov's novel applies a 'double' graphomanic perspective, as the (graphomanic) commentator's indignation is often aroused by his own (graphomanic) style in the narrative part of the novel.[18] In note 242, following several remarks criticising certain clichés in his earlier text, the author laments: (242) Ой, я не могу! Штамп на штампе! Сейчас уже и не понять – кривлялся я или так получилось. Скорее всего – последнее. [. . .][19] A little later he reaches a real outburst, where, for once, there is little room for ambiguity:

Так ли, не так ли, но факт остается фактом: обо всем, кроме литературы, он теперь и думать забыл. А если все ж и думал, то лишь в одной определенной плоскости (329): [. . .]
(329) Штамп на штампе! Все пропитано СОВЕТЧИНОЙ, а ведь казалось, что я – гордый, независимый, все понимаю, веду автономное существование. После того, как по нашей улице проезжал обоз говночистов, «амбрэ» сохранялось еще

дня два-три. А тут – с 17-го года нюхали и к 1974-му окончательно принюхались.[20]

In spite of the prosaic and carnivalesque character of this explanatory note, it is in fact quite serious, highlighting the author's personal experience of the inevitability of the influence of *sovetchina* – his object of criticism throughout the text. Again we can draw a parallel with the post-Soviet philological writings on Soviet newspeak examined in Chapter 1. Gasan Guseinov (2003) argues that Soviet sociopolitical language culture cannot be treated within the narrow confines and genres of official newspeak. He defines it, as we recall, in terms of a particular linguistic experience or competence, with implications even for the language culture of today.[21]

Popov's novel describes and portrays a similar situation, and his strategy for overcoming the influence of *sovetchina*, or at least laying it bare, is that of 'bad writing' (in quotation marks, cf. Borden 1999) – that is, through graphomania. Graphomania exposes itself as bad writing (without quotation marks), thereby transcending the bad style and making a statement about it.[22] It is also in this context that we should understand Popov's ambivalence towards nostalgia. While he cannot himself escape linguistic nostalgia and other nostalgic feelings, his exposure of them and his anti-nostalgic rhetoric nevertheless attack the mythopoetic, imaginary and ahistorical, in short, the *unreflective* nostalgia that is typical of much backward longing in Russia today (Boym 2001).

VLADIMIR SOROKIN: THE DIACHRONIC DIMENSIONS OF LANGUAGE

As we turn now to Vladimir Sorokin, we will confront a writer who is far less explicit, but no less direct and radical, in his manner of tackling language issues. Like many contemporary Russian writers, Sorokin is preoccupied with the past, both the recent, Soviet past and Russia's more distant, pre-Petrine history. At the same time, several of his stories are located in a distant (or not so distant) future, a future which always features a particular linguistic environment. Thus, alongside their frequent combination of elements from quite disparate stylistic and linguistic registers, many of Sorokin's texts exhibit a peculiar mixture of what are usually called 'archaisms' and 'neologisms', that is, elements of language that differ from a diachronic point of view.

The mixture of neologisms (such as the hypertechnological *vestevoi puzyr'* 'news bubble') and archaisms (such as *ud* 'male member') in

Sorokin's novel *Den' oprichnika* (*Day of the Oprichnik*, 2006) has been noted by translators, scholars and reviewers alike. But the diachronic amalgam in this and other of Sorokin's novels is not simply a combination of old and new words, but also a juxtaposition of different styles, syntaxes, and pragmatic and rhetorical structures, that is, a juxtaposition of historically embedded linguistic features that go far beyond the realm of single words. In this section, I aim to identify elements of this 'beyond', while limiting my analysis to the languages of the Soviet era, and to a single short story, since such identification calls for a close reading. Homing in on the short story 'Monoklon' (2010), I will explore the role of Sorokin's 'historical linguistics', with a particular emphasis on the interplay between the text's aesthetics and linguistic make-up, on the one hand, and its political and ethical frame of reference, on the other.

Sorokin's use of the diachronic dimensions of language combines linguistic creativity with recourse to various ideological idioms or styles – the constitutive features of his poetics, according to Dagmar Burkhart:

So wird seine Poetik einerseits von einem ständigen sprachlichen Experimentieren an den Tabugrenzen (Ästhetik des Häßlichen, Turpismus) und andererseits einem imitierenden Zugriff auf totalitäre Weltbilder, konventionelle Rituale und normative Genres, einem tautologischen Nachschreiben von Stilen, Jargons und Prätexten sowie ihrer Zusammenfügung zum Super- oder Megatext (Pastiche) bestimmt. (Burkhart 1999: 5)[23]

Stylistic variety, including the imitative use of clichés, jargon and the like, has been interpreted by Walter Koschmal (1995) and others as one of several strategies employed in post-socialist Russian literature for deconstructing, or at least challenging, the traditional Russian aesthetics of responsibility (*Verantwortungsästhetik*). Distance towards language and its references was famously articulated by Sorokin himself in the early nineties, when he described his writings as лишь буквы на бумаге (Sorokin 1992: 121).[24] While such characterisations are certainly appropriate with regard to Sorokin's early works, one may perceive in his more recent writings, from the novel *Day of the Oprichnik* onwards, a more strongly expressed political undercurrent and ethical concern, raising questions about power structures, social hierarchies and human dignity. The frame of reference has become more time bound than in his earlier works and includes clear pointers to contemporary Russian society. Obviously, Sorokin is not the kind of writer who would express his views on the state of affairs in Russia straightforwardly in his fiction; rather, his concern is conveyed in and by his poetics, through recourse to the grotesque, the absurd and, as I will argue in this section, through the linguistic shape of his text. As I will attempt to show, Sorokin's strategy of employing jargon, particular styles, clichés and other linguistic elements from the past serves to raise the reader's awareness of such concern.

The diachronic dimension of language in Sorokin consists of more than the mere juxtaposition of neologisms and archaisms in one and the same text, however interesting such a juxtaposition might be in itself. This becomes clear when we shift our focus from the linguistic level proper to the historical memory invoked by certain words, phrases, slogans and other linguistic elements. In my reading of the story 'Monoklon', I focus on the diachronic dimensions of Sorokin's language by analysing the historical layers contained in specific words and styles, and on their possible meaning and meaning-generating function. More specifically, I show how the 'linguistic memory'[25] triggered by certain words, quotations or styles combines with other linguistic and poetic features to create perceptions and representations of time, memory and history that encourage the reader to reflect on these topics in ethical and political terms. In so doing, I am less eager to uncover any particular political ideology in Sorokin's work than to explore his aesthetic representations of today's burning linguistic, political and ethical issues. In 'Monoklon', these have to do with the handling of conflicting perceptions of the totalitarian past, seen through the lens of language. My reading is structured according to three lines of enquiry: (1) languages of the past; (2) the discourse of memory; and (3) representations of time.

Languages of the past

'Monoklon' describes one day in the life of an old man, Viktor Nikolaevich, living in an apartment block on Leninskii Prospekt. Having got up and gone through the ritual of his personal hygiene, he is attracted by a noise coming from the street. When he looks out of the window, he sees a shining white crowd of young people dressed in spacesuits and helmets with the inscription SSSR, a celebration of 12 April, Cosmonauts' Day. He becomes entirely absorbed in this wonderful spectacle and equally annoyed when his enjoyment of it is interrupted, first by a phone call from his son, and then by the doorbell. He expects to see Valia, who takes care of his laundry, but the visitors are three men, a man called Monoklon and his two assistants.[26] They come inside; Viktor Nikolaevich recognises Monoklon and is petrified. Monoklon takes out a pickaxe, Viktor Nikolaevich is laid face down on the table, and Monoklon, using a heavy sledge-hammer, forces the pickaxe into Viktor Nikolaevich's anal orifice, penetrating his body. Before leaving the apartment, Monoklon examines closely some photographs hanging on the wall above Viktor Nikolaevich's desk. The guests leave. Viktor Nikolaevich, hardly able to move, drags himself down onto the floor and moves towards the window, manages to rise and lean out, wants to shout, but only blood issues from his mouth. One drop of blood is picked up by the wind and falls onto a young man's helmet. From the explicit temporal references included in the story, we can infer that the action takes place in 2010.

Linguistic elements from the past include, above all, words, phrases and concepts connected with the Soviet era, as well as phrases and fragments of songs that are either Soviet themselves or were included in the Soviet repertoire or school programme:[27]

> – В сто концов убегают рельсы . . . – проговорил он, вспомнив песню Пугачевой. – По рельсам . . . и по шпалам, по шпалам, по шпалам . . . (10)[28]

> – Заправлены в планшеты космические карты . . .
> – И штурман уточняет в последний раз маршрут! – тут же подхватила толпа.
> – Давайте-ка, ребята, покурим перед стартом, у нас еще в запасе четырнадцать мину-у-у-ут! – подпел толпе Виктор Николаевич с шестого этажа. (12)[29]

> За окном пела блестящая толпа:
>   На пыльных тропинках
>   Далеких планет
>   Останутся наши следы! (13)[30]

> За окном пели блестящие:
>   Я Земля, я своих провожаю питомцев –
>   Сыновей, дочерей.
>   Долетайте до самого солнца
>   И домой возвращайтесь скорей. (18)[31]

Particularly noteworthy are the words *kosmonavt* ('cosmonaut') and *Den' kosmonavtiki* ('Cosmonauts' Day'), which in themselves function as signal words for the Soviet celebration of space-related events, evoking images of Iurii Gagarin in his helmet beside his spacecraft.

> День космонавтики. (10, 11, 12)[32]

– Космонавты! – удивленно пробормотал Виктор Николаевич. (10)[33]

– Ничего себе! Космонавты! Космонавтики! (11)[34]

Виктор Николаевич сжал жилистый кулак, выкинул в окно и крикнул:
– Слава героям космоса! (13)[35]

– Ух-ты, ах-ты! – разнесли динамики голос бровастого парня.
– Все мы космонавты! – заревела толпа.
– Ух-ты, ах-ты!
– Все мы космонавты!!
– Ух-ты! Ах-ты!
– Все мы ко-смо-нав-ты!!! (18)[36]

The Soviet-era linguistic elements, together with the general description of the scene, combine to create an audio-visual impression of the radiant crowd of 30,000 young people, where Gagarin's heroic deed is celebrated *today*. This celebratory 'now' is emphasised in the young cosmonaut's address to the crowd, which recalls the anaphoric use of 'today's' characteristic of hymnographical texts used in church: – *Сегодня* двенадцатое апреля. День космонавтики. *В этот день* Юрий Гагарин покорил космос, совершив свой героический полет (11, my italics).[37]

The celebration, full of linguistic fragments reminiscent of another time, brings a glorious past into the present. In some instances, we can see how linguistic elements from the past are combined with those indicating the present, as in the following amalgam of Sovietspeak and present-day patriotism, which also includes contemporary terms referring to the country's tandem leadership: – Каждый патриот России – космонавт в душе! Наш президент – космонавт №1! Толпа зааплодировала. – А уж наш премьер – космонавт из космонавтов! Толпа радостно заревела (12).[38]

During Viktor Nikolaevich's phone call with his son, the identity of the young cosmonauts becomes clear as he paraphrases their name, searching for the right designation: Это эти ... как их ... ну, идут которые? «Мы вместе»? Как их? Да! Да! (12).[39] It is Viktor Nikolaevich's son who obviously suggests their correct name in between this flow of short phrases: *Idushchie vmeste* (Walking together), that is, the pro-Putin youth organisation founded by Vasilii Iakemenko in 2000 and renamed *Nashi* (Ours) in 2005.

To Viktor Nikolaevich, the spectacle represents a hilarious remembrance of the Soviet past. In recognition of the reason for the celebration, he bursts into a combination of Sovietspeak and spontaneous, heartfelt swearing: – Сегодня ж 12 апреля! День космонавтики, сволочи дорогие! Мать честная! (10).[40]

Then he tries to join in, by humming along to the Soviet space song and shouting out a heroic Soviet space-related slogan. He also tries to share his experience with his neighbours, with his son who phones him (shouting slogan-like phrases down the telephone): Готовность – номер один! Выхожу на орбиту! (13),[41] and finally with the arriving guests, in the belief that it is Valia coming to pick up his laundry: Недовольно бормоча и напевая, щелкнул замком, размашисто распахнул дверь: – Валя, быстрей! Я вам щас такое покажу! (13).[42]

Viktor Nikolaevich, however, is struck by the past from two directions: not only by the celebration below his windows, but also by the visit and revenge of Monoklon, whose life path has crossed Viktor Nikolaevich's before, as we learn towards the end of the story. The deep contrast between these two aspects of the past is emphasised by a complex pattern of parallels on the lexical-semantic level. First, we observe a juxtaposition of the collective and the individual: what is going on outside the window is a celebration of the Soviet collective spirit, expressed, for example, in the formulaic 'actions' of the crowd: Толпа радостно зашумела (11); Толпа стихла (11); Толпа зашумела (12); Толпа зааплодировала (12); Толпа радостно заревела (15–16); За окном шумела и смеялась толпа (16); За окном толпа запела песню про Землю, [...] (16); Толпа перестала петь и просто шумела (18).[43]

The melting of the individual into a collective 'self' is made even more explicit in the young leader's address to the crowd, where he urges them to become 'Iuriis' all together. Потому что в душе каждого из вас живет любовь к своей родине, желание сделать ее еще более могущественной, еще более свободной! И мне, из этой ракеты сейчас кажется, друзья, что сегодня каждого из вас зовут Юрий! (11).[44]

By contrast, what goes on inside Viktor Nikolaevich's apartment is a gruesome but solemn act of revenge carried out by one man, Monoklon. Furthermore, the parallel between the two contrasting realms of the past is powerfully reinforced by the abundance of words referring to light, gleaming and radiance based on the verbs *blestat'* ('shine') and *sverkat'* ('gleam', 'flash' [*sverknut'*]). Outside, they refer to the radiant, celebrating crowd, inside to a concrete artefact, the pickaxe, the object with which the act of revenge is perpetrated:

В центре, в мешанине *блестящих* на солнце тел стала приподниматься ракета с гербом России на корпусе. (11)

За окном пела *блестящая* толпа: [. . .] (13)

Но он был идеально отполирован и *сверкал* в солнечном свете, как дорогой японский меч. Валек взял этот *блестящий*, плавно изогнутый кусок железа, [. . .] (15)

Виктор Николаевич уставился на *блестящий* металл. (15)

Моноклон глянул на *блестящий*, прошедший сквозь старческое тело металл, опустил кувалду: [. . .] (16–17)

За окном пели *блестящие*: [. . .] (18)

Лишь одна капля, отскочив, минуя зеленый откос водоотлива, сорвалась вниз, *сверкнула* рубином на солнце, полетела, подхваченная влажным воздухом.
Ветер отнес каплю крови от дома и уронил на толпу *блестящих*. (19, my italics)[45]

The discourse of memory

The linguistic memory triggered by certain words, fragments and phrases is reinforced by what we may call a both implicit and explicit *discourse of memory*. We have seen one example in the young cosmonaut's projection of the historical name and person of Iurii Gagarin onto every individual living person in the crowd's here and now. If this is a straightforward example of collective memory, then we see a more indirect expression of the discourse of memory in Monoklon's string of short utterances in the 'dialogue' between Monoklon and Viktor Nikolaevich, a personal memory. Here are Monoklon's words:

– Хороший день, – [. . .] (14)
– Моноклон. (14)
– Узнал, – [. . .] (14)
– Я же обещал тебе. (14)
– А обещанного ждут не три года, – [. . .] (14)
– Помнит. (15)
– Время, [. . .] (16)[46]

In these short explanatory phrases from Monoklon, we see how personal recollection goes through a number of various stages: recognition, promise, expectance, remembering and actualisation. Finally, the most explicit expression of the discourse of memory is the second of the two inscriptions on the pickaxe: *PROCUL DUBIO* [...] *AD MEMORANDUM* (15).[46] This reflects neither a historical nor a collective memory, nor a personal memory per se. Inscribed on the artefact with which the brutal act is performed, this is a more distant and seemingly objective expression of the memory discourse, which adds to the solemnity of Monoklon's act of revenge by creating the impression of inevitability and historical necessity.

Representations of time

Moving on from languages of the past and discourse of memory to concrete representations of time in the story, one is struck by the number of time-bound references, alluding, above all, to circumstances and events in Viktor Nikolaevich's life. We are told that he is currently eighty-two, a piece of information conveyed by a glimpse of his image in a mirror: Из зеркала на него уставился восьмидесятидвухлетний Виктор Николаевич (9).[48] Scars and tattoos on his body are meticulously described and dated:

> На теле было два старых шрама: на левом бедре, когда в 58-м на охоте его задел клыками раненый кабан и на правом локте, когда в 91-м он сломал руку, поскользнувшись возле своего подъезда. Еще на теле виднелись две татуировки: посередине груди орел, когтящий змею, а на левом плече сердце, проткнутое двумя кинжалами, и еле различимая надпись «Нина». Обе татуировки были старыми, пятидесятых годов. (9)[49]

When he sees the crowd of cosmonauts below his windows, he recalls earlier events, similar to, but not in any way matching, today's celebration:

> За свою сорокалетнюю жизнь на Ленинском проспекте он не видел ничего подобного. Случались здесь демонстрации коммунистов в ельцинские времена, было и знаменитое побоище на площади Гагарина в 1993 году, в трехстах метрах от его дома, когда патриоты из «Трудовой Москвы» схватились с ельцинским ОМОНом. Но такого не было никогда. (10)[50]

We also find other, more indirect 'historical' references, for example in the naming of artefacts that carry a concrete reference to a specific time and place: Потом он долго лежал, глядя в потолок с чешской хрустальной люстрой, купленной покойной женой в середине семидесятых в магазине «Свет» на Ленинском проспекте (7–8).[51] The shop name *Svet* ('Light'), an emblematic example of Soviet language culture, reminds us of typical Soviet shop names such as *Khleb* ('Bread'), *Moloko* ('Milk') or *Miaso* ('Meat').

The most detailed historical references, however, are found in the description of the two photographs which Monoklon examines closely towards the end of the story. These photographs shed light on the prehistory of the last meeting between Viktor Nikolaevich and Monoklon, depicted in the story: a picture from 1949 of graduates at the law faculty of the University of Kazan', with Viktor Nikolaevich standing next to Monoklon, and a picture of Viktor Nikolaevich as a senior lieutenant in the KGB with the inscription 'Norilsk 1952'. Norilsk was famous for its concentration camps, the *Norillag* and the *Gorlag*, where tens of thousands of prisoners were incarcerated. We may infer that Viktor Nikolaevich was a camp guard and Monoklon a prisoner, and that Viktor Nikolaevich showed no mercy towards his former fellow student.

These circumstances are not spelt out in the story. But they are hinted at, partly through these temporal references, but also through meticulous references to concrete traces of brutality on Monoklon's body: Левую бровь пересекал глубокий старый шрам, отчего левый глаз смотрел совсем сквозь щелочку (14);[52] Обе руки его были покалечены: на правой не хватало мизинца, на левой четвертый палец и мизинец не сгибались (17).[53]

Within the timeframe of the story 'Monoklon', the figure of Viktor Nikolaevich represents the *synchronic point zero*. Throughout the narrative, the two realms of 'now' and 'before' are juxtaposed, with Viktor Nikolaevich's perception of them being the link between them. In the first case, the celebration of Gagarin, he is moved and enthused; in the second, the 'revenge', he is petrified, as indicated by his static, death-like responses to Monoklon's act of revenge: Виктор Николаевич замер (14);[54] Но лицо Виктора Николаевича словно окостенело (15);[55] Тело Виктора Николаевича словно окаменело (16).[56]

The most extreme representation of the synchronic point zero follows immediately after this last phrase, when Viktor Nikolaevich, almost dead, lies on the table awaiting the final blow from Monoklon's sledge-hammer: Только нога билась о ножку стола равномерно, будто отсчитывая время (16).[57]

The three main aspects of the diachronic dimension to language that we have observed in this section – languages of the past, the discourse of memory and representations of time – all serve the story's main purpose, which is to bring the past, or rather, two disparate pasts, into the present, in other words, to create a synchronicity of asynchronous historical pasts.

CONCLUSIONS

Popov and Sorokin both address the question of linguistic legacies in present-day Russian society and culture, and they do so in quite different ways. Whereas Popov works through plain exposure, explicit commentary, satire and light irony, Sorokin's technique is one of poetic devices, juxtaposition and subtle allusion. What unites them is a concern for the broader issues implied by the multifarious aspects of 'the language question', in particular in the sphere of ideological language and the Soviet linguistic legacy. Let us look more closely, by way of conclusion, at the interpretive implications of the two approaches.

Evgenii Popov: exposing graphomania

Both in style and content Popov's novel reflects, and reflects on, the language question in post-perestroika Russia. In commenting on a text from the 1970s, the author draws attention at the same time to the linguistic and stylistic heritage from that period still tangible in Russian usage today, contextualising his comments with reference to the major new issues raised by the present-day language debates.

Popov's commentary displays a strong dislike of clichés, stereotypes and conventionalisms. He dismantles dead thinking and dead language, dethrones grand subjects, attacking them through derision and satire. He exposes nonsense and meaninglessness, subtly alluding to the relevance and necessity of such a critique today. Furthermore, he berates what has been called the 'discourse of threat' in the language debates, that is, metaphors of threat and protection, disease, dirt and death (Ryazanova-Clarke 2006a: 34ff.). This is done by playing down the consequences of stylistic promiscuity, promoting the integral place in life and letters of non-standard varieties of Russian, and demonstrating confidence in the ability of the language to take care of itself. As we saw in Chapter 5, Popov shares this confidence with several other contemporary Russian writers, although not many voice it with such clarity in their literary work.

While Popov's critical remarks are passionate and uncompromising, his approving comments reflect liberal and egalitarian views on both the language question and on cultural life in general: (798) [. . .]

И бездуховность решительно не грозит России, которая, даст Бог, непременно впишется в культурное мировое пространство, где мирно сосуществуют «американизм» и эпос, фольклор и постмодернизм, порнуха и романтика, квас и кока-кола.[58] This reconciliation of opposites is reminiscent of Popov's hope for the future of literature, and suggests that Popov's overall idea is one of cultural and linguistic synthesis and pluralism:

> Literature will assume its own modest but lasting, real and meaningful place in that world of literary pluralism where comic books coexist peacefully with loftily intellectual texts and where the novel will finally cease to be perceived as some amalgam of the Bible, a reference book and a manual of etiquette. (Popov 1993: 39, cited in Porter 1994: 97)

How serious is Popov? Jeremy Morris (2013: 85) is right to warn against simplistic readings of this master of irony: 'Almost defying analysis, Popov has a unique ability to point to and then refuse greater "meaning", at the same time as locating potential significance within the most meagre of turn of phrase and gesture.' I would still argue with regard to Popov's axiological stance, however, that there is a clear development in his *oeuvre* from the playful, 'comical irresponsibility' of his earlier work towards what I would call a more 'serious playfulness' in the later. Seen from this perspective, *The True Story of 'The Green Musicians'* signals a new tendency in Popov's work, which, starting from the turn of the century, has become less ironic and more straightforward in its critique of the political, social and linguistic situation in Russia today.[59] In *The True Story of 'The Green Musicians'*, the author's ironic stance gives the commentary an unsettling tone of voice. However, thanks to the critical, humorous, naïve and reconciliatory style, Popov's novel also possesses great didactic potential, inviting the reader to engage in independent reflection on – among other things – language and linguistic usage.

The graphomanic setting of these statements forms a comment in itself, as the author demonstrates to what degree some seventy years of Soviet newspeak have affected Russian and become an integral part of the language, language situation and linguistic competence today. His way of exposing graphomania through graphomania – both in his own linguistic practice and on the metalevel – is a sophisticated and highly original way of responding to the language question, which captures the dual challenges of dealing with Russia's recent linguistic past and of negotiating the language's current state.

Vladimir Sorokin: simultaneity of the non-simultaneous

In his story 'Monoklon', Sorokin creates a synchronicity of asynchronous historical pasts. One is the glorious, celebratory Soviet world of spacecraft and cosmonauts, the other the violent, brutal world of the camps. Formally, the two pasts are divided by strict chronological limits, confining the Norillag and Gorlag to the Stalin period (the camps closed soon after Stalin's death in 1953 – the Norillag in 1956 and the Gorlag in 1954) and the peak of the Soviet space programme to the years before and after Gagarin's famous space flight in 1961 (Cosmonauts' Day was established in 1961 and is celebrated to this day). As the story brings the two pasts together, however, highlighting, through various parallels, the connection between them, it emphasises their being part of one common past, the Soviet era, a fact contemporary Russia still has to come to terms with.

A link between the two worlds is subtly established in the story's conclusion. The closing scene describes an almost symbolic encounter, as a drop of blood from the victim's mouth drips out of the window, is taken up by the air and then falls onto the helmet of a young boy, also called Viktor. The boy is insensitive to the blood. Note, again, the words *sverknut'* ('flash') and *blestat'* ('shine'), underlining the parallel between Monoklon's act of revenge and the celebratory crowd:

> Лишь одна капля, отскочив, минуя зеленый откос водоотлива, сорвалась вниз, *сверкнула* рубином на солнце, полетела, подхваченная влажным воздухом. Ветер отнес каплю крови от домов и уронил на толпу *блестящих*.
> Капля крови упала на шлем хохочущего шестнадцатилетнего парня по имени Виктор. Но он ее не почувствовал. (19, my italics)[60]

If we look back at the opening paragraph of the story, we see that the theme of synchronicity is present from the very start: Viktor Nikolaevich wakes up from a dream in which he sees himself back in 1938, when he was ten years old, but appears in his present form and at his current age (*nyneshnim starikom*), and his own father calls him *dedom Vitei* ('grandfather Vitia', 7):

> Виктор Николаевич проснулся от странного, нелепого сна. Ему приснился покойный отец, довоенный Весьегоньск, свадьба дяди Семена и Анны, на которой он побывал десятилетним мальчиком. Во сне все было почти как тогда, в

далеком 1938-м, но он сам почему-то был уже нынешним стариком и отец звал его дедом Витей. Его посадили во главу стола, отец сидел рядом и все время подливал ему вкусного, легкого, как березовый сок, самогона, от которого дед Витя, будучи по сути мальчиком, сильно захмелел и уже не мог сидеть, а упал под стол и, хохоча, стал хватать всех за ноги, отчего собравшиеся разозлились и принялись сильно пихать и бить его сапогами, галдя, что дед Витя опозорился. Потом его подхватили и поволокли вон из дома, а он от опьянения не мог пошевелить ни рукой, ни ногой, и ему стало так смешно, так весело, что он хохотал, хохотал дико до тех пор, пока не разрыдался. (7)[61]

Setting the tone for the whole story, and indeed for the whole collection of stories in the volume *Monoklon*, this dream may be read as a metapoetic comment on the problem of depicting the 'synchronicity' of contemporary Russia, incorporating, or ignoring, her past. Its main constituents are the absurd (*strannyi* 'strange', *nelepyi* 'odd') and, above all, the grotesque: the heavy drinking, falling under the table, the threefold repetition of the verb *khokhotat'* ('laugh loudly'), echoed, as we saw above, in the story's final passage ('The drop of blood fell on the helmet of a laughing [*khokhochushchego*] sixteen-year-old lad named Viktor').

In an interview following the publication of the *Monoklon* collection, Sorokin spoke of 'the growing concentration of the absurd and grotesque in society', describing the book as 'an attempt to capture this concentration of the grotesque':

И этот сборник как раз попытка нащупать эту самую концентрацию гротеска. Надо сказать, что с каждым годом она увеличивается. [. . .] Здесь плохо приживается человеческое. Громадное место для гротеска, абсурда и все меньше и меньше для обыкновенной человеческой жизни. У нас присутствует тотальное равнодушие к человеческой личности. Человек воспринимается как средство, а не как цель. (Sorokin and Ivanova 2010)[62]

Sorokin's fictional world is less clear-cut in ethical terms. My reading suggests how Sorokin explores poetically the diachronic dimensions of language, in order to draw the reader's attention to the grotesque aspects of contemporary Russian society, where reminiscences of an unsettled and unsettling past are inexorably present.

NOTES

1. For a compehensive study of Popov's *oeuvre*, see Morris (2013).
2. In the spirit of postmodernism, Popov frequently plays with the figures of author, narrator and character, includes many biographical references and creates several alter egos (see Tchouboukov-Pianca 1995: 35–52). In the present context this complex structure is important to bear in mind, but is not essential to my argument; thus 'Popov' will stand for an authorial presence represented also by the figures of narrator or commentator.
3. '"having been expelled" from the institute (412).//(412): A rather awkward expression, which enjoys, at the expense of losing its beauty, the factographic accuracy of *kantseliarit*.' Popov's novel was first published 1998 in the literary journal *Znamia*, before it came out in book form in 1999. Quotations are from Popov [1999] 2003. Page references are not given, since every quotation contains a footnote, which is easy to find in any edition. The sign // marks the division between text and footnote in the translation.
4. '[. . .] afterwards he suddenly took and read it (232)//(232): Soviet *"kantseliarit"*, the language in which educated *"sovki"* expressed themselves. Kornei Chukovskii snatched the moment and concretised his hostility towards Soviet power, when he attacked *"kantseliarit"* for not being worthy of "a builder of communism". However, those in power weren't able to speak in any other language at that time, otherwise it would have been a totally different power.'
5. 'When we manage to abolish completely people's bureaucratic behaviour, *kantseliarit* will disappear by itself.'
6. 'The word "sex", which was allowed to be published at that time in *Literaturnaia gazeta*, the organ of the existing, by permission of the KGB, Soviet liberals, supporters of the "Leninist norms", was nevertheless for many years considered to be a bad word, not sufficiently Soviet. Not without reason some honest woman at the beginning of the end of "perestroika" declared that "in the Soviet Union there was no sex". [. . .] Brezhnev is playing the accordion,/Khrushchev is dancing the Hopak./Russia has been destroyed/By two party idiots. [. . .]'
7. '– Be patient! – said the journalist (377). – Be patient, take heart and write (378).//(378): HERE YOU HAVE IT, COMRADES, POSTMADERNIZIM. MADE IN RASHA.' Popov here plays with the nineteenth-century poet Fedor Tiutchev's famous 'Silentium', which opens with the line Молчи, скрывайся и таи ('Speak not, lie hidden, and conceal' (Nabokov 1944: 33), imitating the postmodernists' playful attitude towards the classics.
8. '[N]obody knows what postmodernism is, but they all pretend that they do . . .'
9. '– he doesn't have this grief, you know, this longing for his literary past, nostalgia so to speak (798)//(798) Just like I myself have absolutely NO nostalgic feelings for those times, the devil take them together with the whole of Soviet power. I would agree to live a far less interesting life than that of those times, if only THERE HAD BEEN LIFE, and not that virtual communist dummy of life with all those "constructions", *"gebukhas* [KGB]", "initiatives", "samizdat", drinking, bravado, fear and shame. [. . .]'
10. '(501) *Zastrozhilsia*" – that's a kind of Siberian, capacious thing, not at all the same as the popular "became serious". In "regional" dictionaries there are many amazing words that should be brought into the Russian standard language, which is becoming

less elastic every year. "*Cho mshish'sia?*" – one muzhik asks another somewhere on the Angara River. This means: "Why are you fussing about [*suetish'sia*] and being nervous, worrying, giving yourself over to pessimism, looking gloomily into the future and coldly at the world, when the world is wonderful, the future – bright, pessimism is not inherent in the Russian mentality, to worry is to harm oneself, nerve cells cannot be restored, and, on the whole, everything on earth is vanity [*sueta*] and vexation of spirit."' (Popov plays on the common root of *suetit'sia* and *sueta*; cf. Eccl. 2: 27.)

11. 'Rubbish (31)!//(31): Now why suddenly this pseudofolklorism again? It's most likely affectation again, being naughty, empty scoffing, though it's unclear at what and what for, thoughtless silliness, limited thinking!'

12. '– But I was making a bet [*po sporu*] (251)//(251) Popular language [*prostorechie*]. The correct way is to say "*na spor*". The inability to use the right preposition is a surviving element of the child's developing mind in the adult's speech, which in this way becomes rich in imagery, living and deep. (A commentary especially for Ms Rosemarie Tietze (Munich), Mr Robert Porter (Bristol) & Comrade Jukka Mallinen (Helsinki), who will translate this "novel", as a result of which we will finally all become not only famous, but also rich.)'

13. '(55) Here again the cultured "either" and the brutal "drunken mug" are combined for pure merriment.'

14. On the term 'uncensored language', see Chapter 6.

15. '(343) The switching to "you" [informal address], as with the use of uncensored language in business conversations, was an easily recognizable sign of a certain favourable disposition on the part of a higher-ranking person towards a lower-ranking one.'

16. 'Ah, ah!... well! – said Ivan Ivanych (376).//(376), but he didn't use at all, as you of course just thought, the bad word starting with the letter "kh" that has been replaced by the three dots. Ivan Ivanych didn't like vulgar language and he was right: even so, everybody was using it all the time – the people, the intellectuals, the party, the government ... Obviously, to swear isn't good in general, it's harmful. For this reason, I'm grateful to a certain extent to the KGB people for confiscating my story "Nevarevalizm" and solemnly burning it in their furnace in accordance with their own resolution, if, of course, they're not lying. [. . .] By the way, everybody in this story loves one another, it's just that they use very bad language, horrible language! It's difficult for a Russian to do without vulgar language. Panteleimon Romanov has a story about how a peasant fighting at the front swore that if he survived, he would give up using bad language. He returned to his native village after the imperialist slaughter of 1914–1917 and soon hanged himself, as he couldn't speak to anybody in the village. And on an expedition we were on to Taimyr there was a certain Sania in our team who knew that it wasn't good to "express oneself" in the presence of ladies, and therefore he was always choked during conversations, like a cat that's overeaten. You could only hear the inarticulate "fck, fck" [. . .]'

17. '– All right, all right. Let's do without hysterics (589), – said the Voice angrily.// (589) Almost graphomania. Romanticism, the fantastic – is, in fact, almost graphomania. And vice versa.'

18. For a detailed analysis of graphomania in Popov's *oeuvre*, see Tchouboukov-Pianca (1995).

19. '(242) Oh, I cannot bear it! One cliché after another! I cannot tell any more whether I was putting it on or it just *came out that way*. Most likely the latter. [. . .]'

20. 'Whatever way it was, the fact remains that he didn't think of anything but literature.

And if he did, then only on one particular level (329): [. . .]//(329) One cliché after another! Everything is soaked in the SOVIET WAY OF THINKING [*SOVETCHINA*], but you know, back then it seemed that I was proud, independent, that I understood everything, led an independent life. Whenever the shit wagon had driven through our street, the 'perfume' lingered for two or three days. But here we'd been sniffing it since 1917, and by 1974 we'd finally got used to the smell.'

21. See in particular Guseinov's preface to his dictionary (2003).
22. Cf. Borden's (1999: 2) distinction between bad writing and 'bad writing'.
23. 'His poetics are informed, on the one hand, by constant linguistic experimentation verging on taboo (the aesthetics of the ugly, anti-aesthetics) and, on the other, by imitation of totalitarian worldviews, conventional rituals and normative genres, a tautological adaption of styles, jargons and pretexts, occasionally combining them into super- or megatexts (pastiche).'
24. 'only letters on a piece of paper'.
25. For research on different aspects of 'linguistic memory' in totalitarian and post-totalitarian societies, cf., for the Soviet case, Mokienko and Nikitina (1998); Sarnov (2002); Guseinov (2003, 2004). Work on National Socialist language is less centred on the post-totalitarian linguistic legacy, but see the classic Klemperer (1947), and Sauer (1995). For a comparative view of post-Soviet literature on the Soviet linguistic legacies and German research on the National Socialist linguistic experience, see Lunde (2008).
26. *Monoklon* is explained in the epigraph to the story: Моноклон - крупный растительноядный динозавр юрского периода мезозойской эры. Передвигался на четырех ногах. На его панцирной голове со щитовидным воротником был один большой рог (7). 'The *monoklon* is a large, plant-eating dinosaur of the Jurassic period of the Mesozoic era. It moved on four legs. On its armour-clad head with a thyroid collar there was one big horn.' Quotations are from Sorokin (2010). Page numbers in brackets refer to the Russian original.
27. An example of the latter is a quotation from Goethe's poem 'Über allen Gipfeln ist Ruh' ('Gornye vershiny spiat vo t'me nochnoi', 'Above all summits it is calm').
28. '– The rails run in a hundred directions, – he said, recalling Pugacheva's song, – Along the rails . . ., and over the sleepers, the sleepers, the sleepers . . .'
29. '– The space maps have been tucked into their cases . . . – And the navigator is checking the route for the last time! – the crowd joined in immediately. – Come on, guys, let's have a smoke before take-off, there's a whole fourteen minutes to go! – Viktor Nikolaevich joined the crowd from the sixth floor.'
30. 'The shining crowd was singing outside the window: On the dusty paths Of distant planets, Our tracks will remain!'
31. 'The shining people were singing outside the window: I'm the Earth, I'm seeing off my children, My sons, my daughters. Fly as far as the sun, And come back home soon.'
32. 'Cosmonauts' Day.'
33. '– Cosmonauts! – Viktor Nikolaevich muttered with surprise.'
34. '– Wow! Cosmonauts! Little cosmonauts!'
35. 'Viktor Nikolaevich clenched his sinewy fist, thrust it out of the window and shouted: – Glory to the heroes of space!'
36. '– Heave-ho, heave-ho! – the loudspeakers spread the voice of the guy with thick eyebrows. – We're all cosmonauts! – the crowd roared. – Heave-ho, heave-ho! – We're all cosmonauts!! – Heave-ho! Heave-ho! – We're all cos-mo-nauts!!!'

37. '*Today* is the 12th of April. Cosmonauts' Day. *On this day* Iurii Gagarin conquered space with his heroic flight.'
38. '– Every Russian patriot is a cosmonaut at his heart! Our president is cosmonaut number one! The crowd applauded. – And as for our Prime Minister, he's the cosmonaut of cosmonauts! The crowd roared with joy.'
39. 'It's those . . . what are they called . . . you know, those who walk? "We're together?" What? Yes! Yes!'
40. '– But today is the 12th of April! The Day of the Cosmonauts, dear bastards! Holy Mother!'
41. 'On immediate standby! I'm going into orbit!'
42. 'Muttering and humming with discontent, he flicked the lock and flung open the door: – Valia, quick! I'm going to show you something marvellous!'
43. 'The crowd stirred cheerfully.'; 'The crowd fell silent.'; 'The crowd stirred.'; 'The crowd applauded.'; 'The crowd roared with joy.'; 'Outside the window the crowd stirred and laughed.'; 'Outside the window, the crowd began to sing a song about the Earth [. . .]'; 'The crowd stopped singing and just stirred.'
44. 'Because in the soul of every one of you lives a love for your country, a desire to make it even more powerful, even more free! And from this rocket I have the impression, my friends, that today each of you bears the name of Iurii!'
45. 'In the centre, in the jumble of bodies *shining* in the sun, a rocket with the Russian coat-of-arms on the hull began to lift off.'; 'Outside the window the *shining* crowd was singing: [. . .]'; 'But it was perfectly polished and *gleaming* in the sunlight, like an expensive Japanese sword. Valek took this *shiny*, gently curved piece of iron, [. . .]'; 'Viktor Nikolaevich stared at the *shiny* metal.'; 'Monoklon looked at the *shiny* metal that had passed through the old man's body, and dropped the sledge-hammer: [. . .]'; 'Outside the window, the *shining* people were singing: [. . .]'; 'Only one drop, bouncing off and passing over the green slope of the drainpipe, fell down, *flashed* like a ruby in the sun, and flew away, caught by the moist air. The wind carried the drop of blood away from the apartment block and let it fall onto the crowd of *shining* people.'
46. '– How do you do, [. . .]'; '– Monoklon.'; '– You've recognised me, [. . .]'; '– After all I promised you.'; '– And promises are not made to be broken [literally: a promise is expected for more than three years], [. . .]'; '– He remembers.'; '– It's time, [. . .]'
47. 'Without doubt [. . .] In memory' (Latin).
48. 'Staring at him in the mirror was the eighty-two-year old Viktor Nikolaevich.'
49. 'There were two old scars on his body: one on the left hip, from 58 when he was struck on a hunting expedition by the tusks of a wounded wild boar, and one on his right elbow from 91 when he broke his arm, slipping outside his door. Furthermore, two tattoos could be seen on his body: in the middle of the chest an eagle with a snake in its claws, and on the left shoulder a heart pierced by two daggers and the barely discernible words "Nina". Both tattoos were old, from the fifties.'
50. 'During his forty years on Leninskii Prospekt, he had not seen anything like this. There had been demonstrations by the Communists here under El'tsin, there was the famous battle on Gagarin Square in 1993, three hundred metres from his block when the patriots of "Labouring Moscow" clashed with El'tsin's OMON forces. But this had never happened before.'
51. 'Then he lay for a long time, staring at the ceiling, with its Czech crystal chandelier, purchased by his late wife in the mid-seventies in the store called "Light" on Leninskii Prospekt.'

52. 'The left eyebrow was traversed by a deep old scar, causing his left eye to see as if through a crack.'
53. 'Both of his hands had injuries: on the right, the little finger was missing, and on the left, the fourth and little fingers did not bend.'
54. 'Viktor Nikolaevich stood stock still.'
55. 'Viktor Nikolaevich's face was as if ossified.'
56. 'Viktor Nikolaevich's body was as though petrified.'
57. 'Only his leg throbbed evenly against the leg of the table, as if marking time.'
58. '(798) [. . .] And a lack of spirituality is definitely not threatening Russia, who, God willing, will certainly inscribe herself on the expanse of world culture, where "Americanism" coexists peacefully with the epic, folklore with postmodernism, pornography with romanticism, *kvas* with Coca-Cola.'
59. Consider, in particular, *Tri pesni o perestroike* (*Three Songs about Perestroika*, 1999); *Master Khaos* (*Master Chaos*, 2002) and *Opera nishchikh* (*The Beggars' Opera*, 2004). Cf. also Raoul Eshelman's (1993) analysis of Popov's early work, which he sees as the modelling of an indifferent stance without any visible axiological position.
60. 'Only one drop, bouncing off and passing over the green slope of the drainpipe, fell down, *flashed* like a ruby in the sun, and flew away, caught by the moist air. The wind carried the drop of blood away from the apartment block and let it fall onto the crowd of *shining* people. The drop of blood fell on the helmet of a laughing sixteen-year-old lad named Viktor. But he did not feel it.'
61. 'Viktor Nikolaevich woke up from a strange, odd dream. He saw his deceased father, pre-war Ves'egon'sk, and the wedding of Uncle Semen and Aunt Anna, where he'd been as a ten-year-old. In the dream everything was almost as then, way back in 1938, but for some reason he himself was already the old man of today, and his father called him grandfather Vitia. He was seated at the head of the table, his father sat next to him and constantly poured him a delicious home-made vodka, light as birch juice, from which grandfather Vitia, in fact a boy, got heavily drunk and became unable to sit, fell under the table and, laughing, started to grab everyone's feet, as a result of which the assembled guests grew angry and began to shove and beat him heavily with their boots, clamouring that grandfather Vitia had disgraced himself. Afterwards they picked him up and dragged him out of the house, and in his drunkenness he couldn't move his arm or leg, and he was so amused, so cheerful, that he laughed, laughed wildly, until he burst into tears.'
62. 'The volume is actually an attempt to capture this concentration of the grotesque. I have to say that it increases with every year. [. . .] The human element has problems holding its own here. There's enormous space for the grotesque, for the absurd, and less and less for normal human life. There's a total neglect of the human personality here. Man is seen as a means rather than a goal.'

CHAPTER 8

Language, Time and Linguistic Dystopia

Tat'iana Tolstaia and Evgenii Vodolazkin

The dynamics between the synchronic state of the language and its diachronic dimension is an issue that informs many of the discussions about the condition of the language in Russia today. Language change is at the heart of the language debates; new words, novel expressions and stylistic variation provoke all kinds of reactions, including nostalgia for earlier states of the language as well as stark prognoses about its future.

In the previous chapter, we looked at the recent linguistic past – the legacy of the Soviet era – and saw how the accumulated implications of languages and styles linked to this legacy are tackled in post-Soviet Russian prose works. In the present chapter, we will look at the diachronic dimension of language in a broader perspective, exploring how prose writers create fictional representations of a past, or a future, where language emerges as an essential theme. I will focus on two main works, one portraying a fictional future for Russian – Tat'iana Tolstaia's 2000 novel *Kys'* (*The Slynx*[1]), and one diving into the language's past – Evgenii Vodolazkin's *Lavr* (*Laurus*) from 2012.

LINGUISTIC DYSTOPIA: TAT'IANA TOLSTAIA

Tat'iana Tolstaia, who published her first literary works in the mid-eighties, had been known mainly as a writer of short stories when her long-awaited novel *The Slynx* – a catastrophe tale – appeared in 2000.

The dystopian (or anti-utopian, the preferred Russian term) novel has become a highly popular genre in post-Soviet Russian prose. While the 1990s brought about a reorientation in the assessment of both the past and the future in a number of cultural practices, the real boom in the literary genre of dystopia came with the turn of the twenty-first century (Chantsev 2009; Ågren 2014: 3; Borenstein 2015). The dystopian genre invites reflection on, and often critique of, contemporary society, largely by exploring possible developments of a future world. Such scenarios may be radical, shocking and extreme, and they often address issues related to language.[2]

Turning to Tolstaia's *The Slynx*, I hasten to say that many critics do not in fact consider the book to be a dystopian novel. Mark Lipovetsky, in his first response to the novel, maintained that: Толстая не прогнозирует будущее (поэтому «Кысь» никакая не антиутопия), а блистательно передает сегодняшний кризис языка, сегодняшний распад иерархических отношений в культуре, когда культурные порядки советской цивилизации рухнули, погребая заодно и альтернативные, антисоветские культурные иерархии (Lipovetskii 2001).[3]

Lipovetsky touches upon the central concerns of *The Slynx*. Still, I agree with Eliot Borenstein (2015: 94–5), who argues that, while perhaps not writing a fully-fledged dystopian novel in the classic sense, Tat'iana Tolstaia uses a number of dystopian tropes – in her own sophisticated way. The lack of clear future scenarios makes any straightforward interpretation of the novel difficult. However, one of the features *The Slynx* does share with the dystopian genre is a strong metafictional component. In my reading, I will focus in particular on the metalinguistic aspects of this quality, and examine Tolstaia's novel with regard to questions of language and style in the wider context of contemporary (to the novel) Russian linguistic and literary culture.

Life of mutants

The Slynx is inhabited by mutants living in the city of Fedor-Kuz'michsk, situated on the site of Moscow some two hundred years after the *Vzryv* ('Blast'), probably a nuclear catastrophe. As a result of the Blast, people suffer from various kinds of *posledstviia* ('consequences'): more often than not, extra appendages of various types, such as claws, a tail, or an unbelievable number of ears or cockscombs.

Fedor-Kuz'michsk, we learn, used to be Ivan-Porfir'ichsk, and before that, Sergei-Sergeichsk, formerly Southern Warehouses and, a long, long time ago, Moscow (18).[4] Life in this society is governed by superstition, the pursuit of food, daily, often slightly aggressive, interactions between the various groups of creatures that inhabit Fedor-Kuz'michsk, and, above all, by the presence of the almighty Fedor Kuz'mich himself and his secret police – the *sanitary* ('Saniturions').[5]

Fedor Kuz'mich – the enunciation of his name is always accompanied by a *slava emu* ('glory to him') or *dolgikh let emu zhizni* ('long may he live') – is the inventor of everything, from the fire to the mouse trap, while the ordinary people – the *golubchiki* ('dear ones') – do not need to bother with knowledge or power. The following passage illustrates the attitude of the novel's main protagonist, Benedikt, and his fellow Golubchiks towards the ruler:

> Принес-то огонь людям Федор Кузьмич, слава ему, а только как дело было, где он тот огонь взял, нам неведомо. Тут хоть три дня думай, не додумаешься, а только разве голова заболит, как если яичного квасу перепьешь. Кто говорит: с неба свел, кто рассказывает, будто топнул ножкой-то Федор Кузьмич, слава ему, и на том месте земля и загорись ясным пламенем. А все может быть. (25–6)[6]

People would seem to have no worries, but then there is the 'Slynx' – *kys'*. The Slynx is introduced very early in the book, and while the creature itself is mysterious and mythological, we get a quite concrete description of her doings: she cries her wild and mournful *ky-ys'*! *ky-ys'*!, and if she catches you, she tears the reason out of you (7). The Slynx *is* what she *says* (*kys'*), and this close link between speech and behaviour, language and identity, is crucial to the novel.

The world of *The Slynx* illustrates, in Helene Goscilo's (2004: 285) words, 'the bewildering disorder within the *perpetuum immobile* endemic to both utopia and dystopia'. Goscilo is one of several scholars to point to parallels between Tolstaia's 1993 essay 'Russkii mir' ('The Russian World') and *The Slynx*. In the essay, Tolstaia describes the current state of post-Soviet Russia in the following terms:

> Россия – это большой сумасшедший дом. [. . .] Единственный абсолют – релятивизм, единственная константа – хаос. Каждый сам устанавливает правила игры, меняя их на ходу по собственной прихоти [. . .] над Россией зависло время мифологическое, застывшее, такое, в котором все события совершаются одновременно. (Tolstaia 2012b: 445–8)[7]

Many elements of this description fit the atmosphere of Fedor-Kuz'michsk perfectly, a world without access to the past and without prospects for the future, a synchronous narrative without real development, 'where all events happen simultaneously'. One dimension of this simultaneity is linguistic.

Linguistic identities

The text combines a great variety of linguistic and stylistic forms: neologisms, colloquialisms and *prostorechie*, dialecticisms, archaic words or word forms, vulgar language, fairy-tale language, semantically reduced speech, and idiosyncratic, 'mutated' words.

Linguistic peculiarities are part of the characterisation of people and, in particular, of groups, such as the *prezhnie* ('Oldeners', survivors of the Blast, with the particular 'consequence' that they do not die of old age), the *pererozhdentsy* ('Degenerators', creatures with both human and animal traits, who also seem to have survived the Blast), the *kokhinory* ('Cockynorks', a people living in a distant suburb of Fedor-Kuz'michsk) and the ordinary Golubchiks themselves. Here is Benedikt's description of the Oldeners, their habits and style of speaking:

> Они по избам своим сидят, а то на работу ходят, а какой и в начальство выбился – все у них, как у нас. Только разговор другой. Повстречается тебе на улице незнакомый голубчик – нипочем не догадаешься, наш он или из Прежних. Разве что спросишь его, как водится: «Хто таков? Почему не знаю? Какого хрена тебя в нашей слободе носит?» – а он нет чтобы ответить, как у людей водится: «А те чо, рыло носить надоело? Ща оборву да об колено» или другое что, – нет, чтобы так понятно, али сказать, вразумительно прояснить, – дескать, ты-то силен, да и я силен, лучше не связывайся! Нет, иной раз в ответ услышишь: «Оставьте меня в покое! Хулиган!» – ну тогда, точно, Прежний это. (126)[8]

In this passage we can observe one of Tolstaia's typical techniques: the combination of explicit and implicit metalanguage. Benedikt's way of describing the speech and attitude of the Oldeners characterises his own way of speaking and interacting, both explicitly, in what he says and does, and implicitly, in the juxtaposition of his own style of speech with that of the Oldeners.

The Oldeners' speech consists of a mixture of clichés, empty phrases and high-style rhetoric, together with a set of terms written in upper-case letters. These words are distorted ('mutated') versions of concepts that have to do, more often than not, with the cultural sphere, and are truly comprehensible only to the Oldeners: ФЕЛОСОФИЯ (52, passim), АРУЖЫЕ (16), ОНЕВЕРСТЕЦКОЕ АБРАЗАВАНИЕ (16), МОГОЗИН (17), ОСФАЛЬТ (17), ЭНТЕЛЕГЕНЦЫЯ (21), ТРОДИЦЫЯ (21), РИНИСАНС (28), ШАДЕВРЫ (37), МЁТ (37), МОЗЕЙ (37), ИЛИМЕНТАРНЫЕ основы МАРАЛИ (80).[9]

Tolstaia adds a satirical dimension to her portrayal of the 'intelligentsia' of Fedor-Kuz'michsk by combining the 'cultural' words in their particular vocabulary with more or less random ones, like 'asphalt' or 'honey'. The same kind of double meaning emerges in Nikita Ivanovich's (the book's central character among the Oldeners) desperate comment on the linguistic situation in the city: – Отчего бы это, – сказал Никита Иваныч, – отчего это у нас все мутирует, ну все! Ладно люди, но язык, понятия, смысл! А? Россия! Все вывернуто! (229).[10] The idea of a 'mutated' or even 'mutating' language is, when viewed from a certain vantage point, equivalent to a diagnosis of the language situation in Russia of the 1990s.[11] At the same time, the words that show the most obvious signs of mutation in *The Slynx* are exactly the upper-case concepts that the Oldeners bemoan the loss of in post-Blast Fedor-Kuz'michsk. We can see in these examples how the linguistic portrayal of the intelligentsia emerges both in the content of what representatives of this group say, and in the way they talk.

While the speech of the common Golubchiks is quite rich in vulgarisms, swear words and a generally rough style, the Degenerators seem to surpass everyone else when it comes to the use of *mat*. According to Benedikt's laconic observation: ругань у них покрепше нашей (116).[12] Degenerators are used by the Golubchiks for transport and harnessed to sleighs, but, as Benedikt explains, you had better keep your distance from them: Ай, ну их к лешему, перерожденцев этих, лучше от них подальше. Страшные они, и не поймешь, то ли они люди, то ли нет: лицо вроде как у человека, туловище шерстью покрыто и на четвереньках бегают (6).[13]

Benedikt's attitude towards the Degenerators is typical of intersubjective relationships generally in the world of *The Slynx*. Other people are, more often than not, met with suspicion, scepticism, or even aggression, and such feelings are frequently expressed also in linguistic terms. Here is Benedikt's description of how he relates to the Cockynorks:

Если кохинорец высунется, кинешь в него камнем для потехи, вроде согреешься, и дальше бежать. А почему кинешь, потому как кохинорцы эти не по-нашему говорят. Бал-бал-бал да бал-бал-бал – да и все тут, да и ничего не разберешь. А почему они так говорят, почему по-нашему не хотят – кто ж их знает. Может, назло. А может, привычка такая вредная, это тоже бывает.

А и то сказать, сами себе вредят. Что они там по-кохинорски-то сказать могут? По-нашему куда сподручней: сел, рассудил не спеша: вот так, дескать, и так; это вот и то-то. И все ясно. (48–9)[14]

In *The Slynx*, verbal interaction lacks both empathy and genuine understanding. Again we see Tolstaia's satirical virtuosity at work: to Benedikt, his own language is perfect and clear, while to the reader, it is obvious that his style of speech is rudimentary: вот так, дескать, и так; это вот и то-то. И все ясно ('such and such and thus and so. And everything's clear as day'). Tolstaia shows this in her portrayal of Benedikt's (and other Golubchiks') language throughout the novel, while in the passage just quoted we also get a semantically reduced metadescription of it.

The linguistic crisis depicted on various levels in the novel is turned, as Christine Gölz (2004: 690) notes, into an epistemological crisis. One of the most famous examples of this is the passage describing Benedikt's self-designed, idiosyncratic cataloguing system which he introduces to the library of forbidden books owned by his father-in-law, Kudeiar Kudeiarych. Before we look more closely at this passage, let us acquaint ourselves with the Kudeiarov family.

Kudeiar Kudeiarych is the head of the Saniturions, the city's secret police, which search people's houses for forbidden books, that is, books from before the Blast, and take people away to cure them of 'the disease'. Benedikt marries Kudeiarych's daughter, Olia, and moves in with the family. He is struck by many aspects of their way of life, including the fact that there are no mice in the building. Mice are important in the life of Fedor-Kuz'michsk, as they are both eaten and used as money. The lack of mice in the house of the Kudeiarovs is explained (by the chief Saniturion himself) by the fact that they lead a *dukhovnaia zhizn'* ('spiritual life'). As it turns out, their lives consist mainly of eating, and their table talk reveals little evidence of a spiritual life. Not only do they talk mainly about food, but the way they speak manifests a total lack of meaningful conversation. Here is just a short passage from a 'dialogue' at the table that goes on for several pages:

– А что блины? Что блины-то?
– А то, что неча!.. Блины!.. Тоже мне!..
– А чего тебе?
– А ничего! Вот чего!
– Ну и ничего! А то: блины!..
– А вот и блины!
– Сама ты «блины».
– Да я-то вот блины. А ты-то что?
– А ничего!
– Ну и молчи!
– Сама молчи!
– Ну и помолчу!

– Ну и помолчи!
– Ну вот и помолчу! «Блины»!
– Ну и молчи! Тише будет! (203)[15]

Tolstaia consistently characterises people through her satirical-hyperbolical play with their linguistic peculiarities. This is also the case with the novel's protagonist, Benedikt. Benedikt is our guide to the world of Fedor-Kuz'michsk, as the book is told as a third-person narration with Benedikt as both the focal and viewpoint character. Similar to the 'double' meaning that we have observed in many examples already – a meaning that emerges in the combination of style and content in the talk of different people – the narrative proceeds in a way that is often more revealing to the reader than to Benedikt himself. As a result, Benedikt emerges as a somewhat naïve, sometimes energetic, but usually dull-witted and slightly sentimental character. His 'explanations' are often tautological: Богатые – они потому богатыми называются, что богато живут (57);[16] Слепцы, они потому и слепцы, что ничегошеньки не видят (92);[17] and above all, he understands everything in its literal meaning: А вот есть «Вопросы литературы». Бенедикт посмотрел: никаких там вопросов, одни ответы. А должно, был номер с вопросами, да пропал. Тоже жалко (195).[18]

Benedikt's lack of understanding is particularly evident in his conversations with the Oldener Nikita Ivanych, who tries to educate Benedikt and pass onto him the cultural tradition from before the Blast. As laconically stated by Benedikt himself: Прежние наших слов не понимают, а мы ихних (27).[19] Benedikt uses here the possessive pronoun *ikhnii* (instead of *ikh*), one of many instances of *prostorechie* forms in the novel. Fedor Kuz'mich's *ukazy* ('decrees') are particularly full of *prostorechie* elements, such as *sekletar'* (*sekretar'*), *entot* (*etot*), or *oposlia* (*posle*). Ironically enough, Fedor Kuz'mich, in the perception of the Golubchiks, is the sole author of everything there is of written texts – of all literature, which plays a crucial role in the novel.

Books and alphabets

Benedikt is initiated into the profession of scribe. He learns the alphabet and the names of the letters (the latter also designate the novel's chapter headings), and is then instructed to copy manuscripts allegedly written by Fedor Kuz'mich. The first four quoted passages tell us that these verses are by Lermontov (his famous translation of Goethe's 'Wandrers Nachtlied'), Mandel'shtam, Pushkin and Blok (22–3).

Benedikt and his fellow scribes are totally ignorant of the realm of culture and literature. They find the verses moving, sometimes clear, sometimes difficult to understand – a biting irony, as they do not understand them at all, or understand them only in a very literal way. They praise the alleged author of all the works, Fedor Kuz'mich, however, for 'knowing many different words' (23), thereby reducing cultural knowledge to the technical size of one's vocabulary.

In the very process of copying texts from what turn out to be pre-Blast books, without contextualising them or preserving the real author's name, the historicity of the texts is lost. 'Literature' becomes something that exists outside of time and history, while all references to (historical) reality are taken to refer to the reality of the Golubchiks. For instance, the unknown word *kon'* ('horse', 'steed') is taken to mean *mysh'* ('mouse') – for how can it be otherwise?:

> – Вот я вас все хочу спросить, Бенедикт. Вот я стихи Федора Кузьмича, слава ему, перебеляю. А там все: конь, конь. Что такое «конь», вы не знаете?
> Бенедикт подумал. Еще подумал. Даже покраснел от натуги. Сам сколько раз это слово писал, а как-то не задумывался.
> – Должно быть, это мышь. [...]
> – Ну а как же тогда: «конь бежит, земля дрожит»?
> – Стало быть, крупная мышь. (41)[20]

The lack of genuine comprehension notwithstanding, books and reading play a central role in the life of Fedor-Kuz'michsk and, in particular, of Benedikt. Benedikt is obsessed with books; he has dreams about them and indulges in rumours about the hiding-places of 'forbidden', 'old-printed' books, that is, books from before the Blast (contemporary books are written in 'bark notebooks').

One of the most striking examples of Benedikt's obsession with books is his cataloguing policy in the library of 'forbidden' books belonging to his father-in-law. Benedikt shelves together books whose titles show a superficial equivalency on the phonetic, lexical, syntactical or rhythmical level: *Evgenii Onegin* is placed next to a book by Evgenii Primakov, then follows *Evgenika – orudie rasistov* (*Eugenics – A Racist's Weapon*); *Gamlet – prints datskii* (*Hamlet – Prince of Denmark*) placed next to *Tashkent – gorod khlebnyi* (*Tashkent – City of Bread*); *Krasnoe i chernoe* (*The Red and the Black*) next to *Goluboe i zelenoe* (*The Blue and the Green*); or, the authors Mukhina, Shershenevich, Zhukov, Shmelev, Tarakanova, Babochkin (all surnames based on words for insects: fly, hornet, beetle, bumble-bee, cockroach, butterfly) placed together (207–8). In Christine Gölz's formulation, Benedikt sees the world as a 'gathering of things and not of signs': 'Diese Dinge setzt er zueinander in Verbindung aufgrund ihrer Ähnlichkeit oder Ikonizität, ohne sie als Verweis auf Absentes, auf die Repräsentanten eines metaphysischen Sinns interpretieren/lesen zu können' (Gölz 2004: 703).[21]

Again we can observe the by now common technique of Tolstaia: by linguistic and stylistic means, she exposes her hero's limited cognitive (and linguistic) capacities in a way that makes reading hilarious. It is also an effective means of inviting the reader to reflect on what language can do. The long section on cataloguing (covering several pages) not only displays the linguistic virtuosity of the author, which goes way beyond the intellectual and linguistic horizon of her protagonist, it also demonstrates the meaning-generating capacities of language itself. What Benedikt does in his cataloguing system is to resemanticise grammatical categories, thereby allowing new combinations and new correlations to emerge. The effect is humorous, as we have seen, but as Mark Lipovetsky (2010: 386) points out, Benedikt's naïve understanding of literature also displays, in an extreme way, the concept of a 'fresh look' at a piece of art or cultural artefact.

In Benedikt's own definition of 'FELOSOFIIA', this attitude emerges quite clearly, but is immediately made fun of by the author in her typical style. She makes Benedikt elaborate on the concept of 'viewing a thing in a new way', adding details that reveal that he has no real understanding of the concept: Смотришь на людей - на мужиков, на баб, - словно впервые видишь, словно ты другой породы, али только что из лесу вышел, али, наоборот, в лес вошел (52–3).[22] The 'fresh look', alas, does not lead to any new meaning or discovery. The long catalogue of books in Benedikt's narrative is followed by his statement that he has now read them all – but what is he to do next? His immediate solution to the problem is to throw himself into a week of love-making with his wife Olia. The reading pleasure obviously lasted only for as long as he was reading.

The absence of cultural transmission

In a wider context, the theme of books, alphabets, culture and learning comes to a head in the abyss that blocks any meaningful access to pre-Blast culture. Nikita Ivanych accuses Benedikt of knowing only the letters on paper, not the real 'alphabet of life': Читать ты по сути дела не умеешь, книга тебе не впрок, пустой шелест, набор букв. Жизненную, жизненную азбуку не освоил! (263).[23]

When he learns from Nikita Ivanych that he should seek the Book of Life, the book where it is written how he should live, Benedikt immediately starts looking for one particular, concrete book. He asks Nikita Ivanych again about the book as the latter stands tied to the stake, waiting to be burned alive at the command of the new ruler, Kudeiar Kudeiarych, and Nikita Ivanych repeats his point about the alphabet: – Никита Ива-а-аныч! Дедушка! Книга где-е-е? Быстро говорите-е-е! – Азбуку учи! Азбуку! Сто раз повторял! Без азбуки не прочтешь! Прощай! Побереги-и-ись! (314).[24]

Benedikt, for his part, demonstrates his simplistic conception of the alphabet by likening the form of the letters to concrete objects: «Ци» и «ща» – с хвостами, как Бенедикт до свадьбы. «Червь» – как стуло перевернутое. «Глаголь» – вроде крюка (273).[25] A little later, at home, he experiences a kind of revelation, thinking about the whole structure of society, including the role of books, and claims to understand how everything makes sense – things like 'the disease', 'reading', 'the Book'. Obsessed with the idea of finding 'the Book', he recalls everything Nikita Ivanych and his fellow Oldener Lev L'vovich have said about it. But again, Benedikt interprets everything in the most concrete sense, failing to really grasp the meaning of anything. In particular, he is unable to see meaningful connections such as causal relations. His lack of genuine understanding is paralleled in this section by the quality of his speech, which contains ever more disconnected fragments of other texts in the form of literary quotations and allusions.

Tolstaia demonstrates in this way not only Benedikt's lack of understanding, but also his lack of originality. The idea that he himself, or other Golubchiks, could write their own books, new books, does not occur to Benedikt; indeed, the whole idea of cultural transmission is absent: Древние люди, что книгу эту написамши, сошли на нет, вымерли, и тени не осталось, и не вернутся, и не придут! Нету их! (216).[26]

Nikita Ivanych is the chief stoker (the Golubchiks are dependent on him, as they do not know how to make fire) and the only person who tries to convey some pre-Blast culture to the 'new' society. He does this by erecting pillars to commemorate former streets and places, as well as cultural figures, for example Strastnoi bul'var, Kuznetskii most, Volkhonka and, above all, Pushkin. In her usual style, Tolstaia makes fun of Benedikt's ignorance of Pushkin, but there is also a deep critique in her portrayal of the Oldeners' concept of culture. А ведь Пушкин, Беня, Пушкин – это наше все! Все! Вот ты об этом подумай, запомни и усвой . . . (226).[27] The representation of the Oldeners does much to discredit their views and values. Their speech and thoughts are expressed in stereotypes. They use the same words and concepts over and over again and their culture is a static one. Dwelling in remnants of the past, they seem unable to imagine transformation and development within culture.

The funeral of one of the Oldeners (even if they do not die of old age, they are not immortal) is a key episode that adds to this mocking image. The people present are asked to bring 'instructions' from Soviet times, and one of the mourners delivers instructions на мясорубку. Со сменными насадками (129),[28] which are then laid on the pillow of the deceased. Later during the funeral, in one of the speeches by the mourners, these instructions are referred to as a 'spiritual heritage': Главное же – сберечь духовное наследие! Предмета как такового нет, но есть инструкция к пользованию, духовное, не побоюсь этого слова, завещание, весточка из прошлого! (132).[29] Culture is conceived of as something that *was*, that *took place*, that can be commemorated and that stands in stark contrast to life as lived by the Golubchiks. From the point of view of the Oldeners, the life and society of the Golubchiks are defined not in terms of culture, but as absence of culture.

Even as he is about to burn at the stake, Nikita Ivanych does not cease to educate his surroundings: – Пинзинчику плеснуть, – заговорили в толпе, – пинзинчику надоть ... – БЕНзинчику, – закричал с верхотуры рассерженный Никита Иваныч, – сколько раз повторять, учить: БЕН, БЕН, БЕНзин!!! Олухи! (313).[30] The use of gasoline eventually leads to a massive 'blast'. After this new 'end of the world', the only survivors are Benedikt, Nikita Ivanych and Lev L'vovich. Nikita Ivanych, seemingly unimpressed by the events, just goes on where the old world left off, calling upon Lev L'vovich to continue their endless discussions about Russia, the West and the 'cursed questions': – Левушка! Подите сюда. Так на чем мы остановились? (316).[31]

Characteristically, reference to the lack of forward movement, development, and transmission of past culture to a meaningful future is made by Benedikt in a way that reveals more to the reader than to the protagonist, by employing a decontextualised quotation from the poet Natal'ia Krandievskaia-Tolstaia (1888–1963): Господи! Да ведь так же всегда и было: и в древности то же самое! «Но разве мир не одинаков в веках, и ныне, и всегда?..» Одинаков! Одинаков! (279).[32]

Catastrophe follows catastrophe, while the cyclical time frame that structures the novel on both the macro- and the micro-level (Gölz 2004: 692) becomes more and more explicit: – Кончена жизнь, Никита Иваныч, – сказал Бенедикт не своим голосом. Слова отдавались в голове, как в пустом каменном ведре, как в колодце. – Кончена – начнем другую, – ворчливо отозвался старик (316).[33] The lack of continuity is reinforced by Benedikt's feeling of total emptiness in a situation where even his own words seem to come not from himself, and to resonate only in a void.

Tolstaia leaves us at this 'point zero', giving few clues, it would seem, suggesting hope. The main targets of her criticism are quite clear: the intelligentsia, logocentrism, linguistic decay and cultural muteness. Yet, by writing itself into the tradition of the *azbukovniki* – the alphabetical explanatory encyclopedias of the sixteenth and seventeenth centuries (Gölz 2004) – *The Slynx* is also an edificatory text. Wherein lies its explanatory, constructive potential, if there is one? We will return to this question in the final section of this chapter, but let us first consider Evgenii Vodolazkin's version of an 'alphabetical novel', *Lavr*.

EVGENII VODOLAZKIN: A NON-HISTORICAL RESPONSE TO LANGUAGE HISTORY

Evgenii Vodolazkin, born 1964 in Kiev, works in the famous St Petersburg Department of Early Russian Literature at the Russian Academy of Sciences. As a philologist, he is known in particular for his work on medieval historiography. He made his debut as a writer of fiction in 2009 with the novel *Solov'ev and Larionov*, which was nominated for several Russian literary prizes. In 2012 his novel *Lavr* was published, shortlisted for both the NOS (*novaia slovesnost'* – 'new writing') and the Russian Booker Prize, and awarded the Big Book Prize 2013. Since then, he has published a volume of short stories (2016) and a new novel, *Aviator* (also 2016).

Laurus is a modern hagiographic account of Arsenii, a doctor living in fifteenth-century Russia. In the course of the book's four parts, we learn about Arsenii's childhood spent in the village of Rukino with his grandfather Khristofor, his relationship with the young girl Ustina, who becomes pregnant and dies in childbirth because Arsenii hesitates to call for a midwife, his life as a wandering doctor and later holy fool (*iurodivyi*) in Pskov, his friendship with the Italian Ambrogio and their pilgrimage to Jerusalem during which Ambrogio is killed, before Arsenii becomes a monk at the Kirillo-Beloozersk monastery and finally a receives the tonsure of the Great Schema – the mark of the highest degree of spiritual excellence – living alone in a cave. As *iurodivyi* he takes on the name Ustin, to honour the deceased Ustina; as monk he receives the name Amvrosii, the Slavic variant of Ambrosius (Italian Ambrogio); and finally as *skhimnik* he is called Lavr. Possible hagiographic prototypes for Arsenii include St Kseniia of St Petersburg and St Varlaam Keretskii. Kseniia became a *iurodivaia* after her husband's death, wandering around the streets of St Petersburg wearing her deceased husband's military uniform; Varlaam murdered his own wife in an attack of jealousy, later repented, dug up her dead body and sailed with it on a small boat until it dissolved.

Drawing on a long cultural history of sainthood in Russia, the novel is extraordinarily rich in terms of interpretive possibilities. I shall limit myself, however, to the role and theme of language in the novel, asking how the linguistic make-up of the text may be interpreted in the context of the language discussions taking place in Russia today.

If we were to characterise the language of the novel in one keyword, it would probably be diversity. The novel displays a peculiar kind of linguistic amalgam, where its diversity is primarily related to temporality, but also includes elements of style and sociolect. The main linguistic ingredients are, apart from standard literary Russian, Church Slavonic and early or middle Rus(s)ian elements[34] (words, word forms, syntax, style), officialese and profanity. Let us first look at the instances and contexts where we find Church Slavonic elements.

Slavonicisms

Slavonicisms appear mainly in the speech of particular characters, such as Khristofor (Arsenii's grandfather) and Arsenii himself, both as a child and as an adult, but also in that of many people whom he meets, for example monks and elders, the young boy Silvestr, the tavern keeper's wife, sailors, pilgrims and even his Italian friend Ambrogio. We also find such language in passages written in birch-bark letters by Khristofor, in quotations from the Bible and historical chronicles, as well as in quoted passages from the Kievan Caves Paterikon which Arsenii is ordered to copy in the monastery. Let us look first at an instance of dialogue between the young boy Arsenii and his grandfather: Что убо чтеши, Христофоре? Книги Авраамовы не от Священных Писаний. Чти же в голос, да и аз послушаю (55).[35]

The two of them do not always speak in this manner. In fact, more often than not, instances of Church Slavonic appear in the midst of standard literary Russian. Here Khristofor tells Arsenii about mythological birds, such as the phoenix and the caladrius:

Есть, наконец, птица харадр, вся сплошь белая. *И аще кто в болезнь впадет, есть от харадра разумети, жив будет или умрет. Да аще будет ему умрети, отвратит лице свое харадр, аще ли будет ему живу быти, то харадр, веселуяся, взлетит на воздух противу солнца* – и все понимают, что харадр взял язву болящего и развеял ее в воздухе. (31, my italics)³⁶

We see that Church Slavonic elements appear when Khristofor explains the options of death and life, that is, at the most solemn point of his utterance. A similar pattern may be observed in the meeting between Arsenii and the young boy Silvestr: Когда он подошел, Арсений увидел, что это мальчик лет семи. *Аз есмь Сильвестр, сказал мальчик. Се придох, яко болеет моя мати. Ты же, Арсение, помози нам.* Он взял Арсения за руку и потянул его в сторону берега (136, my italics).³⁷ Here the use of Church Slavonic indicates the young boy's holiness with a reference to the hagiographic *puer senex* topos – the young boy as an old man – as he solemnly states his name and mission and instructs Arsenii to come to the house of his sick mother. In a similar manner, quotations or stock phrases from saints' lives may motivate the switch from standard Russian to Church Slavonic within a passage, sometimes affecting only parts of a sentence. Consider, for instance, this address by Arsenii to (the dead) Ustina: Веришь ли, сказал он Устине, я стал привередлив и боюсь кровососущих. *Живя яко в чуждем телеси, я* никого не боялся. Вот это-то, любовь моя, и путает. Не растерял ли я в одночасье того, что собирал для тебя все эти годы? (253, my italics).³⁸

The relationship between form and content is not always so straightforward, however. Sometimes the switch between registers occurs in the middle of a sentence or passage without any accompanying change in subject matter. Slavonicisms may even occur in instances where one would not expect them, if they were reserved for topics of dignity and solemnity. Here are the tavern keeper's wife's words, falsely accusing Arsenii, who stays overnight in the tavern keeper's house, of attacking her sexually: Жена корчмаря окинула его [i.e. the tavern keeper] строгим взглядом: Эх ты, Черпак. *Сей же рече ми: наслажуся красоты твоея. Аз же ему возбраних.* Если не золотой, дайте хоть что-нибудь (256, my italics).³⁹

Even Arsenii's friend Ambrogio, a young Italian who becomes obsessed with the question of the end of the world and travels to Russia in order to find out more, occasionally speaks in Church Slavonic: Мню, яко единому Богу се ведомо есть, уклончиво отвечал Амброджо. В чтомых мною книгах многдажды о сем речено, обаче несть в них численного согласия (243).⁴⁰

Arsenii's fellow *iurodivyi* in Pskov, Foma, is probably the most 'extreme' user of Church Slavonic, both in the sense of his style of speech and in the manner in which he mixes Slavonicisms with other linguistic registers. We shall return to the latter below; consider here a typical outburst of Foma's: *Тьма смертная объя мя, и отиде свет от очию моею*, закричал, обойдя полгорода, Фома (357, my italics).[41]

The use of Slavonicisms is not confined to the realm of direct speech, however. There are noteworthy examples of *visual* uses of Church Slavonic, especially in the section where Arsenii teaches Ustina to read and write. She is surprised when she learns that the letters have names (*az*, *buki*, *vedi* . . .) and charmed by the 'independent life' and 'unexpected meanings' these names give the letters (85–6).[42] The letters furthermore have numerical values, Ustina learns, a fact Vodolazkin illustrates visually by numbering the individual chapters of the novel with Church Slavonic letters.[43] The ancient and traditional role of the Church Slavonic alphabet in the teaching of reading and writing is furthermore thematised in Khristofor's *gramoty*, the small pieces of birch bark which he uses for all kinds of writing and which are quoted throughout the novel. In this particular section, Ustina reads a *kolorodstvo*, a pattern of the seven stages of a human life symbolised by the seven days of the week, often provided in the Slavic *Azbukovniki*, the 'alphabetical encyclopedias':

а҃-й день рождение детища, [Arsenii's birth and early life with Khristofor]
в҃-й день юноша, [young Arsenii]
г҃-й день совершен муж, [Arsenii's union with Ustina]
д҃-й день средовечие, [Arsenii as holy fool; Arsenii and Ambrogio]
е҃-й день седина, [Arsenii as monk]
ѕ҃-й день старость, [Arsenii as *skhimnik*]
з҃-й день скончание. [Arsenii's death and the posthumous miracles] (86)[44]

It is not difficult to divide, as I have done here, the different stages of Arsenii's life according to the seven 'letters', and this clear parallel points to the significant interconnections in this novel between the concepts of language, time and a human life. Before we go any further in analysing the philosophical and epistemological aspects of these interconnections, it is essential to get a firm grip not only on the novel's use of older forms of Russian, but also on its peculiar mix of the old and the new, the high and the low.

The blending of languages and styles

The way Church Slavonic elements are used in the text is indicative of the general style of the novel, which may be summed up by two keywords that bring us back to the concept of diversity: variation and flexibility. We find patterns of flexible variation on all levels, from the orthographic to the lexical and stylistic. Consider the following short dialogue between Arsenii and a woman who has come to see him and be treated by him: Впусти ее, Мелетий, говорит Амвросий, не оборачиваясь. Чего ты хочешь, жено? Жити хощу, Врачу. Помози ми. А умереть не хочешь? (379).[45] Whereas Arsenii uses the modern Russian *khochesh'* ('wish' second person singular) twice, the woman uses the Church Slavonic *khoshchu* ('wish' first person singular), which we also find in the orthographic variant *khoshchiu* a few pages earlier. This kind of flexible variation, as well as switching of stylistic and linguistic register, so typical of medieval text culture (Cerquiglini 1989), can be found in abundance throughout the novel.

In addition to archaic language, we also encounter markedly contemporary uses of language, most notably a matter-of-fact style bordering on officialese. It is the holy fool Foma, in particular, who uses this mixture of styles, while also adding the occasional *mat* word to his speech: Посмотри на себя, Арсение. Ты и есть юродивый, иже избра себе житие буйственное и от человек уничиженное. [. . .] Ты кто? Хуй в пальто, ответил Фома (179).[46] The mix of languages adds to the mildly ironic portrayal of the holy fool, who is as serious and sincere about his foolish behaviour as he is eager to demarcate the geographic space of his performance territory: Любезный друг, граница между частями города ныне стерта естественным путем. Следует констатировать, что разделявшая нас преграда скрылась на время под невиданно толстым льдом. Если желаешь собирать замерзающий элемент и на моей территории, ничтоже вопреки глаголю (201).[47] The amalgam of officialese, plain matter-of-fact language and high-style Slavonicisms reaches its climax in Foma's last speech:

> Неужели же вы думаете, что я изгнал их [бесов] навеки? Ну, лет на пять, максимум – на десять. И что вы, спрашивается, будете делать дальше? А теперь пишите. Вас ждет великий мор, но вам поможет раб Божий Арсений, вернувшись из Иерусалима. А потом уйдет и Арсений, ибо ему понадобится покинуть град сей. Вот тогда-то вам придется проявить крепость духа и внутреннюю сосредоточенность. В конце концов, вы сами уже не дети.
>
> Проследив, чтобы все было записано, юродивый Фома закрыл глаза и умер. Затем он открыл на мгновенье глаза и добавил:

Постскриптум. Пусть Арсений имеет в виду, что его ждет монастырь аввы Кирилла. Всё.
Сказав это, юродивый Фома умер окончательно. (357)[48]

The elements of this mixture range from the solemn to the humorous; they add to the stylistic variety of the book and make it entertaining to read. This diversity in terms of linguistic layers, but also of different periods of time, is not only a literary device, but a quality of utmost importance to Vodolazkin, which becomes evident if we examine more systematically the patterns of variation.

From a contemporary point of view, our speech may contain elements from all layers attested in the history of a given language. The characters in Vodolazkin's novel, however, are supposed to live and speak in fifteenth-century Russia. How can they be using styles and words from the twentieth century? How can a fifteenth-century monk speak of *avtomatizm* (399) or Arsenii's grandfather cite Saint-Exupéry's *Little Prince* (33)? The seeming (or real) anachronisms are not confined to language; we also stumble across plastic bottles appearing under the melting snow in front of Arsenii's house. Vodolazkin's subtitle to the novel, *neistoricheskii roman* (*non-historical novel*) may turn out to mean more than a statement about genre.

A philosophy of language

The actual uses of historical linguistic elements are supplemented by what I would call fragments of a linguistic philosophy, ideas about language that emerge in single comments throughout the novel. These ideas are linked furthermore to (fragments of) a philosophy of time, as we shall see in the next section.

First, we may note a strong belief in the written word, as exemplified in the role of Khristofor's birch-bark letters, which accompany Arsenii throughout his life. Khristofor writes down his words of wisdom, recipes and biblical quotations not because he is afraid of forgetting, we are told, but because слово записанное упорядочивает мир. Останавливает его текучесть. Не позволяет понятиям размываться (40).[49] At the same time, the idea about the (written) word's power to represent, and even structure, reality is paired with an equally 'logocentric' idea about the primacy of silence. In my next example, the reader's attention is drawn towards the sounds that arise when people do not speak:

Они поздоровались, и из уст их изошло четыре струйки пара. Больше за всю дорогу они не произнесли ни звука, храня слова для грядущей исповеди. *Эхом их безмолвия по мерзлой земле звенели копыта.* Под ободами колес хрустел наст. Мороз ударил накануне, и *грязь смерзлась бороздами и комками, превратив дорогу в стиральную доску*.[50] (52, my emphasis)

I call the focus on silence in *Laurus* 'logocentric' because in many of the scenes where silence is central, the power of language is still underlined. In such passages we find sections of rhythmical prose and poetic devices, for instance (see my emphasis in the passage just quoted), demonstrating the wide range of linguistic functions that go beyond the referential in creating meaning. In the scene where Ustina learns to read and write – a chapter full of visual representations of Church Slavonic letters and talk about their names and meanings – the dialogue between Arsenii and Ustina evolves into a silent conversation, a dialogue without spoken words, before ending with the statement that, Важно, что мы с тобой уже понимаем друг друга без слов (87).[51] Later on, in Arsenii's encounter with a young Italian girl, Laura,[52] there is a similar instance of dialogic understanding, where the actual words spoken are seemingly of no relevance: Меня зовут Лаура, и я не понимаю твоего языка. Я вижу, что ты чем-то подавлена, но не знаю причины твоей скорби. Иногда легче говорить, когда тебя не понимают (311).[53] There follows a long dialogue, where the two speak to each other, without understanding the pronounced words, but in some sense still receiving the meaning. Laura tells him that she has been diagnosed with leprosy. Arsenii apparently heals her with a formula-like sentence (Пребуди, чадо, в здравии [313]),[54] and then disappears: Лаура не смогла бы повторить его слов, но они наполнили ее бесконечной радостью, ибо главный их смысл был ей уже открыт (313).[55]

When Arsenii returns to Pskov from his dramatic pilgrimage to Jerusalem, having suffered the loss of his true friend Ambrogio, he is said not to tell anyone anything and to speak little in general, but his silence is of a special kind: Вернувшись, он никому ничего не рассказывал. Он вообще говорил очень мало. Не так, может быть, мало, как в бытность свою юродивым, но теперешние его слова звенели такой тишиной, какая не свойственна самому глубокому молчанию (356).[56] In such instances, silence (or the lack of plain communication, as above) is valued more than speech, but it is a particular kind of silence, one that is intimately linked to the effect of words, to the power of language.

A philosophy of time

The philosophy of language sketched above is explicit enough to tell us that language is an important theme in this novel. The historical dimension of language as particularly significant becomes clear when we look at the focus on language in conjunction with the reflections on time found in the text, above all in the dialogues between Arsenii and his Italian friend Ambrogio. Ambrogio is obsessed by the idea of the end of the world, which was expected to occur in 1492. The young Italian has dreams and visions in which he foresees both historical events and everyday episodes just a few years – or hundreds of years – ahead, from Columbus's discovery of America in 1492 to scenes from city life in the Russia of 2012, the year the novel was published.

Absorbed in this free flux of time, Ambrogio comes to realise that, in fact, there is no such thing as time (279). Our concept of time is merely something that helps us structure our lives, just as writing down words does, according to Khristofor.[57] The parallel between language and time has already been established earlier in Arsenii's discussion with Ambrogio, where the former points out that, as letters indicating years alter their form in the manuscript (as time passes), so they become (or are interpreted as) different letters representing years other than those originally intended – and this may change our concept of history altogether. With its growing distrust in the ability of time to fixate history, and (written) language to fixate time, the narrative increasingly focuses on cyclical time:

> Начиная с той зимы Лавр потерял счет времени, устремленного вперед. Теперь он чувствовал только время круговое, замкнутое на себе, – время дня, недели и года. [. . .]
> События в его памяти более не соотносились со временем. Они спокойно растеклись по его жизни, выстроившись в особый, со временем не связанный порядок. (412)[58]

As it turns out, the end of the world does not happen. Life goes on, while on the novel's philosophical level, time is increasingly conceived of not as a constraint, but as a creative force. The cyclical character of life and history is finally confirmed in Arsenii's own life when, as the novel draws to a close, he saves the lives of the orphan Anastasia and her baby, thereby implicitly obtaining forgiveness for his sin committed against Ustina and their child.

Time and narration

We saw earlier, especially in the representation of the holy fool Foma's speech, that there is a significant element of (sympathetic) irony in the depiction of the characters of the novel. This tone of voice also emerges in the narrator's comments, for instance when he describes the encounter between Ambrogio and the people of Pskov. The people first look at Ambrogio with a degree of scepticism, before they understand that indeed, his only interest is the end of the world. Such a respectable endeavour, we are told, they can appreciate, ибо на Руси любили масштабные задачи (242).[59]

The tone of voice in this and similar examples saves the book from becoming obsessed with national identity and the heroic past, as is the case in many 'historical novels' from which Vodolazkin disassociates himself in his subtitle *non-historical novel*. Still, it becomes apparent in many instances that the author of the novel is a specialist in Rus' medieval culture, as for instance when he describes how Khristofor does not pick up the birch-bark letters if they fall on the ground: смутно предвидя их позднейшее обнаружение в культурном слое (40).[60] Vodolazkin's narrator even uses the word 'medieval' in many instances, clearly stepping out of the narrated situation and taking a retrospective glance:

> Развешивал [одежду] на кустах шиповника и молодых сосенках, которые сгибались под тяжестью мокрых средневековых одежд. (261)[61]

> Средневековье редко имело возможность дважды свести людей в течение земной жизни. (308)[62]

> Деньги в Средневековье не были бумажными, и спрятать их было очень непросто. (350)[63]

> Берестяные грамоты дитя читало вслух. В Средневековье вообще читали преимущественно вслух, на худой конец просто шевелили губами. (41)[64]

In such instances the reader, who is otherwise drawn smoothly into the narrative by an omniscient but not conspicuously present narrator, is reminded both that what is being told belongs to times long gone, and that we, as readers, live in very different times.

In other words, we can note a change of register in the voice(s) of the narrator, which is so strong in some cases that we may speak of a change of genre. Thus the fourth and last part of the novel opens with the words: Принято считать, что на Русь Арсений вернулся в середине восьмидесятых годов (355),[65] thus switching, as it were, from the fictional to the historiographical genre. The effect is the same as with the use of markers such as 'the Middle Ages': the narrator establishes a new 'now' and the reader, reminded of being situated far away in time and space, is invited to reflect on this fact.

CONCLUSIONS

When commenting through their artistic works on the language question, writers tend to present their views less straightforwardly than in the official debates, and frequently by means of ambiguation and, not least, humour. Occasionally, the recurrent themes of the language debates are given a philosophical or epistemological interpretation. With both Tolstaia and Vodolazkin, we are still dealing with authors from whom we can expect a certain underlying didactic 'message'.

Both writers challenge the language of literature by stretching its potential and including a wealth of elements taken from non-standard varieties and archaic layers. They are very different, however, in their style and method. In Tolstaia, we find a radical juxtaposition of not only words but also values, in order to portray a destructive, brutal 'truth' about contemporary society. Vodolazkin's verbal style is a more smoothly created amalgam that displays flexibility and multifunctionality. In Tolstaia there is no future and no past, and the author shows this situation with all its destructive consequences. Vodolazkin's stance is, perhaps, more constructive, highlighting the creative forces of disruption and diversity.

In both novels, the reader is invited to reflect, engage and take responsibility for the language. Let us look more closely at the ways in which the two writers approach this topic.

Tat'iana Tolstaia: discursive critique

Tolstaia is known to have been very critical of the evolution of linguistic standards during late perestroika and early post-Soviet times, bemoaning the lack of stylistic and lexical nuance, the uncritical use of foreign loanwords, the rough style of speech (Tolstaia 2012a). In *The Slynx*, she portrays, of course, a much more radical linguistic situation – a true linguistic crisis with far-reaching consequences. Tolstaia 'attacks' in particular the connections between language and tradition, language and identity, language and history – she exposes their crisis at a time when such connections were frequently being made in the language debates.

Innerfictionally, the lack of literacy – what we might call, in this context, the language culture or language situation– is associated with a de-humanisation and degradation of society. Tolstaia attacks the logocentric tradition, the very meaning of words, books and culture. At the same time, however, through her linguistic inventiveness, sophisticated play on words and broad orientation in the literary tradition, she clearly demonstrates her own mastery of language. The novel, among many other things, is a celebration of stylistic diversity. Not, to be sure, the individual variety used by particular individuals in the novel, such as *prostorechie*, archaic forms or vulgar language, but stylistic diversity as such, and above all, Tolstaia's own stylistic virtuosity. We have seen many examples of how she uses linguistic techniques to characterise her protagonists, in ways that are more revealing to the reader than to the persons described. There is a cynical attitude in this. As a result, the novel represents a fundamental critique of the language that it portrays (and of its users) – in particular, the capacity of language to make sense of the world. Yet at the same time, the text emerges as a playful experiment demonstrating and celebrating the multifarious functions and meaning-generating capacities of language as such.

We have seen how cyclical time contributes to portraying a world without forward movement, with ever new beginnings and ever new catastrophes. Benedikt's frequent digressions, lists and catalogues mirror this situation on the narrative level, whereas on the syntactic, we can observe a similar predominance of parallel constructions, synonyms and repetitions. Here is a typical descriptive passage by Benedikt, as he characterises Nikita Ivanych:

> Пожелает – костерок запалит, сядет к огню, подбрасывая сухой бурелом, веточки, дрянь лесную, опадыши чащобные; станет глядеть в красно-желтое, живое, шевелящееся, теплое, пляшущее. Ни просить не надо, ни кланяться, ни челом бить, ни пугаться – ничего. Свобода! Вот бы Бенедикту так! Вот бы так!.. (71)[66]

With Benedikt as focal character, the story moves in a horizontal plane of narration within clear confines. The perspective is introduced by Tolstaia's ironic, sarcastic, at times cynical stance, and – not least – by the potential involvement of the reader. By consistently revealing more to the reader than to her characters, Tolstaia invites the reader to reflect, and in this lies the strong metafictional, and possibly didactic, element of the novel. Understood in this light, the representation of linguistic culture in *The Slynx* may be read as a challenge to language users to take responsibility for their own 'verbal life'.

Evgenii Vodolazkin: be mindful of the past

I disagree with literary critic Petr Basinskii, who maintains, in his review of *Laurus*, that 'language cannot be the theme and goal of prose writing' (Basinskii 2013). Language is not the only theme of Vodolazkin's book, of course, but it is, I would argue, a main theme. We have noted how the speaking characters, as well as the narrator, move freely between different layers of language, style and even genre. Tat'iana Morozova, in her review of the novel, calls the language in *Laurus* an *obshchechelovecheskii iazyk* ('one that is common to all mankind') (Morozova 2013), and in an interview Vodolazkin himself points out that the novel is neither about the Middle Ages nor about contemporaries, but about the *vnevremennik*, a person 'situated outside of time' (Vodolazkin and Luchenko 2014).

What are we, then, to make of the voice of the philologist which comes through clearly from time to time? When the fictionally represented time is occasionally labelled as 'medieval', we are reminded of the fact that we do not live in medieval times, but 'now'. The explanatory voice of the narrator at such moments serves to remind us of the great time span between Arsenii's time and our own. It might be read as a 'warning' not to live (and speak) in such a way that is confined only to the present, but rather to be mindful of the past, just as we should be mindful the future – to the extent that we can do so at all, not being endowed with the gift of foreseeing the future, as is Ambrogio. Vodolazkin's own comments on this point confirm that the narrator's fluctuating perspective is, indeed, a conscious device:

> У меня в романе два сознания: одно средневековое, одно – современное. Это редкий случай для современной литературы, когда не автор, а повествователь способен переходить с одного сознания на другое: то есть, когда он пишет как средневековый человек, а потом распрямляется и бросает взгляд из современности. (Vodolazkin and Luchenko 2014)[67]

What Vodolazkin does not comment on is the irony that often accompanies the perspective of the medieval historian or even philologist. Here are two examples from Arsenii's pilgrimage, where he is confronted with unknown languages and dialects: В Жешове Арсений сказал Устине: В *речи жешовцев, здешних жителей, очевидно учащение шипящих.*

Подчас ощущаешь пресыщение (291, my italics).[68] The point is typically reinforced by poetic devices, demonstrating on the phonetic level the 'surfeit' of sibilants in the statement describing it. Likewise, when reaching Austria, the narrator notes that the Austrians 'already tried to speak their own particular variant of German': В конце XV века австрийцы еще в точности не знали, отличаются ли они от немцев и если отличаются, то чем. Особенности произношения в конце концов дали им ответ на оба вопроса (292).[69]

As Morozova (2013) notes, the irony saves Vodolazkin's book from becoming too full of pathos. Indeed, in this novel, the use of Church Slavonic linguistic elements are not linked to any particular nationalist, orthodox or patriotic stance. Quite the opposite. As several reviewers have pointed out, Arsenii lives most of his life outside of established institutions such as the church. When he enters the monastery towards the end of his life, it is only to leave it again in order to become a hermit.

'Russianness' is treated with irony in *Laurus*, as in the oft-quoted ending, where the dead body of Arsenii is dragged along the ground, according to his own pre-death request. A foreigner, the merchant Siegfried, is horrified, but is told by the local blacksmith Averkii that he does not understand the Russian people. Siegfried replies: А сами вы ее понимаете? спрашивает Зигфрид. Мы? Кузнец задумывается и смотрит на Зигфрида. Сами мы ее, конечно, тоже не понимаем (441).[70]

In *Laurus*, the historical dimensions of language receive a philosophical interpretation related to the meaning of time in the life of an individual, in history and in reality as such. When Arsenii, or Lavr, spends his last days in a lonely cave, people and all their once-spoken words come together and fill him with new words, and new life:

> Ему не было одиноко, потому что он не чувствовал себя оставленным людьми. Все когда-либо встреченные им ощущались им как присутствующие. Они продолжали тихую жизнь в его душе – независимо от того, отправились ли в иной мир или были всё еще живы. Он помнил все их слова, интонации и движения. Их старые слова рождали новые слова, они взаимодействовали с позднейшими событиями и словами самого Лавра. Жизнь продолжалась во всем своем многообразии. (407–8)[70]

In an ever changing amalgam of linguistic elements, of stylistic and historical variation, time and language are brought together in the fictional representation of a simultaneity that demonstrates the inexhaustible richness of the language, on the one hand, and the individual human being's endless potential for linguistic creativity, on the other. The language of *Laurus* beautifully illustrates the point made explicit in one of Vodolazkin's interviews, that 'our language is richer than we think, and it did not originate today' (Vodolazkin and Luchenko 2014).

NOTES

1. Jamey Gambrell's rendering of the title (Tolstaya 2003).
2. This concerns, of course, not just Russian literature; see, for example, Meyers (1980), Sisk (1997) and Mohr (2009) for studies of the role of language in non-Russian utopias and related genres. For a discussion of the role of language in a number of recent Russian conservative dystopias, see Bodin (2016).
3. 'Tolstaia is not forecasting the future (therefore *The Slynx* is not at all anti-utopian) but she brilliantly conveys the present-day crisis of language, the present-day collapse of hierarchical relationships in culture, when the cultural orders of Soviet civilisation have come tumbling down, burying at the same time alternative, anti-Soviet cultural hierarchies' (Lipovetskii 2001).
4. Page numbers in brackets refer to Tolstaia (2005).
5. I follow Jamey Gambrell's (Tolstaya 2003) rendering of the 'Golubchiks', 'Oldeners', 'Degenerators', and so forth.
6. 'It was Fyodor Kuzmich, Glorybe, brought fire to people. Only how it all happened, where he got the fire, we don't know. You could think on it for three days and you wouldn't figure it out, you'd just get a headache, like you'd drunk too much egg kvas. Some say it was from the sky, some say that Fyodor Kuzmich, Glorybe, stamped his foot and the earth flared up in a clear fire right then and there. Anything could be true' (22). English translations are taken from Tolstaya (2003), with page numbers in brackets.
7. 'Russia is a huge asylum [. . .] the one and only absolute is relativism, the one and only constant – chaos. Everyone establishes the rules of the game for herself, altering them along the way according to her own moods [. . .] time in Russia is mythological, frozen, one where all events happen simultaneously.'
8. 'They sit in their izbas or go to work, and some have made it into the bosses – same as with us. Only their talk is different. If you run into a Golubchik stranger on the street, you could never say whether he's one of us or an Oldener. Until you ask him the usual: "Who are ya? How come I don't know you? What the heck you doin' in our neck of the woods?" An Oldener doesn't answer like other people do: "Whassit to ya, tired of lugging that mug around? Just wait, I'll rip it offa ya," or something like that. No, they don't answer so's you can make sense of it, so to speak: You got muscles and I got muscles so don't mess with me! No, sometimes you'll get an answer like: "Leave me be, you uncouth hooligan!" Then you know for sure the guy's an Oldener' (115).
9. 'Philosophy, weapon, university education, shop, asphalt, intelligentsia, tradition, renaissance, chef d'œuvres, honey, museum, elementary moral principles.'
10. '"Why is it," said Nikita Ivanich, "why is it that everything keeps mutating, everything? People, well, all right, but the language, concepts, meaning! Huh? Russia! Everything gets twisted up in knots"' (211).

11. Tolstaia herself encourages this interpretation in an early interview about the novel: А это ведь и есть главное последствие описанной в романе катастрофы. Мутация языка ('This is in fact the main consequence of the catastrophe portrayed in the novel. The mutation of the language') (Tolstaia and Zimin 2000).
12. 'They swear a sight better than we do' (106).
13. 'To hell with them, those Degenerators, better to keep your distance. They're strange ones, and you can't figure out if they're people or not. Their faces look human, but their bodies are all furry and they run on all fours' (4).
14. 'If a Cockynork sticks his head out you throw a rock at him to warm yourself up, and keep running. You throw the rock because the Cockynorks, they don't talk like us: all they say is blah-blah-blah and blah-blah-blah – you can't understand a thing. Why do they talk like that, why don't they want to talk like we do? Who knows. Maybe on purpose. Or maybe it's just a bad habit, that kind of thing can happen. They're just cutting off their noses to spite their faces. What can they say in Cockynork? Our language is handier any way you look at it: you can sit down, talk things over, discuss them: such and such and thus and so. And everything's clear as day' (44).
15. '"Bliny, so what? What about bliny?" "What about, nothing about! Bliny! What'll it be next?" "What's it to you?" "Nothing! That's what!" "Well, then, don't say nothing. But I say: bliny!" "I'll give you bliny!" "You're a real blin yourself." "That's right, I'm a blin. So what does that make you?" "Nothing!" "Then shut up!" "Shut up yourself!" "I'll just shut up, then!" "So just go ahead and shut up!" "So there, I'll shut up! Bliny!" "Then just shut up! Give us some peace and quiet!"' (186–7).
16. 'Rich people are called rich because they live rich' (51).
17. 'Blind people are blind because they can't see a darn thing' (83).
18. 'Then there's *Questions of Literature*. Benedikt took a look at it: no questions at all, only answers. The issue with questions must have got lost. Too bad' (179).
19. 'Oldeners don't understand our words, and we don't understand theirs' (23).
20. '"I've been meaning to ask you, Benedikt. I'm copying poems by Fyodor Kuzmich, Glorybe. And I keep coming across the word 'steed,' 'steed.' What is a steed, do you know?" Benedikt thought for a moment. Then another. His face even reddened from the effort. How many times he'd written that word himself, and had never thought about it. "It must be a mouse." [. . .] "Well, then, what about 'The steed races, the earth trembles'?" "It must be a big mouse"' (36).
21. 'He combines these things on the basis of their similarity or iconicity, without being able to read them as referring to something absent, to the representatives of a metaphysical meaning.'
22. 'You look at people – men, women – like you're seeing them for the first time, like you're a different creature, or you just came out of the forest, or the other way around you just walked into the forest' (47).
23. 'You don't really know how to read, books are of no use to you. They're just empty page-turning, a collection of letters. You haven't learned the alphabet of life. Of life, do you hear me?' (244).
24. '"Nikita Ivaaaaanich! Grandfather! Where is the booook! Tell me quiiiiick!" "Study your letters! The ABCs! I've told you a hundred times! You can't read it without your letters! Farewell! Take ca-a-aaaa-re!"' (294).
25. 'Ц, Tsi, and Щ, Shcha, have tails, like Benedikt before his wedding. Ч, Cherv, is like an upside-down chair. Г, Glagol, is shaped like a hook' (254).
26. 'The ancient people who wrote these books have turned to dust, they've died out,

not a shadow remains. They won't return, they'll never come back! They don't exist anymore!' (199).
27. 'And Pushkin, you know, Benya, Pushkin is our be all and end all! He's everything to us. You just think about it, remember, and assimilate it . . .' (208).
28. 'for a meat grinder. With attachments' (118).
29. 'The most important thing is to preserve our spiritual heritage! The object itself may not exist, but there are instructions for its use, we have its spiritual – no, I do not fear that word – will and testament, a missive from the past!' (121).
30. ' "Splash a little guzzelean," the crowd muttered, "it needs a little guzzelean." "*Gas-o-line*," shouted an angry Nikita Ivanich from above, "how many times do you have to be told, to be taught: GAS-O-line, or, as it is occasionally referred to, petrol, or benzine, that's B-E-N-zine, you blockheads!" ' (293).
31. ' "Lyovushka! Come over here. So, where were we?" ' (296).
32. 'Good Lord! That's how it always was, in ancient times too! "But is the world not all alike . . . Throughout the ages, now and ever more?" It is! It is!' (260).
33. ' "Life is over, Nikita Ivanich," said Benedikt in a voice that was not his own. The words resounded in his head, as though spoken in an empty stone bucket or a well. "It's over . . . so we'll start another one," the old man grumbled in reply' (295–6).
34. The 'registers' of Church Slavonic and early or middle Rus(s)ian overlap and are sometimes difficult to separate. For simplicity's sake, in the following discussion, I term such elements in *Laurus* 'Church Slavonic' or 'Slavonicisms'.
35. ' "What readest thou, O Christopher?" "Books of Abraham not from the Holy Scriptures." "Go on, reade it out loud, I shall listen" ' (44). Page numbers in brackets following the Russian original refer to Vodolazkin (2012), translations are taken from Vodolazkin (2016). I have indicated, in the translations, the alternation of direct speech in dialogues by inserting double quotation marks. Note that the translation anglicises Russian names (Christopher) and that spellings of names may vary slightly from the conventions used in this book (Arseny).
36. 'Finally, there is the caladrius bird, which is completely white. Yf one falls into illness, he can learne from the caladrius yf he will live or die. And yf he will die, the caladrius will turn his face away but yf he will live, the caladrius will merrily fly up into the air against the sun – and everyone will understand the caladrius took the sick person's sore and scattered it in the air' (24).
37. 'When the boy approached, Arseny saw he was around seven years old. "I am Silvester," said the boy. "I have come, for my mother is sicke. Helpe us, O Arseny." He took Arseny by the hand and pulled him in the direction of the shore' (111).
38. 'Can you believe, he said to Ustina, that I have gotten squeamish and am afraid of these bloodsuckers? I feared nothing *when I was living as if in the body of another*. And that, my love, does frighten me. Did I lose in an instant what I was gathering for you all those years?' (205).
39. 'The tavern keeper's wife cast a stern look at him: "Oh you, Ladle. This one sayde to me, I will revell in youre beauty. And I did denye him. At least give me something, even if it is not gold coin" ' (208).
40. 'Me thinketh it be knowne only to God, Ambrogio answered, evading. I have ofte read in books of what is sayde, moreover, there is not any numeric agreement within them' (197).
41. 'The dark of death has taken me, and the light wente awaye from myne eyes, Foma began shouting as he circled half the city' (292).
42. Больше всего Устине нравилось, что у букв есть имена. Она произносила

их про себя, и губы ее постоянно шевелились. Аз. Буки. Веди. [...] Имена давали буквам самостоятельную жизнь. Они давали им неожиданный смысл, который завораживал Устину (85–6). 'More than anything Ustina liked that letters had names. She pronounced them to herself, her lips constantly moving. *Az. Buki. Vedi.* [...] The names gave the letters independent life. They gave them an unexpected meaning that bewitched Ustina' (69, slightly amended).

43. Whereas both Tolstaia's and Vodolazkin's chapter titles are inspired by the use of Church Slavonic and pre-revolutionary letters, their individual approaches differ: Tolstaia writes out the Church Slavonic names of the letters and the chapter titles follow the established order of the pre-revolutionary Russian alphabet. The letters, however, appear in a modern typeface. Vodolazkin employs the letters according to their numerical value and keeps the Church Slavonic typeface.

44. 'The first day is a childe's birth, the second day is for a yonge man, on the third day he is a growne man, the fourth day is for the middle of the lyfe, fifth is the day of graying, the sixth day is for old age, and the seventh day is for the ende' (70).

45. '"Let her in, Melety," says Amvrosy, not turning. "What do you want, O woman?" "I want to lyve, O Doctor. Helpe me." "And you do not want to die?"' (311).

46. '"Look at yourself, O Arseny. You really are a holy fool, for thou hast chosen a life for yourself that is wild and disparaged by people." [...] "Who are you? Who?" "A prick wearing one shoe [that's none of your fucking business]," answered Foma' (146).

47. 'My kind friend, the border between the city's various parts has now been erased by natural means. It should be stated that the barrier that divided us is hidden temporarily under ice of an unprecedented thickness. If you wish to gather up these frozen elements on my territory, too, I shall saye nothinge against it' (164).

48. '"You don't really think I drove them out forever, do you? Maybe about five years, ten maximum. And what will you do then? you might ask. Well, write this down. A great pestilence awaits you but God's servant Arseny will help you, when he's back from Jerusalem. And then Arseny will leave, too, for he will need to leave this burg. And then you'll have to display some spiritual fortitude and internal focus. You're not children anymore yourselves, after all." Holy fool Foma closed his eyes and died after he had made sure everything had been written down. Then he opened his eyes for a moment and added: "*Postscriptum.* Arseny should keep in mind that Abba Kirill's monastery is expecting him. That's all." After saying that, holy fool Foma died forever' (292–3).

49. 'the written word seemed to regulate the world. Stop its fluctuations. Prevent notions from eroding' (31–2).

50. 'Four plumes of vapor flowed from their lips when they greeted the new passengers. They did not utter another sound for the rest of the journey, preserving their words for the impending Confession. Hooves rang out on the frozen earth, echoing their silence. The thin crust of ice covering the snow crunched under the rims of the wheels. A frost had hit the night before and the mud had frozen into furrows and clods, turning the road into a washboard' (41–2).

51. 'What is important is that you and I already understand each other without words' (70).

52. In addition to being the female variant of Laurus, the name Laura also reminds us of Petrarch's encounter with his muse Laura in the church of Sainte-Claire d'Avignon.

53. '"My name is Laura, and I do not understand your language." "I see you are

somehow dispirited but I do not know the reason for your sorrow." "Sometimes it is easier to speak when people do not understand you"' (254).
54. 'Be in good health, childe' (255).
55. 'Laura could not have repeated his words but they had filled her with endless joy, for their main meaning had already been disclosed to her' (256).
56. 'He did not tell anyone anything after he returned. He generally spoke very little. Not as little, perhaps, as in his time as a holy fool, but his words these days rang with a quietness that was not characteristic of even the deepest silence' (292).
57. Я скажу странную вещь. Мне все больше кажется, что времени нет. Все на свете существует вневременно, иначе как мог бы я знать небывшее будущее? Я думаю, время дано нам по милосердию Божию, чтобы мы не запутались, ибо не может сознание человека впустить в себя все события одновременно. Мы заперты во времени из-за слабости нашей (279). 'I am going to tell you something strange. It seems ever more to me that there is no time. Everything on earth exists outside of time, otherwise how could I know about the future that has not occurred? I think time is given to us by the grace of God so we will not get mixed up, because a person's consciousness cannot take in all events at once. We are locked up in time because of our weakness' (228).
58. 'Beginning that winter, Laurus lost track of forward-moving time. Laurus now sensed he felt only cyclical time, which was a closed loop: the time of a day, of a week, or of a year. [...] The events in his memory no longer correlated with time. They quietly spread through his life, falling into a distinct order unconnected with time' (339).
59. 'for people in Rus' loved large-scale tasks' (196).
60. 'he vaguely anticipated their discovery, much later in a cultural stratum' (32).
61. 'He hung it [i.e. the clothes] on rosehip bushes and pine saplings that bent under the weight of their wet medieval clothes' (212).
62. 'The Middle Ages rarely presented opportunities that brought people together twice during the course of an earthly life' (252).
63. 'Money was not made of paper in the Middle Ages and it was not at all simple to hide' (285).
64. 'The child read the birch-bark manuscripts out loud. Basically, during the Middle Ages people read predominantly out loud, at the very least simply moving their lips' (32).
65. 'It is generally held that Arseny returned to Rus' in the mid eighties' (291).
66. 'If he wants, he can start a campfire and sit down by the flames, tossing on dry storm kindling, branches, forest garbage, fallen thicket rubbish; he can stare into the live, reddish-yellow, flickering, warm, dancing flame. He doesn't have to ask, or bow, or scrape, or be afraid – nothing. Freedom! Benedikt would like that! Yes, he would! ...' (64).
67. 'There are two kinds of perception in my novel: one is medieval, one is contemporary. This is a rare instance in contemporary literature when, not the author, but the narrator, is able to switch from one kind of perception to another: that is, when he first writes as a medieval person and then takes a step back and casts a glance from the present.'
68. 'In Rzeszów, Arseny said to Ustina: "In the speech of these Rzeszów people, the local inhabitants, you note a higher frequency of sibilants. Sometimes you feel a surfeit of the same"' (my translation). Lisa C. Hayden renders this passage elegantly, mirroring the playful phonetics of the original: 'In Zheshov, Arseny said to Ustina:

"These Zheshovites' speech surely does shine with shushing sufficient for the inspiration of sensations of sheer satiation"' (238).
69. 'At the end of the fifteenth century, Austrians still did not know for sure if they were different from Germans and – if they were – how. In the end, the specifics of pronunciation gave them answers to both questions' (239).
70. '"And do you yourself understand it [i.e. the Russian people]?", asks Zygfryd. "Do we?" The blacksmith mulls that over and looks at Zygfryd. "Of course we, too, do not understand"' (362).
71. 'He was not lonely because he did not feel that people had abandoned him. He sensed everyone he had ever met as if they were present. They continued a quiet life in his soul, regardless of whether they had gone off to another world or were still alive. He remembered all their words, intonations, and movements. Their old words gave rise to new words and integrated with more recent events and Laurus' own words. Life continued on, in all manner of variety' (335).

CHAPTER 9

Language Ideologies and Society

Valerii Votrin and Mikhail Gigolashvili

Since the turn of the century the public debates on language have increasingly focused on the need to 'protect' the language. This tendency has been accompanied by greater state involvement in the domain of language regulation and legislation. The much-debated Law on the Russian Language of 2005 is a key text in this regard, while recent prohibitive laws, such as the ban on profanity in art (2014), the fourth successive renewal for 2016–20 of the Federal targeted programme 'Russian language' and the emphasis on 'the role of the Russian language' in various governmental policy documents, indicate both that language cultivation is of concern to the authorities and that there is a belief, or ideological conviction, that language *can* be regulated through political initiatives.

In Chapter 6 we looked at reactions to state involvement in linguistic questions of writers and intellectuals, including protest actions such as Abanamat. In the present section we turn again to the writers' primary domain, their artistic and linguistic practice. Questions concerning language legislation, linguistic ideologies and, more broadly, language and power, are central to a number of recent Russian novels. We shall take a closer look at two novels from 2012, Valerii Votrin's *Logoped* (*The Speech Therapist*) and Mikhail Gigolashvili's *Zakhvat Moskovii: natsional-lingvisticheskii roman* (*The Occupation of Muscovy: A National-Linguistic Novel*), and see how these topics are treated.

VALERII VOTRIN'S *THE SPEECH THERAPIST*

Valerii Votrin was born in Tashkent and studied Romance languages at Tashkent university. In 2000 he moved to Brussels, where he went on to study ecology. He now lives in Bath in the UK and works both in the field of ecology, and as a translator and writer of fiction, having published, since his debut in 1995, a number of stories and three novels: *Zhalitvoslov* (*The Book of Prayers and Complaints*, 2007), *Poslednii magog* (*The Last Magog*, 2009) and *Logoped* (*The Speech Therapist*, 2012). Several of his books have been nominated for Russian book prizes.

The Speech Therapist portrays a society governed by strict orthoepic laws: a set of rules for pronunciation meant to preserve the standard language. Although this language is called 'bookish' in the novel, the focus is, and this is quite original, on the spoken language. The sanctioned standard language is constantly challenged by the vernacular spoken by most people, and labelled variously *rodnaia rech'* ('vernacular'), *razgovornaia rech'* ('colloquial speech') or *narodnyi iazyk* ('popular language').

The orthoepic laws are supplemented by all the essential ingredients of a repressive society, both with regard to language use: censorship (*logopedicheskaia tsenzura*), state institutions linked to speech cultivation (*raionnaia logopedicheskaia kommisiia, Uprava, Glavnyi Logoped, Sovet logopedov*), a whole army of speech therapists, speech-improving institutes and speech correctors (*recheispravitel'nye instituty, recheispraviteli*), a speech therapy police (*logopedicheskaia militsiia* or *lomilitsiia*); and more generally: closed power structures, a considerable distance between the people and the centre of power, a past containing revolution and war, and even an opposition in emigration.

Within this world, we follow the fate of two protagonists. Speech therapist Iurii Petrovich Rozhnov is a liberal member of the speech therapy commission that tests the speech standards of people called to work for the party. If the candidates do not pass the examination, they are sent off to speech-improving institutes from where many, rather than improving their speech, return as *nemtyri* ('mutes'). Lev Pavlovich Zablukaev stems from a family of teachers, but has an ardent wish to become a speech therapist (a profession one is born into). He studies journalism and publishes fierce articles on speech culture and speech cultivation. Zablukaev takes a particular interest in 'unsuccessful candidates' and investigates the stories of those who return from the speech-improving institutes as broken people. After a brief involvement with the *lingvari*, one of the two main oppositional groups in the country, he is arrested and exiled, but continues to write articles for the émigré press on the need for speech cultivation.

Meanwhile, there are stark tensions within the different factions of power within the society portrayed. The speech therapists are divided among themselves: there are liberals and conservatives. There are those who are open to reform, and those who adhere to the rules and regulations, with the 'Law on the Purity of Language' enjoying pride of place. There are those with a more pragmatic and descriptive attitude towards language, and those with a strictly prescriptive approach.

Liberal-minded speech therapists like Rozhnov eventually help to uncover the cruelties committed by the speech correctors, and begin to advocate the need for reforms. Just as with the perestroika programme of the late 1980s, the reforms, however, lead to the break-up of the state. The government is overthrown and a coalition of oppositional movements seizes power. Behind all this, there lurks a mysterious, frightening and, in the end, triumphant creature, reminiscent of the 'Slynx' we encountered in Tat'iana Tolstaia's *Kys'*. Votrin's creature is no 'Slynx', however; its name is *Iazyk* – 'Language' or 'Tongue'.[1]

A mirror of the language debates

Linguistic ideologies, speech cultivation and the role of the state in such matters define the main focus of Votrin's novel. In addition to highlighting the topic of language legislation and control, the book also plays with central concepts that we recognise from the discourse on language in post-Soviet Russian society, from the conservatives' focus on preservation (*sokhranenie*) and purity (*chistota*) of language, or the 'discourse of threat' (Ryazanova-Clarke 2006a: 34) warning of damage and contamination (*porcha, zasorenie iazyka*), to the more liberal-minded language mavens speaking of the natural and necessary development (*razvitie*) of language. Thus, every session of the speech therapy commission begins with the solemn declaration of the speech therapist's oath: Я, [. . .] , обязуюсь соблюдать чистоту языка и образцово следить за священными нормами . . . (12).[2]

Rozhnov himself shows liberal tendencies and defends the point of view that language must evolve and change. To him, language is 'pure from its very beginning', while the issue of 'purity' in the language of the party appointees is rather 'a question of personal hygiene' (9). His 'dynamic' take on the question of linguistic purity, and in particular his views on linguistic development are shared by other characters in the novel. 'Language doesn't stand still' is a mantra repeated three times in the text. In the following passage it serves to characterise the liberal views of Zablukaev's mother, the schoolteacher Natal'ia Mikhailovna, in contrast to those of his father, Pavel L'vovich. The passage describes their individual reactions to a pronunciation error heard on the radio, which again reflects the new trend of allowing *variants* in pronunciation: Павел Львович приходил в ужас, на что Наталья Михайловна, его жена, спокойно замечала, что язык не стоит на месте, он развивается и прекрасно, что правительство это понимает (25).³ Natal'ia Mikhailovna refers here to the constant stream of circulars that have recently begun to be issued by the Ministry of Education and that introduce ever more recently accepted variants (24). We can easily recognise in this episode an echo of the lively discussions that took place in the Russian media in response to the Ministry of Education's *prikaz* of 1 September 2009 accepting as correct a number of variant forms, such as the neuter gender of the noun *kofe* ('coffee', thus allowing for the use of *chernoe kofe* alongside the established standard *chernyi kofe* 'black coffee') or 'alternative' patterns of stress placement (*dógovor*, *iogúrt* and others).

As we can see from these introductory examples, Votrin's novel reflects particular aspects of the post-Soviet linguistic condition on several levels. The novel portrays an oppressive society with its prime focus on language cultivation, within a framework reminiscent of the powerful utopian trend in contemporary Russian literature. Within this fictional world, Votrin highlights a number of central issues in the language debates. So far, we have looked briefly at his often playful treatment of notions such as 'purity', 'linguistic development' and 'variants'. Let us now move to the more overarching concepts of 'norms' and 'language'.

Sacred norms

In the previous section we came across the notion of 'sacred norms' in the oath recited by members of the speech therapy commission at the start of every session. This conception of norms is the institutionalised one, nurtured already in the schools for speech therapy students, where they sing hymns to the various sounds and their corresponding orthoepic norms. In fact, their attitude to the norms is what distinguishes the ruling elite from the people: Логопеды стали нормоблюстителями с тех самых пор, когда народ перестал обращать внимание на нормы. От нас, и только от нас, зависит теперь спасение языка. Ибо народ не с нами. Народ – против нас! (63).⁴

The different viewpoints regarding the status of linguistic norms are illustrated by the narrative perspective: the chapters that tell of Rozhnov, the reform-friendly speech therapist, are entitled in such a way that reflects the vernacular, or popular speech, with spellings such as *Glava pelvaia* (instead of *pervaia*), *tlet'ia* (instead of *tret'ia*) and *shed'maia* (instead of *sed'maia*); chapters that tell of Zablukaev, the conservative guardian of the standard language, are labelled *vtoraia*, *chetvertaia*, *piataia*, in full accordance with standard norms.

If we look more systematically into the characteristics of this 'popular speech', we see that the novel starts out by describing two major 'errors', the pronunciation of [r] as [l] – as in *poliadok* (for *poriadok* 'order') – and the inability to pronounce fricatives and affricates like [sh], [zh], [ch] or [shch] (pronounced like [s], [z] or [f]). Rozhnov, who speaks standard Russian, typically thinks in his own version of popular speech, which features only the r/l error: Юрий Петрович идет и думает с негодованием: «Неполядок. Где дволники?Ублать мешок! Лазвелось мусола, хоть сам бели метлу в луки и убилай. И это на плавительственной улице! [. . .] Полядка не стало (7).⁵

After a while, we are introduced to new types of error: [d] for [r] and [v] for [r]; both seem to be variants of the r/l error (people seem to follow one). Rozhnov's attempt to summarise the variants captures some, but not all, of these: Они говорят: «Просу просения». Они говорят: «Пвощу пвощения». Говорят, наконец: «Плошу площения», – так что же, нужно их за это гнать? (9).⁶ Towards the end, the various errors are compounded, occurring more and more frequently in conjunction with one another. As a result, the speech becomes hard to understand. Here is a brief dialogue between Rozhnov and Parin, a representative of one of the new parties in power:

> – Вот! Мы слываем покловы лзивого языка с насих имен, весей и слов! Тепель люди и веси называются своими истинными именами!
> – Но, позвольте, а нормы? – слабо возразить [sic] Рожнов, но Парин в ответ, плюясь бешеной слюной, закричал:
> – Нет больсе никаких сталых лзивых плогнивсих нолм! Свобода языка – свобода налода! Где вы были в последнее влемя, товались?! (215)⁷

Rozhnov is shocked by the style of speech of the new authorities. His liberal views are guided, after all, by the majority's right to define the norms: only norms that contradict the linguistic practices of the majority should be reformed, Rozhnov believes. For example, the pronunciation of [r] as [l] is widespread and should be allowed, Rozhnov judges, while the inability to pronounce affricates and fricatives is not widespread enough to justify a reform.

'The new language' is not just a problem for Rozhnov, it turns out. People speak with so many deviations from the standard norms that they no longer understand each other. The language question has become a political problem and Rozhnov is invited to the ministry to discuss the matter during a special session 'on language': Все по-своему пишут и говолят. Нисего не понятно. Один говолит так, длугой – эдак,

будто языки им подлезали. Плислось плиостановить лаботу (229).⁸
Rozhnov gives his advice, but it becomes clear to him when speaking that his speech – standard Russian in accordance with the norms – is no longer comprehensible to the people around him. He acts out, in a way, the repeatedly voiced concern of many language mavens of the late 1990s and early 2000s, that the dominant tendencies in contemporary Russian language culture – the huge influx of foreign loanwords and the spread of non-standard varieties – would lead, in the end, to a situation where people would no longer understand each other.

We see how Votrin challenges central concepts in the language debates, stretching their potential and experimenting with 'extreme versions' of notions such as *variants*, *norms* or *purity*. So far, however, we have dealt with such concepts mainly from the point of view of language legislators, language mavens and ordinary language users. What is truly original in the novel is the role played by language itself.

Language: a frightening creature

There is a third main protagonist in Votrin's *The Speech Therapist*, a mysterious creature by the name of Language or Tongue (*Iazyk*) which becomes intertwined with the lives of both Rozhnov and Zablukaev. While the portrayal of the society, its people, groups and factions is from the point of view of humans and (human) linguistic ideologies, the introduction of *Iazyk* introduces the point of view of language itself. The 'liberalisation of language' – a catchphrase of the language debates of the 1990s – is interpreted quite literally as the liberation of a frightening creature that lurks around outside windows in the dark and acquires ever more grotesque features. For *Iazyk*, norms are just a disturbing hindrance to the free flow of language, or the Rule of Language.

Iazyk makes its first appearance early in the novel as a friendly creature in Rozhnov's dream. It appears in the form of letters that surround and caress Rozhnov like kittens. Rozhnov offers it milk and feels safe and protected. He likes to think that *Iazyk* knows about his efforts to expose the wrongdoings of the speech correctors and that he paves the way for it, sets it free: Юрий Петрович был уверен, что гнев Языка не тронет его (8).⁹ It takes a while before Rozhnov understands that he needs to surrender totally to Language, in order not to disturb it:

> Он мешает выдвиженцам, он мешает языку. Да, он мешает Языку. И он больше не будет ему мешать.
> Именно с той ночи он стал видеть сны – он играет с буквами, наливает им в блюдце молока и получает ласковый,

одобрительный взгляд из темноты. Рожнов знает – это Язык. (108)¹⁰

More often than not, however, the 'gaze of Language' is not approving, but threatening. There is much talk about the 'wrath of Language', as in the stories that Zablukaev gathers about the unsuccessful party candidates, the *nemtyri*: выяснилось, что по ночам Пискунова терроризирует Язык. Страшные глаза заглядывают по ночам в квартиру Пискунова (75).¹¹ It is Iubin, Zablukaev's main informant, that explains the true goal of Language to Zablukaev: – Язык – это, Лева, Язык! Ты ведь не говоришь на нем? – Как не говорю? Говорю! – Да нет, ты по книжкам говоришь. А он этого не любит. Он любит, когда все на нем говорят (43).¹² In a later conversation with Iubin, the contrast between Zablukaev's conception of language and Iubin's view of the situation becomes even more explicit: А Он совсем не такой, как в книжках. Он другой, Левка. Он стра-ашный! (73).¹³ *Iazyk* is here identified with the popular language spoken by the people and promoted by reform-friendly speech therapists like Rozhnov. Zablukaev's mission, however, is to preserve the standard language, to fight against what he sees as its corruption (*porcha*). This battle is the main topic of his articles for the émigré press and his position on this point is very radical: Однако порча языка, дозволяемая обществом, может привести к большему, чем просто потеря свободы. Запятая, поставленная не там, или орфографическая ошибка могут привести к войне (148).¹⁴

From Zablukaev's perspective, the popular language is a result of corruption. His choice of terms reflects his view of the state of the language, which he paraphrases as *l'zheiazyk* ('false language'), *durnoe porozhdenie negramotnogo plebsa* ('bad creation of the illiterate plebs') and *psevdoiazyk* ('pseudolanguage'). The image of *Iazyk* becomes, for him, a frightening creature which acquires, towards the end of the novel, truly grotesque dimensions:

Это был он, Язык. Невозможно описать его. Он весь вихрился, брезжил, менял очертания. [. . .] Он владычествовал. Склонив бесформенную голову над страной, он глядел, слушал, подчинял. Под ним сновали микроскопические людишки, но их почти не было видно. Он сам был ими. И он не мог говорить. Да, Заблукаев сразу понял, что Язык – немой. (205)¹⁵

While Zablukaev is able to withstand the evil gaze of *Iazyk*, he is, paradoxically, convinced that were he to die, it would be by 'a word from the old books':

По непонятной причине он знал, что убить его может только слово – острое, заточенное. И не из народного языка должно быть оно – слишком жидок был этот псевдоязык, – нет, слово это должно было быть взято из старых книг. Да, только там возможно было отыскать такое пронзающее, как дротик, слово, обладающее страшной поражающей силой, слово-боек, слово-чекан, слово-кистень. (161–2)[16]

Zablukaev gives up his dream of becoming a speech therapist and decides to return to 'post-revolutionary' Russia and become a teacher. When he returns, he is in fact killed as soon as he steps out of the train. We learn of this when Rozhnov and his wife, a day later, are expelled from the country as 'enemies of the language'. As they arrive at the train station, Rozhnov's glance is caught by the new signboards, featuring spellings such as *Bivetnye kashshy* (instead of *Biletnye kassy*), *Lestolan* (instead of *Restoran*), *Gavety i vulnaly* (instead of *Gazety i zhurnaly*):

И тут Рожнов застывает на месте. Что за наваждение! Краем глаза он замечает, что в ряду других световых вывесок пылают буквы, которых не должно, не может здесь быть. Среди жалких изуродованных слов сияет слово – нетронутое, настоящее, всесильное слово из старых книг, и грозный смысл исходит от него. (241)[17]

They learn from the guard that the day before, another fellow who had stared at the same signboards had fallen down dead as if shot. It was Zablukaev, hit by the all-powerful word. Уситeлиска какой-то,[18] says the guard. Rozhnov replies: – Не учитель [. . .] Логопед. Истинный логопед (241).[19]

Rozhnov and Zablukaev never meet, although their paths cross when the material about the fate of the 'mutes' gathered by Zablukaev and confiscated by the secret police comes to light as Rozhnov prepares his final blow against the speech correctors, a process that gets out of control and leads to great turmoil and the eventual overthrow of the authorities. In this way, Zablukaev, just like Rozhnov, contributes unwillingly to the upheaval; one ends up dead, the other is expelled from the country. The triumphant one is *Iazyk*. Once the train has left and the platform is deserted, it starts to move as 'a huge, horned shadow': Медленно, точно потягиваясь, встает она, глядя вослед уходящему поезду, а потом, когда огни его скрываются из виду, удовлетворенно поднимается вверх и растворяется над городом (242).[20]

The fates of both Rozhnov and Zablukaev may leave the reader puzzled. While Rozhnov is initially in favour of reforms, once the process takes off, it is clear that 'perestroika' leads to disintegration, that is, the process has gone way too far. When he returns to the ministry, warning against linguistic anarchy and propagating the need for norms after all, it is equally clear that, as a hero of yesterday, he comes too late. But why is Zablukaev killed by a word 'from the old books', associated with the correct, or standard language? In Zablukaev's own explanation, only such a word is powerful enough to kill, an idea that plays in a grotesque manner on the traditional logocentricity of Russian culture. The irony of his death is also, however, part of a pattern of destabilisation at work in the novel, that renders all concepts, positions and ideologies ambiguous.

Language ideologies and linguistic cultivation

Rozhnov is not the only 'latecomer' in the novel. One of the oppositional movements in emigration is the *tarabary*, named after Vasilii Tarabrin, the first and only Procurator General of the country to have spoken officially in the popular language. Since Tarabrin's days, the *tarabary* have been preparing for the advent of the 'Empire of the True Language' (*Tsarstvo Istinnogo Iazyka*). With the collapse of the old regime, they return to Russia to take part in the new government. The other oppositional group, however, the *lingvary* (or 'babblers' as they are also called), likewise aspire to power. This is a conservative group with mystical religious overtones, presented in the novel as: приверженцев мистического учения, считающего язык богом, а непрекращающееся болтанье – жертвой ему (50).[21] Interestingly, the *lingvary* usually speak not the popular language, but standard Russian, and so it was obviously not their speech that was a problem to the (old) regime, but their linguistic ideology. When Zablukaev makes his first acquaintance with the *lingvary*, he meets a man with the telling name of Brother Palimpsest, who explains:

> – Вы скоро поймете, – ответил он, – что правильной или неправильной речи нет. Богиню Норму выдумали логопеды. Есть один бог – Язык, и он требует одного – чтобы говорили. Можно говорить даже без слов, можно – любыми словами, даже неизвестными. Главное – говорить. Потому что только это Ему любезно. (79)[22]

The language ideology of the *lingvary* implies a total discrediting of all speech cultivation measures and in this way questions the legitimacy of the ruling elites, both before and after the upheaval. This critique is partly mirrored in Zablukaev's stance. Radical himself in his linguistic ideology (he sees himself as someone chosen to protect the standard language), in his articles for the émigré press he lays bare the ideological impact of the belief in popular language: Их язык [that is, the popular language] [...] есть инструмент порабощения общества, который тиранит похуже самого лютого тирана-человека, потому что обитает в головах (159).²³

The *tarabary*'s seizure of power is followed by a bloody war between the speech therapists and the oppositional groups before the former are killed, expelled or arrested, while the latter form a coalition government. During this time, Zablukaev's articles about the 'correct language' become immensely popular and are even distributed among the speech therapists fighting on the front lines. To Zablukaev, this is a war about language, not about power. When he is eventually asked to join forces with the defeated speech therapists in exile, he renounces the concepts of control and monitoring and switches to what turns out to be his 'true profession' after all: teaching. Yet Zablukaev, who criticises the ideological aspect of *Iazyk* 'inhabiting people's minds', is also literally filled with his own ideal of a correct language from early in life: Чтение он воспринимал как наращивание мускулов, боевую подготовку, ибо чувствовал, как сила старых правильных слов вливается в него (29).²⁴

These last examples reveal a fundamental aspect of Votrin's novel, a poetics of ambiguity that serves to undermine all ideologies, concepts, stances and positions affecting the language question.

Destabilisation

Votrin's poetic treatment of the language question in *The Speech Therapist* destabilises a number of terms, conceptions and ideological notions. From early on we sense a blurring of borderlines between 'liberals' and 'conservatives' in questions of language cultivation. The speech therapist Rozhnov, whose task it is to maintain the standard language, is *very* liberal in his language attitudes and understanding of norms: [...] язык должен развиваться бесконтрольно. Раз народ так говорит – так оно, значит, и должно быть (8–9).²⁵ Правильным слово делаете вы – ваше произношение (15).²⁶

The linguistic varieties themselves are also destabilised, or change connotations: as a result of Zablukaev's rhetorical persuasion in his articles promoting the 'correct language', speaking in this manner becomes a fashion among young people in the émigré society, which is dominated by the *tarabary*, that is, speakers of the popular language: Эмигранты среднего возраста изводились по поводу того, что их дети не желают говорить на простом языке и переходят на «книжную» речь. Это стало в среде молодежи модой. Правильная речь превратилась в своего рода молодежный жаргон, ей стало принято щеголять (158).²⁷

'Order' – *poriadok* – is a catchword throughout the novel, but is mostly spelled and pronounced *poliadok* (apart from by Rozhnov's parrot, which pronounces it in a grotesquely hypercorrect version: – Порррядок! Порррядок! – радостно вопит Ломуальд (6).²⁸ Its opposite, *proizvol* – 'lawlessness' – appears in the correct spelling.

Also, we should not forget that, to the reader, the 'correct' speech is the unmarked standard Russian, while for most of the inhabitants of this country, it is not. In the eyes of the reader, the 'natural', popular speech (*narodnaia rech'*), comes through as not only flawed and imperfect, but rather infantile, as is evident from publication titles such as *Olfoglafiia: inoi vzgliad na problemu* (instead of *Orfografiia* . . .), party names like *Istinno-Nadodnoe Delo* (instead of *Narodnoe*), or character descriptions such as the following, of Natal'ia Mikhailovna, Zablukaev's mother: В школе ее любили, считали своей. «Уситека нафа нифего тетка, понимаюсяя», – говорили про нее. И она втайне гордилась приобретенным уважением (25–6).²⁹

On the ideological level, the linguistic conservatives are depicted initially as repressive and totalitarian in their outlook, whereas later, when the proponents of reform and popular language come to power, they turn out to be just as brutal and unscrupulous as their predecessors: Теперь на улицах стали хватать за услышанный разговор с правильным выговором, и сотни логопедов и обычных интеллигентов угодили в тюрьму, откуда выбрались немногие (219).³⁰

Rozhnov warns the new authorities: Мы на грани гибели языка, товарищи (231).³¹ A moment later, however, he starts speaking with numerous errors, until his speech turns into completely incomprehensible gibberish:

– Товались Ковопенькин, – втолковывал ему Рожнов, с ужасом слыша свой голос, – я ве ошполяю вазнофть басего доквата. До вы доздны бонядь, фто сейфяз гвавдое – явык. Пойбите, фто ствада де мовет вазвиваться вде явыка. Мы доздны бовоться ва его фястоту.
«Боже, что я говорю! – в ужасе думал он. – Что со мной?» (237)³²

He wants to convince the authorities of the need for linguistic control, but loses control over his own speech: he becomes a *nemtyr'*, – but not as a result of the measures of the speech correctors.

> Он раскрыл рот, чтобы предупредить Конопелькина, отвлечь его, срочно поведать о необходимости ввести языковой контроль, но из его рта вырвалось бессвязное мычание. Язык не слушался Рожнова. Он пытался выговорить слова, но язык его не слушался.
> – Ы! Ы! – в ужасе мычал Рожнов.
> Он понял, что его постигла кара. Язык его оставил. В наказание его поразила немота. Кажется, с ним случился удар. От дикого страха Рожнов замычал еще сильнее. Он звал Ирошникова, всегдашние рассудочность, спокойствие того были нужны ему как воздух:
> – Хафа! Саза! Бафа! Таса! (237)[33]

We see in these examples how the protagonists move in and out of linguistic ideologies and practices, and in and out of different relationships to the personification of Language, before the title of the novel, finally, shifts its reference from Rozhnov to Zablukaev, who is designated by Rozhnov to be 'the true speech therapist', having just been killed by 'the evil word' of the language he believed in.

On the surface, *The Speech Therapist* is quite explicit and straightforward in its treatment of central ideas and concepts of the language debates. As we have seen, however, there is a certain irony at work in the novel, expressed by means of a poetics of ambiguity and destabilisation, which makes the novel stand out as a sophisticated discussion of current conceptions of *norms*, *language* and *linguistic ideologies*. Before we relate this discussion to the most complex questions raised by the novel, that of language and power, and of language and identity, let us turn to Mikhail Gigolashvili's less serious, more humorous, but equally ironic treatment of the language question in his *Occupation of Muscovy: A National-Linguistic Novel*.

MIKHAIL GIGOLASHVILI'S 'OCCUPATION OF MUSCOVY'

Like Valerii Votrin, writer, artist and university teacher Mikhail Gigolashvili lives and works outside Russia, in Saarbrücken, where he moved in 1991 to teach Russian at the University of Saarland. Born in Tbilisi in 1953, he studied Russian literature in Georgia and wrote his PhD dissertation on Dostoevskii's narrative techniques. His debut as a writer came in 1978 with the novel *Judea*, while most of his literary production stems from the 2000s. In particular, his book *Chertova koleso*

(*The Devil's Wheel*, 2009) – a novel portraying corruption and crime in Georgia in the late 1980s – has been widely read and much praised in Russia, while his most recent novel, *The Occupation of Muscovy* (2012) has received more mixed reviews (Bavil'skii 2012; Birger 2012; Kucherskaia 2012).

A core theme of Gigolashvili's writing is the confrontation between cultures – national, social, historical – in times of social and political upheaval. The author of a series of scholarly articles on foreigners in Russian literature, Gigolashvili is also interested in representations of 'the other' from a professional point of view. Finally, as a Georgian writing in Russian and living in Germany, it is clear that the theme of cultural encounters is also part of the writer's own personal experience.

In *The Occupation of Muscovy*, which bears the subtitle *a national-linguistic novel*, he frames the theme of cultural encounters within the larger theme of language culture. *The Occupation of Muscovy* tells the story of Manfred Bommel, German student of Russian, and his adventures during his first trip to Russia. The novel is set in 2009 and the core of the plot takes place between 19 and 30 September of that year. Manfred is passionately interested in everything Russian. He also has family ties to Russia, having grown up with his Russian grandmother, who had conveyed to him not only some colloquial Russian but also much Russian-style 'folk wisdom'. What is more, one of his ancestors is claimed to be the sixteenth-century historian and adventurer Heinrich von Staden, who travelled to Russia, worked in Ivan the Terrible's *oprichnina* and wrote an account of his travels, *Aufzeichnungen über den Moskauer Staat*.[34] Excerpts from this text are inserted into Gigolashvili's novel in seven separate instalments.

The story is told from Manfred Bommel's perspective and thus provides a constant view from the outside on contemporary Russian society. This perspective is informed by Manfred's family bonds with Russia, his naïve love of everything Russian and, not least, the seminars of his Russian professor on topics ranging from traditional food to 'sacred language' (profanity).

Gigolashvili himself has named language as the true hero of the novel (Gigolashvili and Besedin 2013). Indeed, this is justified. Language plays a central role on several levels: in the linguistic practices with which Manfred is confronted; in his own peculiar style of Russian; in his reflections and thoughts about language, people and society including the interrelationship between them; as well as in the plot, where Manfred's encounter with the grammar nazi movement leads to a series of events that ends with his being arrested at Munich airport on his return. Finally, and most significantly, language is demonstratively foregrounded as being the main prism through which Manfred 'reads' Russian culture and society.

A linguotrip to Russia

Young Manfred exposes himself to the Russian language with all his mind, body and soul, and is surrounded by a plurality of varieties: slang, criminal jargon, regionalisms, bureaucratic speech, Sovietspeak, profanity, as well as different languages: apart from Russian itself, German, Georgian and Bulgarian are most vividly present. Manfred is eager to learn and – not least – understand, not only Russian, but the Russians. He is constantly confronted with words, situations and people he does not understand, and much of the comic qualities of the book stem from his attempts to 'translate', as it were, what he hears and sees and adapt it to his own linguistic worldview: Это очень интересно, я же в первую очередь лингвист, а потом всё остальное (75).[35]

Manfred's optimistic and open attitude towards Russia and the Russians is indomitable. Even at the very end, when everything has gone wrong, he is positive about his experience and 'true' exposure to the language: Но зато какая была практика!.. Как это полезно!.. Со сколькими носителями языка я вступал в диалог! (591).[36] True, Manfred has interacted with war veterans, the police, prostitutes, criminals, taxi drivers, mafiosi, bureaucrats and many others. He has been exposed to unknown words, constructions and expressions which leave him bewildered, but which spur his own linguistic creativity, as he eagerly uses them as hermeneutic tools to learn and understand. Here is a typical example of his attitude, wholly dominated by his linguistic take on everything he encounters: Пока ехали, шофер долго и фонетически отчетливо ругал правительство, я почти всё понимал, а кое-что даже успевал записывать в мой электронный словарик [. . .] (16).[37] Meanwhile, Manfred's misunderstandings are a constant source of comic episodes:

– [. . .] Немець . . . Откуда? Не из-под Нюрнберга, чай?
– Чай? – не понял я, но на всякий случай подтвердил, что да, хочу пить чай с моим товарищем. (19)[38]

– Умный мужик, уважают его ребята, ушлый . . .
– Ушлый – который ушёл?
– А куда он ушёл?
– Он? Никуда не ушёл. Наоборот, пришел. Куда ему уходить?
[. . .]

– Но вы говорите «ушлый». Это же тот, кто ушёл? [...] (133)[39]

The portrayal of Manfred as slightly naïve is reinforced by the occasional use of the third person by the first-person narrator: (Чего они хотят от Фреди?.. Почему не отдают Фреде паспорт?.. [261]).[40] His own Russian is characterised by his inability to understand slang expressions and colloquial speech, his struggle with Russian verbal aspect leading to his frequent use of both forms (Виталик Иванов меня в гости звал-позвал (я часто употребляю обе формы глагола, потому что не знаю, какая будет правильной) [19][41]), his love of Russian suffixes (in particular diminutives) and his linguistic creativity, in particular in the fields of word formation and interpretive etymology.

Manfred is hypersensitive towards language and overeager to interpret the linguistic phenomena he encounters. This, and his way of linking language to other notions, such as countries, people or morals, is a typical folk linguistic attitude. In addition to the folk linguistic framing of Manfred's encounter with Russia, we also find more concrete references in Gigolashvili's novel to particular subdisciplines of linguistics. In one of the passages where Manfred praises the richness and variety of the linguistic experience to which he has been exposed, he explicitly notes the variation in age and gender, a standard concern in quantitative sociolinguistics: Зато сколько разных нарраторов было со мной в диалогах?.. Разных возрастных групп и полов! Очень интересно. Настоящая практика языка на базе жизни (177).[42]

Like all true philologists, Manfred has his linguistic darlings. He is confronted with a great variety of colloquial Russian styles, with foreign languages and accents, with bureaucratic speech and police jargon, and he is excited about the richness of the language. But what he loves most are the diminutives, which he has also studied with his Russian professor in a special seminar: Помню Ваши спецзанятия по уменьшительным суффиксам, таким милым и ласковым в русском ... «У маленькой свинюшки – розовые ушки» ... Я их обожаю – ими можно играть, как угодно, свобода, креативитет ... О, все эти Енька, Онька, Улька, Алька!.. (79).[43] Again, Manfred's excitement is ridiculed, as in his own tautological self-designation as маленький лингвистик (143)[44] or in his habit of adding diminutive suffixes in awkward places:

> Я молча взял ключи и пошел, удивляясь – он же меня совсем не знает, кто я ему, чужой, а ключи дает ... Какой наш немец сделал бы так?.. Вот она, загадочная душа ... нараспашку ... нет, нараспашонку ... (210)[45]

Водка оказалась хорошей, в голове начал буркать адренали-
нушко. (215)[46]

Manfred's excessive use of diminutives might also reflect the current online trend of 'new sentimentality', one of the hallmarks of which is the extraordinarily rich use of diminutives. As Maksim Krongauz explains, some of the signal words of this tendency were known earlier, but from the second half of 2010 they quickly gained in popularity. Examples of this trend include such words as *pechal'ka* (or *pichal'ka*) – 'little-pity', used in the sense of 'what a pity' – and *niashka* (or *niasheshka*), stemming from Japanese *nia* ('miaow') and expressing tenderness and emotion towards someone, more often than not, a girl. The word first became popular among Russian anime fans, but gained great popularity in 2011 (Krongauz 2013: 310). In other words, like the grammar nazi movement, this 'new sentimental' style emerged at the time when Gigolashvili was writing his novel, and Manfred's extensive use of diminutives may be taken as the author's playful response to this online trend – as it is to a number of other styles.

More often than not, Manfred's 'linguistic' analysis of what he hears and sees leads to stereotypical conclusions about the Russian people and interpretations of Russian society:

А сколько свободы в русском языке!.. У нас, немцев, на всё регламент, у французов – на всё запрет, англичанин только шипит и морщится, а русский человек великодушен, и язык его ничего не боится, потому что его язык широк, глубок, высок, снисходителен, по-женски податлив для носителя, но по-мужски неприступен для чужака … И в этой свободе – суть величия души бескрайнего народа! (490)[47]

In this and numerous other passages, Manfred refers to romantic concepts about Russians (and other peoples), culminating in such stereotypical notions as *velichie dushi* ('greatness of the soul'), *beskrainii narod* ('boundless people'), *zagadochnaia dusha* ('enigmatic soul') and similar. *The Occupation of Muscovy*, it could be argued, is a novel about cultural stereotypes viewed through the lens of language.

Linguistic and cultural stereotypes

Manfred's observations about language tend to lead to ideas about people, with the comparative view on Russians and Germans as a major topic. While the various romantic and traditional conceptions about

'Russians' and 'Germans' are apparently taken seriously by Manfred himself, for the reader they come across as hyperbolic and slightly ridiculous:[48] Они все постоянно употребляют совершенный вид прошедшего времени: «Сделал! Сел! Встал! Принес! Замолк!» Есть в этом что-то очень неприятное, фамильярное, грубое, наглое ... И интонации голоса при этом такие ... недружественные ... грубые ... язык – зеркало социума ... (151).[49]

In addition to general cultural myths, we also find specific references to particular interpretations of 'Russian mentality' in Russian cultural history. Thus, in one of Manfred's reflections on the phenomenon of foreign loanwords – but here from the unusual perspective of Russian loans in Western European languages – we clearly hear an echo of Chaadaev's famous 'Philosophical Letter' of 1836,[50] lamenting Russia's meagre contribution to world history and culture and, above all, the lack of originality in Russia's own cultural tradition.

> А есть ли они вообще в европейских языках, русские слова? Я стал вспоминать, но ничего, кроме «бистро», «бефстроганов», «балалайка», «водка», «икра», «матрешка», «рубль», «перестройка», «гласность», «калашников» и «молотов-коктейль», не вспомнилось ... Значит ли это, что русскими не было создано ничего принципиально оригинального, нового, чему не было бы еще имени и что надо было как-то называть, как Рентген, Порше, Ватт и так далее? ... Очевидно, так ... (205)[51]

Many of the cultural stereotypes linked in Manfred's reflections to Russia, Russians and Russian culture are concepts which are frequently discussed in the popular Russian subdiscipline of (cognitive) linguistics known as the study of the 'linguistic world view' (*iazykovaia kartina mira*), or, more broadly, in Russian ethno- or psycholinguistics, where the focus is on such concepts as, for example, *prostor* ('wide open space'), *dolia* ('lot', 'fate'), *avos'* ('perhaps'). In Manfred's naïve conception, the interrelationship between words, concepts, peoples and mentalities is simplified, however, to such a degree that they stand out as comic and purely as stereotypes:

> я зафиксировал пару новых глаголов, «стибрить», «стырить», «слямзить». Тибра! Лямза! Тыра! Где в немецком такая россыпь оттенков?.. Одно «stehlen» – и всё. А тут!.. Эльдорадо для психолингвистов, которые утверждают: где каких глаголов много, тем народ в этом речевом поле в основном и занимается. (274)[52]

This simplified identification of linguistic features and mentalities is, of course, also part of Gigolashvili's mockery of the whole concept of interpreting peoples through language, as we can see from the way in which this link is sometimes developed ad absurdum. In the 'manifesto' of the grammar nazis, for example, the Russian verbal aspect is taken to explain 'all misfortune' in Russia because nothing can be accomplished (i.e. *perfective aspect*) in the present (tense) (324),[53] as the present tense excludes the use of perfective verb forms. The grammar nazis, we sense, are the main target of Gigolashvili's mockery in *The Occupation of Muscovy*.

Manfred and the grammar nazis

The grammar nazi movement, as outlined in Chapter 2, is a Russian virtual community employing Nazi symbols and vocabulary in its fight against linguistic errors. In Gigolashvili's novel, the grammar nazis have left the online sphere and entered the real world.

Manfred has three encounters with the grammar nazis. He is introduced to them by his friend Vitalii and immediately intrigued by the attention paid to language that mirrors his own, albeit in a very different way. He is immediately surprised, however, and even shocked, by their radical proposals for linguistic reforms. As described in Chapter 2, the grammar nazi movement is characterised by a peculiar combination of aggressive, radical symbolism and style (slogans such as Грамматик махт фрай – 'Grammar sets you free'), on the one hand, and a sense of entertainment or play, on the other. In Gigolashvili's hyperbolic representation of the grammar nazis, this paradoxical approach is very pronounced. Gigolashvili combines elements of the grammar nazis' self-representation with fake stories and commentaries on the phenomenon, in order to create a fictional world wherein the grammar nazis become flesh-and-blood people, who collect money to buy a seat in the Duma (29), carry out actions against people who do not master the Russian standard language to a sufficient degree (42), and propose radical linguistic reforms. Here is an example of the latter: Сейчас декрет об отмене глаголов готовят . . . Я удивился: – Не может . . . Какая это глупость? Как можно . . . глаголы? – А междометиями заменить: вместо «нырять» – «бултых», вместо купаться – «чупи-чупи», вместо «включить» – «щёлк», вместо «целовать» – «чмок», вместо «трахаться» – «шпок» или «чих-пых»!.. (29).[54]

While the grammar nazis' proposals are radical, there is always more than a tint of absurdity about them, of course, in Gigolashvili's rendering. The same may be said of certain concrete issues central to the post-Soviet language debates that come up during Manfred's encounters with the grammar nazis, for example the question of foreign loanwords. The grammar nazis have committed themselves to not using foreign loanwords (37), but as it turns out, they have great problems in keeping to their own rules. Russian is a language which, in the course of its history, has generally been open to foreign loans. Thus, when speaking Russian, you do not get very far without using a minimum of loanwords, a fact which Isidor, one of the grammar nazis Manfred meets up with, learns the hard way: – Почему же так категори . . . отрубно? . . . Это честь . . . Впрочем, как хотите. Нас интересует выход на Европу. Могли бы вы помочь нам наладить контакты с коллегами . . . то есть касания с содругами?.. (196).[55]

Gigolashvili's portrayal of the grammar nazis extends to exposing their lack of etymological knowledge, as they come up with far-fetched interpretations of loans in order to make them appear as Russian words: – А вот опять слово – аристократ! – заметил Фрол. Исидор на секунды две воззрился на него с вызывающим презрением: – А вот и нет! Это сложное слово, боец: ария – сто – крат! Стократный ария, значит, самый что ни на есть чистый ариец . . . (195).[56]

The grammar nazi fellows, in particular Isidor, are additionally made fun of in Gigolashvili's 'poetic' supplement to his portrayal of the movement, the presentation of Isidor's poetry. The texts Isidor gives to Manfred to read and possibly translate into German turn out to consist of a mixture of obscure Russian words and platitudinous rhymes. A similar unprofessional attitude emerges from their enthusiastic response to Manfred's suggestion about 'more freedom in language', which is consistent with Manfred's own linguistic attitude, but would seem to run counter to the grammar nazis' ideals of linguistic purity and correctness. During their first meeting, Manfred suggests to Isidor and Frol that they claim 'full freedom' concerning suffixal derivation in Russian and receives a positive response, upon which he immediately elaborates: – А что, можно подумать, идея здравая . . . Чем больше свободы – тем лучше! Я с воодушевлением поддержал его: – Да. Полно свободы! Свободище! – и стал доказывать, что всегда должно быть место для импровизации [. . .] (41).[57]

I mentioned above the tension in the grammar nazi movement between seriousness and play. In Gigolashvili's own rendering, this question becomes even more pronounced, and is actually posed by Manfred himself: – Я растерялся, вдруг не понимая, всерьез это всё или так, шутка [. . .] (37);[58] Они это всерьез или в шутку? (81).[59]

The explicit ambiguity is further mirrored in the ironic stance evident in the way in which common positions or concepts are represented in the language debates, as when the grammar nazis interview Manfred and ask, echoing the Turgenevian phrase, – Откуда вам известен наш великий язык? (37).⁶⁰ Or when the grammar nazis' analysis of the Russian language is linked to stereotypical concepts, as in the case of verbal aspect in the example quoted above. Such cases caricature the tendency in the language debates of linking linguistic questions to broader issues of identity, tradition and ethical values.

CONCLUSIONS

Both Votrin and Gigolashvili deal with questions related to language cultivation and language legislation, in particular the monitoring and control of linguistic usage. Their approaches are radically different, and refreshingly so, I would say. Against the background of Gigolashvili's playful, mocking style, which exposes the fallacy of naïve, interpretive philology, the absurdity of the grammar nazi movement, but also the richness of 'linguistic experience' as seen from the perspective of a foreigner, the philosophical dimensions of Votrin's novel, its questioning of both the overt and hidden interrelationships between language and power, and language and identity, become all the more apparent. Let us look in more detail at the individual treatments of these questions.

Valerii Votrin: ideology, power, identity

It is easy to read Votrin's *The Speech Therapist* as a political allegory of the perestroika years and subsequent break-up of the Soviet Union. After the 'revolution', there is a need to handle the past, a classic question in post-totalitarian societies: Самое опасное – замалчивать историю, заглушать ее честный голос (145).⁶¹ The focus on language, meanwhile, allows Votrin to pose a number of more specific questions related to the post-totalitarian condition. The close connection between language and power is emphasised in the very structure of the quasi-totalitarian state, where language legislation is seen as the foundation of the state, and later in the break-up and democratisation of both state and language: – Наше общество, решительно двинувшееся по пути демократического обновления, остро нуждается в реформировании самого главного – языка, нашей с вами родной речи. [. . .] Будущее нашего свободного общества – в свободном языке (145).⁶²

As we have seen, the metaphor of a 'free language' is materialised in the liberalisation of Language, which, in the course of the novel, comes to be associated with power. In Rozhnov's words to the new regime: Вы думаете, что вы власть. Вы считаете, что правите страной, сидя здесь. Но вы ошибаетесь. Не вы правите страной. Не вы – власть. Власть – Он, ваш Язык (232).⁶³

The representation of Language as an acting figure in its own right may be interpreted on several levels. It acts out the 'liberalisation of language' mantra in a grotesque manner (reminiscent of Sorokin's radical materialisation of metaphors, cf. Uffelmann 2006), but it is also a playful response to the typical assurances expressed in the language debates by linguists and other language professionals (even writers) that the language is strong enough to take care of itself. Furthermore, it turns the institutional view on norms and language legislation on its head, by introducing the radical perspective of language itself on these matters: norms are just a hindrance to the free flow of language. By implication, it also questions the legitimacy of the ruling power with reference to the significant role played by linguistic regulation in society.

The topic of language and power is further highlighted through the issue of language ideologies. From the outset, linguistic ideologies are represented as being related to groups, rather than to individuals. The topic of variation, for example, is treated in relation to various groups or factions, or to types of people, who react differently; popular speech is spoken by the abstract notion of *narod* ('the people'), and so on. Most vividly, the tension between individuals and ideologies comes to the fore in Zablukaev's stories about the 'mutes'. Since the manuscript was confiscated by the authorities before Zablukaev emigrated, he must evoke the individual stories from memory when he intends to use them in his writings about speech cultivation for the émigré press. It turns out that he can remember only the facts, and not the individuals and their particular speech habits:

> Удалось ему и восстановить большую часть историй из утраченного сборника о немтырях. Он опубликовал некоторые из них, самые, на его взгляд, важные, но присовокупил, что в этих сделанных по памяти публикациях отсутствует главное – язык. Цепкая память Заблукаева помнила факты, помнила канву и сюжет, но язык ... – Заблукаев не мог упомнить речевых особенностей всех рассказчиков, и поэтому все истории утратили индивидуальность. (162–3)⁶⁴

A similar flash of insight occurs into the complex relationship between language, power and identity in Rozhnov's personal dealings with the language. At the beginning of the novel, he has a habit of thinking in popular language and speaking in correct language: he adheres to the rules set by the authorities and is himself part of the monitoring and control system. Later, he makes a conscious decision to speak (his moderated version of) the popular language, before, again, he switches back to the correct language towards the end of the novel. The pivotal moment is the scene in the ministry, where he discovers his name on a sheet of paper spelled as Iulii Lozhnov.

> – Простите, – начал Рожнов, возвращаясь к столу.
> – Сто такое?
> – Вот здесь написано: «Ложнов». Это какая-то ошибка, моя фамилия Рожнов.
> На лице Парина появилась неприятная улыбка.
> – Никакой осибки нет. Это ланьсе вы так назывались, пли сталом лезиме. А так будете называться пли новом. Это тепель васа настоясяя фамилия. (214–15)⁶⁵

Struck by this attack on his own identity, he decides to abandon popular speech, as becomes apparent in a dialogue with his wife: – Ты сто, Юлочка? – попятилась она. – Ты зе сам так говолил! – Я не Юлочка! – продолжал бушевать Рожнов. – Все, с этой дрянью у меня в доме покончено! Отныне – только чистый правильный язык! (216).⁶⁶

In the end, Rozhnov gives up popular speech because of the problematic link between language and power. He realises that he cannot speak the language of those now in power, who are burning books, persecuting people who speak the correct language, and changing the names of people in order to conform to the new norms. Whereas to Rozhnov, the question of language and language cultivation was initially a pragmatic question of complying with the speech practices of the majority, it now becomes a personal decision linked to identity and moral convictions, rather than to abstract notions of power and ideology.

Mikhail Gigolashvili: a folk linguistic analysis of Russian society

Several ideologies come together in Gigolashvili's portrayal of the grammar nazis – racist nationalism, including Nazi slogans and symbolism, and linguistic purism being the most prominent. Gigolashvili radicalises the already extremely aggressive style of the grammar nazis. He takes them seriously, on the one hand, but on a parallel level, he questions their right to be taken seriously by constantly exposing and ridiculing their lack of linguistic knowledge and inability to follow their own rules.

The grammar nazis of *The Occupation of Muscovy* are not just more radical, but also more hands-on, than the Runet grammar nazis: – Они сейчас деньги собирают, хотят место в Думе купить, чтобы потом там шороху навести, всех депутатов на чистоту языка проверить . . . (29).⁶⁷ This is but one example of the ways in which the topic of language in Gigolashvili's novel allows him to make numerous satirical references to present-day Russian society, and allude to important problems such as corruption, organised crime and social hardships, but also to less weighty challenges such as the low level of linguistic competence among politicians and officials.

As we have seen in many examples, language is understood, especially by Manfred, to carry more meaning than is usually assumed. Verbal aspect, verbs of motion, suffixes, profanity – these and many other linguistic elements are not only interpreted as having an impact on the 'mentality', people, country and society as a whole; language is also foregrounded as the main interpretive framework for experiencing and understanding reality. 'There is no reality in *The Occupation of Muscovy* other than the linguistic one', holds literary critic Dmitrii Bavil'skii (2012). Compared with 'Language' as a powerful agency or a philosophical perspective on the relationship between language and power, as we saw in Votrin's *The Speech Therapist*, the foregrounding of language as the 'main protagonist' in Gigolashvili's novel is of a different kind. Gigolashvili invites us to experience Russian, Russia and the Russians through Manfred's linguistic lens, a lens that often assumes the character of a magnifying glass, thus offering a satirical perspective on the implications of linguistic epistemology.

Within this framework, a major topic more directly linked to the language debates is linguistic creativity and adaptability versus linguistic monitoring and control. [Г]де грань между ошибкой и импровизацией? (41),⁶⁸ Manfred asks at the beginning of the novel. And later on: Можно-нельзя – кто решает? Комиссия? Вот эту диктатуру надо уничтожить! Пусть все говорят как хотят, язык развиваться будет . . . (223).⁶⁹

During the course of events, linguistic improvisation (*and* the making of mistakes) is exactly what Manfred is engaged in. His often very peculiar Russian is an unceasing source of new, often unexpected meanings – or interpretations by his interlocutors. If Manfred's stance demonstrates the dynamic character of spoken Russian, its elasticity, as well as the proclaimed right of every human being to talk as he or she pleases, the grammar nazis, by contrast, promote a very static view of language, fixated on details such as punctuation and orthography.

Gigolashvili gives a sympathetic representation of the richness of contemporary Russian, simultaneously highlighting, in his hyperbolic and comic way, the decisive role of language in understanding and interpreting reality in general, and Russian contemporary society in particular. He questions particular linguistic, interpretive methods, such as (quantitative) sociolinguistics and Russian ethnolinguistics. Likewise, he ridicules the lack of linguistic knowledge, inconsistent attitude and problematic ideology of the grammar nazis.

Taking a critical stance, one could argue that Gigolashvili's agenda is one that limits itself to the exposure of weaknesses, failures, absurdities, various linguistic attitudes, and so forth, while no alternative vision is presented. Admittedly, linguistic creativity, or even linguistic anarchy, is portrayed in more positive terms than strict linguistic monitoring and regulation, but in the end, these features too are made fun of – though with much love and sympathy.

Votrin's and Gigolashvili's novels show us two very different interpretations of one of the catch phrases in the language debates of the 1990s, the 'democratisation of language'. In Votrin's treatment, a philosophical perspective goes hand in hand with grotesque devices, questioning the legitimacy of power structures that get involved in linguistic regulation. Gigolashvili shows us the 'democratic' face of language by immersing Manfred in all kinds of linguistic varieties, by celebrating linguistic diversity and creativity, and by exposing linguistic control through satire and ridicule.

NOTES

1. *Iazyk* can mean both 'language' and 'tongue' as organ of speech. This double meaning is relevant for the novel's focus on *spoken language*; also, it clearly comes into play in some of the descriptions of the physical forms and movements of this creature, especially towards the end of the novel. In the quoted passages that follow, I keep 'Language' as the main translation of *Iazyk* but invite the reader to keep the broader meaning of the Russian word in mind.
2. 'I, [. . .] promise to observe the purity of language and follow the sacred norms in an exemplary way . . .' Quotations are taken from Votrin (2012), with page references in parentheses.
3. 'Pavel L'vovich would freak out, while his wife, Natal'ia Mikhailovna, would calmly observe that language doesn't stand still, it evolves, and it is excellent that the government understands this.'
4. 'The speech therapists became guardians of the norms from the very moment when people stopped paying attention to the norms. The salvation of language now depends on us [i.e. the speech therapists], only on us. For the people are not with us. The people are against us!'
5. 'Iurii Petrovich walks and thinks with indignation: "It's a *mess*. Where are the

janitors? That bag needs to be *removed. Garbage all over the place*, one should *take* a broom in *hand* and *clean up*. And this on the street of the *government*! [. . .] There's no *order*."' (Deviations from the standard language, here and in the following quotations, are indicated by italics.)

6. 'Some people say "I apologise [*Prosu proseniia*]". Others say "I apologise [*Pvoshchu pvoshcheniia*]". Still others say: "I apologise [*Ploshu ploshcheniia*]". So what, are we going to chase them off for that?'
7. '– That's it! We *tear the cover of the false language* off *our* names, *things* and words! *Now* people and *things* are called by their real names! – But what about the norms? – Rozhnov protested faintly, but Parin responded, furiously spitting saliva: *There are no old false rotten norms* any more! The freedom of language is the freedom of the *people*! Where have you been *lately, comrade*?!'
8. 'Everyone writes and speaks in his own manner. You don't understand a word. One speaks this way, another that way, as if they've had their tongues cut off. We've had to suspend work.'
9. 'Iurii Petrovich was certain that the wrath of Language wouldn't touch him.'
10. 'He gets in the way of the [party] nominees, he gets in the way of language. Yes, he gets in the way of Language. But he won't get in its way any longer. From that night on, he started to have dreams: he plays with the letters, offers them milk in a bowl and receives an affectionate, approving look out of the darkness. Rozhnov knows: this is Language.'
11. 'it turned out that Piskunov was being terrorised at night by Language. Scary eyes look into Piskunov's flat at night.'
12. '– It's language, Leva, Language! You don't speak it yourself, do you? – Why shouldn't I? Of course I do! – Oh no, you speak according to the books. And it doesn't like that. It likes it when everyone speaks it.'
13. 'But It isn't like the one in books. It's quite different, Levka. It's terrifying!'
14. 'The corruption of language that is permitted by society can lead to worse things than just the loss of freedom. A comma in the wrong place or a spelling error can lead to war.'
15. 'There it was, Language. It was impossible to describe. It was all swirling, glimmering and changing its shape. [. . .] It ruled. It bowed his shapeless head over the country, watched, listened, subdued. Below it scurried tiny little people, but they were almost impossible to see. It itself was them. And it couldn't speak. Yes, Zablukaev immediately realised that Language was mute.'
16. 'For some incomprehensible reason he knew that he could be killed only by a word – a sharp, honed one. And it would not be one from the popular language – this pseudolanguage was far too fluid, – no, this word would need to be taken from the old books. Yes, only there would it be possible to find a word, piercing as a dart, a word with a terrifying destructive power, a hammerhead word, a chisel word, a bludgeon word.'
17. 'And then Rozhnov freezes on the spot. What a delusion! From the corner of his eye he notices that in between other neon signboards there are some glowing letters, that should not, that cannot be there. Among the miserable mutilated words, shines one word – an untouched, genuine, all-powerful word from the old books, and a terrifying meaning pours out of it.'
18. '*A kind of teacher* he was . . .'
19. 'Not a teacher [. . .] A speech therapist. A true speech therapist.'
20. 'Slowly, as if stretching, it stands up and looks behind the departed train, and then,

when its lights are hidden from sight, it rises in satisfaction and dissolves over the city.'
21. 'adherents of a mystical doctrine where language is considered to be a god, and continuous babbling – a sacrifice to this god'.
22. '– You will soon understand, – he replied, – that there is no correct and incorrect language. The Norm goddess was invented by the speech therapists. There's one god – *Iazyk*, and he requires one thing: that we speak. You can speak even without words, with any words, even with unknown words. The main thing is to speak. That's the only thing that pleases him.'
23. 'Their language is an instrument for society's enslavement that tyrannises more cruelly than the most cruel human tyrant, because it inhabits the heads of people.'
24. 'He took reading as a flexing of muscles, a preparation for battle, for he felt the power of the old, correct words streaming into him.'
25. 'Language must evolve without any control. If the people speak this way, it has to be like this.'
26. 'It is you who makes the word correct – your pronunciation.'
27. 'Middle-aged emigrants were tormented by the fact that their children did not want to use plain speech and switched to the "bookish" language. This became a fashion among young people. Correct speech became a kind of youth slang, something with which to show off.'
28. '– Orrrrder! Orrrder! – Lomual'd cried out joyfully.'
29. 'In school they loved her, reckoned her among their own: "*Our teacher is great, she understands*", they said about her. She was secretly proud of her acquired respect.'
30. 'Now they started to arrest people heard talking with correct pronunciation, and hundreds of speech therapists and ordinary intellectuals went to prison, from where only a few returned.'
31. 'We are on the verge of language's demise, comrades.'
32. '– *Comrade Kovopen'kin*, – Rozhnov hammered on to him while listening to his own voice with disgust, – *I don't argue against the significance of your address. But you must understand that the main thing now is the language. You need to understand that the country cannot develop independently of the language. We have to fight for its purity.* "God, what I am saying!" he thought in horror. "What's happening to me?"'
33. 'He opened his mouth in order to warn Konopel'kin, to distract him, to let him know urgently about the need to introduce linguistic control, but incoherent grunting rushed out of his mouth. Rozhnov's tongue did not obey him. He tried to pronounce words, but his tongue did not obey him. – Ugh! Ugh! – Rozhnov roared horror-stricken. He understood that retribution had befallen him. His language had left him. Muteness had struck him in retribution. It seemed as if he had suffered a stroke. From wild terror Rozhnov "ugh-ed" even loader. He called for Iroshnikov, whose customary voice of reason and calm were as necessary to him as air: – Khafa! Saza! Bafa! Tasa!'
34. Translated into English as *The Land and Government of Muscovy* (von Staden 1967).
35. 'That's very interesting, after all, I am first of all a linguist, and then everything else.' Quotations are taken from Gigolashvili (2012), with page references in parentheses.
36. 'But then, what a [linguistic] practice it has been! . . . How useful! . . . And all the native speakers that I've been interacting with!'
37. 'Along the way, the driver railed against the government – at length and in a phonetically distinct way, so that I understood almost everything and even managed to take down this or that in my electronic dictionary [. . .]'

38. '– German ... From where? Not incidentally [*chai*] from the Nuremberg area? – Tea [*chai*]? – I didn't understand, but just to be on the safe side confirmed that, yes, I would like to drink tea with my friend.'
39. 'He's a clever guy, the boys respect him, he's smart [*ushlyi*] ... *Ushlyi* – is that someone who has left [*ushel*]? – Where did he go? – He? He didn't go anywhere. On the contrary, he has arrived. Where should he go? [...] – But you say "*ushlyi*". Is that someone who has left?'
40. 'What do they want of Fredia?.. Why don't they return Fredia's passport?'
41. 'Vitalik Ivanov invited-has invited me (I often use both forms of the verb, not knowing which one is the right one).'
42. 'But then how many different narrators were in dialogue with me?.. Of different age groups and gender! Very interesting. Real linguistic practice on a life basis.'
43. 'I remember your special course on diminutive suffixes, which are so sweet and gentle in Russian ... "The little piggy had little pink-coloured ears" ... I adore them – you can play with them as you like, freedom, creativity ... Oh, all these En'ka, On'ka, Ul'ka, Al'ka!..'
44. 'little little-linguist'.
45. 'I took the keys without a word and went away, astonished: he doesn't know me at all, what am I to him, a stranger, and he gives away his key ... What German would do that?.. There it is, the enigmatic soul ... wide-open ... not, a-little-wide-open ...'
46. 'The vodka turned out to be good, and the-little-adrenalin started to growl in the head.'
47. 'How much freedom there is in the Russian language!.. With us, the Germans, everything is regulated, with the French, everything is forbidden, the Englishman just hisses and wrinkles his nose, while the Russian is generous and his language afraid of nothing, because his language is broad, profound, indulgent, pliant like a woman to its native speaker, but inaccessible like a man to intruders ... And in this freedom is the essence of the magnitude of soul of this boundless people!'
48. This trait is, of course, reinforced by the insertions of the passages from Heinrich von Staden's sixteenth-century account and the genre of travel literature that frames the novel as a whole.
49. 'All the time they use the perfective aspect of the past tense [in the imperative mood]: "Done! Sat down! Stood up! Brought this! Shut up!" There's something highly unpleasant in this, unceremonious, coarse, impudent ... And the intonation of the voice ... unfriendly ... coarse ... the language is the mirror of society ...'
50. Incidentally, the 'fables' of Isidor (one of the grammar nazis Manfred encounters) also have an epigraph by Chaadaev.
51. 'Do they exist at all, Russian words in European languages? I searched my memory, but couldn't come up with words other than "bistro", "beef stroganoff", "balalaika", "vodka", "ikra" [caviar], "matroshka", "ruble", "perestroika", "glasnost", "kalashnikov" and "Molotov cocktail" ... Does this mean that the Russians haven't created anything truly original, new, something that didn't yet have a name and that had to be given one, such as Röntgen [who has given his name to terminology related to X-rays and radiography in many languages], Porsche, Watt and so on? ... Obviously yes ...'
52. 'I have noted a couple of new verbs, "filch", "snaffle", "snitch". Filcher! Snatcher! Snaffler! Where in German would you find such a distribution of nuances?.. Just "stehlen" [steal] and that's it. And here!.. An eldorado for psycholinguists, who maintain that, where there is a wealth of a particular kind of verbs, that's the speech field within which people are anyway engaged.'

53. This particular passage from the grammar nazi manifesto is taken almost verbatim from a 'Manifesto of the Party of the National Linguists' by Evgenii Lukin (2012) that can be found on various online literature sites, for example at Maksim Moshkov's Library, one of the greatest and oldest Runet library sites.
54. 'Now they're preparing a decree on the replacement of verbs . . . I was surprised: – That can't be . . . what kind of nonsense is that? How can you . . . the verbs? – Replace them with exclamation words: instead of "dive into" – "splash", instead of "swim" – "splat-splat", instead of "switch on" – "click", instead of "kiss" – "smack", instead of "fuck" – "bonk" or "chop-chop!" . . .'
55. 'Why in such a categori . . . chopped-off way? . . . It's a question of honour . . . Well, as you like. We're interested in outreach to Europe. Would you be able to help us in establishing contact with colleagues . . . that is, touching mutual friends?..'
56. 'Again such a word – aristocrat! – Frol noted. Isidor looked at him for two seconds with challenging contempt: – This time you're wrong! That's a composite word, dude – *ariia* [aria] – *sto* [hundred] – *krat* [times]! A hundred times aria, that is the purest Aryan there can be . . .'
57. 'Why not, we'll think about it, the idea makes sense . . . The more freedom, the better! I enthusiastically supported him: Yes. Full freedom! Dear little freedom! – and I began demonstrating that there always has to be room for improvisation [. . .]'
58. 'I was confused and all of a sudden I didn't understand whether this was serious or just a joke [. . .]'
59. 'Are they serious or are they joking?'
60. 'From where do you get your knowledge of our great language?'
61. 'The most dangerous thing is to keep the history secret, to silence its honest voice.'
62. 'Our society, which is definitely moving towards democratic reform, is in great need of a reformation of the main thing: language, our vernacular speech. [. . .] The future of our free society depends on the freedom of language.'
63. 'You think that you are in power. You think that, sitting here, you rule the country. But you are wrong. It is not you who rule the country. It is not you who are in power. It is in power – It, your Language.'
64. 'He was able to recall a large number of the stories from the lost collection about the mutes. He published a few of them, the most important ones in his view, but added that these publications based on memory lacked the main thing: the language. Zablukaev's tenacious memory had retained the facts, retained the outline and the story, but the language . . . – Zablukaev couldn't remember the speech characteristics of the storytellers, and therefore all the stories lost individuality.'
65. '–Excuse me, – began Rozhnov and returned to the table. – *What* is it? – Here there's written "Lozhnov". That's an error of some kind, my surname is Rozhnov. An unpleasant smile appeared on the face of Parin. – *No error at all.* You had that name *earlier, under the old regime*. This is how you're called *under* the new one. *Now* that's *your real* surname.'
66. '– *What* is it, *Iulochka*? – she moved back. – *But* you *talked* that way yourself! – I'm not *Iulochka*! – Rozhnov continued to roar. – Enough of this rubbish in my house! From now on – only the pure, correct language!'
67. '– They're collecting money to buy a seat in the Duma, in order afterwards to knock some heads together there and to check the linguistic purity of all deputies . . .'
68. 'Where is the line between error and improvisation?'
69. 'Allowed-forbidden – who's to judge? A commission? This dictatorship has to be abandoned! Let everyone talk as they like, and language will develop . . .'

CONCLUSION

Towards a Theory of Performative Metalanguage

A number of sociopolitical changes during late perestroika, including the fall of censorship and the policy of glasnost, led to a plethora of styles in official speech culture, but also in printed texts of all genres, allowing for a wider range of possibilities and choices with regard to not only topic, but also language and style. This development, in turn, inspired fervent language debates, with the participation of institutions, groups and individuals. In this book, the linguistic condition of post-Soviet Russian society, on the one hand, and the language debate – the linguistic metalevel – on the other, have provided a dual background, against which every literary 'utterance' – every text – may be read and interpreted. I have argued that these dimensions to what we termed sociolinguistic change – linguistic change as well as changes in society's life with language, including linguistic reflexivity – may have an impact on how language is represented, used or thematised in a given literary text, thus allowing us to read the literary work as a possible contribution to the language debate itself. As we have seen in the analyses undertaken in Chapters 7–9, such contributions differ in form, argumentation, and most probably also in impact, from the public debates on language, but also from the more explicit involvement in the debates by writers when they are interviewed or participate in surveys and round-table discussions on linguistic matters.

We saw in Chapters 5 and 6 that writers are still included in discussions about the state of the language. Naturally, their views range from the conservative to the liberal. In the surveys and interviews examined in Chapter 5, we observed a relatively relaxed attitude among writers towards the issue of norms and a highly sceptical view of political involvement in questions of linguistic regulation and legislation. We also sensed that many writers respond to 'the language question' with a natural authority, consciously or unconsciously perpetuating the earlier tradition where writers offered guidance and opinions on linguistic matters. In writers' reactions to the law banning *mat* from literature, theatre, film and performances (the 'Abanamat' protests), we observed how political involvement in linguistic regulation is felt to be particularly unjustified when it targets the realm of culture and art. An interesting aspect of the reactions to the 2014 anti-obscenity law was that they took on a quasi-artistic, performative form. There was more showing than telling in the artists' and activists' performance of poems, songs and readings containing *mat*. Still, the message was clear: it was directed both against the concrete legislative measure of banning *mat* from artistic realms, and also against the very idea of defining *mat* and setting up constraints for its use. The way in which participants acted and spoke revealed a conception of *mat* and its range of linguistic and cultural functions that was far broader than the notion of obscene language as expressed in the text of the law and accompanying parliamentary discussions. The reactions questioned, in a humorous and sometimes artistic form, the legitimacy of defining, by means of a political, top-down initiative, a linguistic stratum and of devising limitations for its usage, thus emphasising the urgency of such questioning when the legislative measures target the realm of art.

Even if we stress the *performative* aspect of the Abanamat protests, it is important to realise that, when we turn to the prose texts, we are dealing with an altogether different kind of linguistic commentary, a different type of metalanguage, or 'talk about talk'. In this final chapter I will explore this *difference* in more detail. First, I will summarise the main topics and issues related to language treated in my readings of the six prose works and try to determine the authors' and works' individual ways of dealing with 'the language question' in their artistic practice. We will then proceed to a theoretical discussion of the particular form of metalinguistic commentary employed in literary fiction, a form of metalanguage that combines the metalevel proper with the linguistic and artistic practice itself. I have coined the term *performative metalanguage* (Lunde 2009) for this kind of linguistic commentary, and will discuss the term in more detail below. Finally, I will map the different types of performative metalanguage that the six writers employ in their prose works and discuss briefly their interpretive potential.

THE RESPONSE OF LITERATURE

The six writers address a range of issues connected with the language of literature, the standard language, or the language situation in a broader sense. If, for a start, we return to Monika Wingender's (2003, 2013) standard language model, we can see that, taken together, they address all four components – the *linguistic, functional, social* and *situative* – of the standard language, but to different degrees. The *linguistic* component, we recall, has to do with the heterogeneity of the linguistic basis, the influence of varieties and (other) languages, and the standardisation and codification process itself. Of these issues, *linguistic diversity* is the one most foregrounded in the prose texts examined. It is a prominent feature of the texts of Popov, Tolstaia, Vodolazkin, Votrin and Gigolashvili. In Popov and Gigolashvili, the topic of linguistic diversity is linked to issues of identity and social differentiation in depictions that embrace both the uses and the users of non-standard varieties. In Tolstaia, by contrast, linguistic diversity reflects a fragmented, post-catastrophic society, while the link between language and identity is employed by the author as a way of characterising her literary personae. Vodolazkin creates a synthesis of different linguistic strata that demonstrates the richness of the language, also in a diachronic perspective, while the issue of language and diversity is further linked to philosophical questions of time, language and life. Votrin plays with the question of norms, standardisation and codification in a depiction that also touches upon broader questions of identity and power, while Gigolashvili has his protagonist interpret linguistic diversity with reference to 'mentality' and national identity.

With several of these latter concepts, we have come close to the *functional component* of the standard language, which relates to the 'extension of the functional spheres', 'vitality' and 'official attitudes'. Votrin's treatment of linguistic ideologies and language policies clearly addresses this aspect, while Gigolashvili's portrayal of the grammar nazi movement tackles the theme of language attitudes and linguistic cultivation within the framework of a typical folk linguistic setting. It is no coincidence that both Votrin's and Gigolashvili's books came out in 2012, when questions of linguistic legislation and language cultivation had been on the political agenda for a decade.

Linguistic attitudes in turn bring us to the *social component* of the standard language, embracing 'user attitudes', 'tradition and history' and 'symbolic value'. All writers discussed in Chapters 7–9 address this realm. While we may observe, in the public language debates, that the question of linguistic culture is frequently linked to broader issues of national identity, tradition, history and culture, in literary fiction such connections are even more wide-ranging and pronounced. Popov and Sorokin focus in particular on the question of linguistic legacies and their symbolic and ideological value, Tolstaia challenges concepts of linguistic and cultural tradition and transmission, Vodolazkin explores the philosophical dimension of language's diachronic aspect, Votrin treats the complex interrelationship between language and (symbolic) power and Gigolashvili plays with popular conceptions of languages, peoples and national identities.

The *situative component*, which has to do with the degree of 'autonomy' and 'sociolinguistic embeddedness', is an element of the standard language in Wingender's model that is less frequently addressed, but both Tolstaia's portrayal of the complex relationship between languages, varieties and groups of people (creatures) and Votrin's of the roles in society of the sanctioned language, on the one hand, and the vernacular, on the other, touch upon questions related to the sociolinguistic embeddedness of any language.

The six writers' engagement in linguistic questions is not exhausted by the above examples and, of course, not confined to the realm of the standard language. On the contrary, all the books that I have analysed stretch the potential of the standard language, at times challenging or breaking its limits, thereby clearly demonstrating that the language of literature has a broader basis than the strictly codified 'standard language'. Still, it is interesting to note how questions related to the standard language – and Wingender's perceptive model helps us include its essential aspects – are so central to the works analysed here. At the same time, the 'classic' topics of the language debates – linguistic diversity, norms, linguistic regulation and legislation – are frequently given a broader, more philosophical and less clear-cut interpretation. Naturally, this is a consequence of the genre of literary fiction itself, which, as a self-contained artistic verbal universe, is essentially different from a critical essay, journalistic article or political treatise. In addition, I would argue that the more profound and in many senses richer interpretation of 'the language question' in these works of literature has to do with the fact that, in literary prose, metalinguistic reflexivity is expressed by a whole range of different means, including the combination of explicit metacommentary with linguistic and artistic practices – again, a combination of 'telling' and 'showing'. In various ways, language is *pointed at*, or *put on display*. In this sense, the literary work may function as an invitation to the reader to be aware of the language and to reflect on linguistic issues.

PERFORMATIVE METALANGUAGE

A common and simple way of paraphrasing metalanguage is 'talk about talk'. We use language to reflect on language, to say something about language. Sociolinguists argue that we do so, in fact, all the time when we speak, when we use language (Lucy 1993; Cameron 2004). In other words, metalanguage is much more than just 'talk about talk'. The fact that we use language in order to say something about language itself is challenging for linguistic research. How can we pin down and describe the reflexive dimension of language? Moreover, how can we account for it, if it is not expressed explicitly? Because it may be, but does not have to be. In order to capture the kind of metalanguage that is not expressed explicitly, I have proposed the term *performative metalanguage*. It may be defined as follows: 'Performative metalanguage amounts to statements about language communicated through a concrete linguistic practice, a display or representation of language.'

Performative metalanguage as 'linguistic practice' means that we are talking about any kind of language use where a reflexive attitude towards language comes into play, such as quotation, imitation, stylisation, word play, irony, the sudden insertion of a dialect word, an unexpected turn of phrase, a distorted idiom, and so on. We are dealing with a 'display' or 'representation' of language when the language, or aspects of it, becomes an object of (artistic) representation and interpretation.[1]

Metalanguage has received considerable attention within various branches of linguistics, semiotics, anthropology and psychology over the past few decades (Gumperz 1982; Lucy 1993; Schieffelin et al. 1998; Silverstein 1998; Jaworski et al. 2004, among others). Even just within sociolinguistics, metalanguage is a broadly applied concept. It comprises straightforward remarks about language as, for example, in a discussion about the spelling of a word; simple mentioning of one's own language while speaking, in such expressions as 'in other words', or 'what I'm trying to say is . . .'; but also guidelines for interpretation that arise through the framing of speech, its formal or semantic structure, or intonation. In some of the latter, more 'implicit' forms of metalanguage, we are not far from the realm of performative metalanguage. Many fields have contributed to understanding the concept of metalanguage: functionalist approaches, linguistic pragmatics and anthropology, studies of reported speech, the poetics of speech style and stylisation, language ideology and others. Put in greatly simplified terms, we could say that these are scholarly traditions that study contextual meanings in language use and their social and ideological underpinnings.

Within the various subdisciplines of sociolinguistics, scholars have tried to determine the degree of explicitness of such contextual meanings and to establish categories in which they can be placed. In some contexts, these 'meanings' include 'received, taken-for-granted, normative and sometimes repressive assumptions' about language (Coupland and

Jaworski 2004: 20) – here we approach the field of language ideologies (Schieffelin et al. 1998).

Let us return to the concept of 'performative metalanguage' and look in more detail at its meaning. What does 'performative' mean in this composite term? Performativity and performance are interdisciplinary concepts that have emerged in theories of culture and identity, theatre and performance studies, anthropology, linguistics, law, and a broad range of adjacent disciplines. The origin of the term 'performative' is usually associated with philosopher of language John Austin's speech act theory, as formulated in a series of Harvard lectures delivered in 1955 and published posthumously in what has now become a classic, *How to Do Things with Words* (1962). Austin challenged current philosophies of language that focused on language's abilities to *state* and *assert* by pointing out that using words can also imply *doing* something. Performatives, in Austin's terms, are utterances that *perform an action*, such as the words 'I do' spoken as part of the marriage service (Austin 1975: 6).

Since Austin, the concept of performativity has undergone several stages of critique and reformulation.[2] One might indeed argue that there are parallel histories of the concept in the various disciplines.

In my first definition of performative metalanguage, I explained that 'performative' describes a particular type of metalanguage. Performative metalanguage amounts to utterances on language that are stated in the linguistic performance itself: in the manner you speak, in the way you use, represent or display language. While performative utterances, in terms of speech act theory, amount to doing something by saying something, performative metalanguage, it would seem, is the opposite: to say something by doing something: to state something *about* language by using language. To *show* rather than to *tell*, to use another pair of established terms. *Doing* and *saying*, however, do not mean exactly the same thing in these two statements, so we need to be a little more precise: (1) *performative utterances*: to act (perform) by speaking; (2) *performative metalanguage*: to state by acting (or, performing linguistically).

My reformulation detaches the term 'performative' from many current uses of 'performativity' in cultural theory, while it brings us closer to understandings of 'performance' that convey the dual sense of artistic action and artistic event.

What does it mean to perform linguistically? In his classic *Verbal Art as Performance*, Richard Bauman (1977: 11) treats performance as a particular mode of speaking and suggests that it sets up an *interpretive frame* that focuses on the means and expressive force of the utterance. The interpretive frame carries additional layers of meaning that may relate to the 'explicit message' or content of the utterance in a number of ways. It may reinforce it, help interpret it, or even contradict it. In sociolinguistics, one speaks rather technically of a metapragmatic frame that gives the receiver the necessary instructions so that he or she can understand the message. But the meaning – or 'meta-meaning' – that arises through the various uses of verbal performance need not be connected to the 'plain message' of a given statement at all, though more often than not, it may well be. For instance, you can express your positive view on the English standard language using English slang or other non-standard language. It will certainly increase the level of ambiguity and multiple meanings in your statement as a whole. This would be an example of a combination of explicit metalanguage and performative metalanguage that points in two different directions at the same time and results in an ironic statement.

The specificity of performative metalanguage lies in the concept of performance that I have tried to outline above. It includes an element of playful creativity that manifests itself in verbal practices that draw attention to the linguistic metalevel. Elements of playful creativity are highly characteristic of post-Soviet Russian literature as a whole and indeed, the term 'performative metalanguage' has been to some extent inspired and shaped by my readings of contemporary Russian authors. While this does not confine its potential to the study of texts and language usage within only a limited range of genres, let us return again to our six prose authors and briefly sum up some of the ways in which they employ performative metalanguage in their works of literary fiction.

LANGUAGE ON DISPLAY

In our readings of the six prose works, we have come across a number of different types of performative metalanguage. A common pattern is the combination of *representations* of particular styles or varieties with performative devices on the level of detail (single words, word-forms, or phrases). These features in turn interact with explicit commentary related to linguistic issues, in the characters' direct speech, in the narrator's account, or in the depicted events. In this way, the particular linguistic features of the represented languages or styles serve to characterise the language itself, while, within the fictional framework, the writers lay bare the conditions for the individual language's functioning in the society portrayed. This allows them to link their representations of languages, or concrete linguistic practices, to particular topics connected to language ideology, aspects of language history, language culture, and so on – topics that we recognise from the language debates.

Sorokin explores the linguistic memory of specific words, concepts and phrases and combines the historical realities invoked by these elements with poetic devices in order to create a synchronicity of asynchronous historical pasts. He shows, by so doing, that language is a bearer of historical memory and points to the need to deal with this legacy in today's society. Popov likewise creates a reflexive space that underlines how crucial it is to be aware of linguistic legacies and their ideological underpinnings. His main performative device is his use of humour to expose the grand style, on the one hand, and to praise linguistic diversity, on the other. Vodolazkin's approach is likewise a playful one. Historical layers of the language are evoked in order to create an amalgam of styles, and are combined with a philosophical interpretation of time so as to display the richness of the language. His novel's verbal structure thus creates room for reflection where the reader is invited to be mindful of his or her own language. Tolstaia's novel employs a combination of satire and verbal virtuosity in order to expose the lack of culture, tradition and true knowledge in the fictional world she portrays. On the level of detail, the performative element emerges in the juxtaposition of the individual linguistic phenomena and features represented, from semantically reduced language and 'mutated words' to *prostorechie* and archaic elements. In addition, Tolstaia consistently characterises her literary personae through their speech, thus playfully invoking the close connection between language and identity that features frequently in public discussions about 'the state of the language'. Votrin portrays two linguistic varieties and links them to particular ideologies. Here, the performative device lies in the juxtaposition and evolution of the varieties and their accompanying ideologies, which fluctuate between different axiological stances. Furthermore, Votrin playfully displays, or 'acts out', central metaphors of the language debates in all their grotesque realisations. Gigolashvili, finally, portrays the linguistic diversity of contemporary Russian and shows us the interpretive capacities of a 'linguistic view on things' through his slightly mocking representation of young Manfred, German student of Russian. He also links concrete grammatical categories to particular conceptions of people and countries in the style of folk linguistics, and displays the ideology of the grammar nazis through their manner of talking and acting.

The six writers employ a great variety of devices in order to turn our attention to linguistic matters. The main themes are easily recognisable from the public language debates: linguistic diversity, the standard language and non-standard elements, language regulation and legislation, and the role of language in the broader context of history, culture and identity. The performative approach to these topics allows the authors to give them a broader, more nuanced and less clear-cut interpretation, as opposed to the more rigid stances adopted in the public debates. Devices such as language play, deviations from the norm, or the unexpected juxtaposition of styles establish a space for metalinguistic reflection which the reader is invited to join. Performative metalanguage thus creates a particular relationship between author and reader, one of proximity and shared understanding. As such, it is a less pretentious and more inclusive manner of engaging in linguistic debates.

NOTES

1. It is important to stress that performative metalanguage is not confined to the realm of literary fiction, but may in principle take place in all types and genres of communication.
2. Most notably by John Searle, Jacques Derrida, Stanley Fish, Judith Butler and Eve Kosofsky Sedgwick. For an informative review of the concept, see Loxley (2007).

References

'"Abanamat" – vserossiiskaia aktsiia' (2014), '"Abanamat" – vserossiiskaia aktsiia v zashchitu kul'tury proshla v Kazani', *Biznes-Online TV*, 1 July, <http://www.youtube.com/watch?v=lPQGXhW-XaI#t=15> (last accessed 30 June 2016).

'Abanamat: kak v Barnaule' (2014), 'Abanamat: kak v Barnaule proshchalis' s maternymi slovami', *Politsib.ru*, 1 July, <http://www.politsib.ru/news/72278> (last accessed 30 June 2016).

'Abanamat: reaktsii' (2014), 'Abanamat: reaktsii na sanktsii', *Fontanka.ru*, 1 July, <http://www.fontanka.ru/2014/07/01/184/> (last accessed 30 June 2016).

Ågren, Mattias (2014), *Phantoms of a Future Past: A Study of Contemporary Russian Anti-Utopian Novels* (Stockholm Studies in Russian Literature 43), Stockholm: Stockholm University Press.

Aksenov, Vasilii, Andrei Bitov, Viktor Erofeev, Fazil' Iskander and Evgenii Popov (eds) (1979), *Metropol': literaturnyi almanakh*, Ann Arbor: Ardis.

Amelin, Maksim, Boris Ekimov, Oleg Ermakov, Vitalii Kal'pidi, Svetlana Kekova, Igor' Klekh, Vladislav Otroshenko, Oleg Pavlov and Aleksei Tsvetkov (2006), 'Iazyk nash svoboden', *Znamia* 12, <http://magazines.russ.ru/znamia/2006/12/ia9.html> (last accessed 30 June 2016).

Andersen, Henning (1989), 'Understanding linguistic innovations', in LeivEgil Breivik and Ernst H. Jahr (eds), *Language Change: Contributions to the Study of Its Causes*, Berlin/New York: De Gruyter, pp. 5–28.

Andersen, Henning (2009), 'Living norms', in Ingunn Lunde and Martin Paulsen (eds), *From Poets to Padonki: Linguistic Authority and Norm Negotiation in Modern Russian Culture* (Slavica Bergensia 9), Bergen: Department of Foreign Languages, pp. 18–33.

Androutsopoulos, Jannis (2014), 'Mediatization and sociolinguistic change: Key concepts, research traditions, open issues', in Jannis Androutsopoulos (ed.), *Mediatization and Sociolinguistic Change*, Berlin/Boston: De Gruyter, pp. 3–48.

Arkhipova, Aleksandra, Anton Somin and Alesandra Sheveleva (2016), 'S ekrana na plakat: diskurs vlasti v iazykovoi igre oppozitsii', in Ekatarina Lapina-Kratasiuk, Oksana Moroz and Evgeniia Nim (eds), *Nastroika iazyka: upravlenie kommunikatsiiami na postsovetskom prostranstve*, Moscow: Novoe literaturnoe obozrenie, pp. 175–94.

Austin, John (1975), *How to Do Things with Words*, Oxford: Clarendon Press.

Babenko, Natal'ia (2010), *Iazyk i poetika russkoi prozy v epokhu postmoderna*, 2nd edn, Moscow: Librokom.

Bak, Dmitrii, Gasan Guseinov, Maksim Krongauz, Mikhail Epshtein and Marina Adamovich (2010), 'Russkii iazyk v sovremennom mire', *Novyi zhurnal* 208, <http://magazines.russ.ru/nj/2010/258/ru19.html> (last accessed 30 June 2016).
Bakulina, Ol'ga (2014), '"Panikhida po matu" sobrala v Barnaule bol'she uchastnikov, chem ozhidali organizatory', *Komsomol'skaia Pravda*, 1 July, <http://www.alt.kp.ru/daily/26249/3130106/> (last accessed 30 June 2016).
Baranov, Anatolii (2007), *Lingvisticheskaia ekspertiza teksta: teoriia i praktika*, Moscow: Flinta.
Basinskii, Pavel (2013), 'Svetiashchaiasia t'ma', *Rossiiskaia gazeta*, 26 November, <http://www.rg.ru/2012/11/26/basinskij.html> (last accessed 7 September 2016).
Baumann, Richard (1977), *Verbal Art as Performance*, Prospect Heights, IL: Waveland Press.
Bavil'skii, Dmitrii (2012), 'Zalivnoi iazyk', *Topos: literaturno-filosofskii zhurnal*, 28 June, <http://www.topos.ru/article/literaturnaya-kritika/zalivnoi-yazyk> (last accessed 30 June 2016).
Becker, Joern-Martin (2001), *Semantische Variabilität der russischen politischen Lexik im zwanzigsten Jahrhundert*, Munich: Otto Sagner.
Berdicevskis, Aleksandrs and Vera Zvereva (2014), 'Slangs go online, or the rise and fall of the Olbanian language', in Michael S. Gorham, Ingunn Lunde and Martin Paulsen (eds), *Digital Russia: The Language, Culture and Politics of New Media Communication*, London/New York: Routledge, pp. 123–40.
Birger, Liza (2012), 'Ment zhivotvoriashchii', *Gazeta.ru*, 27 March, <http://www.gazeta.ru/culture/2012/03/27/a_4106141.shtml> (last accessed 30 June 2016).
Bodin, Per-Arne (2016), 'The Russian language in contemporary conservative dystopias', *The Russian Review* 75 (4), pp. 579–88.
Bogdanov, Sergei, Petr Bukharkin, Kirill Kopeikin, Natal'ia Rogozhina and Evgenii Iurkov (eds) (2006a), *Besedy liubitelei russkogo slova: pravoslavnoe dukhovenstvo o iazyke*, St Petersburg: Osipov.
Bogdanov, Sergei, Petr Bukharkin, Natal'ia Rogozhina and Evgenii Iurkov (eds) (2004a), *Besedy liubitelei russkogo slova: pisateli o iazyke*, St Petersburg: Politekhnika.
Bogdanov, Sergei, Natal'ia Rogozhina and Evgenii Iurkov (eds) (2006b), *Sovremennaia russkaia rech: sostoianie i funktsionirovanie: sbornik analiticheskich materialov*, vol. 2, St Petersburg: Filologicheskii fakul'tet SPbGU.
Bogdanov, Sergei, Liudmila Verbitskaia, Leonid Moskovkina and Evgenii Iurkov (eds) (2004b), *Sovremennaia russkaia rech: sostoianie i funktsionirovanie: sbornik analiticheskich materialov*, vol. 1, St Petersburg: Filologicheskii fakul'tet SPbGU.
Bondareva, T. B. and Alla Latynina (1974), *Pisateli o literaturnom iazyke*, Moscow: Znanie.
Borden, Richard C. (1999), *The Art of Writing Badly: Valentin Kataev's Mauvism and the Rebirth of Russian Modernism*, Evanston, IL: Northwestern University Press.
Borenstein, Eliot (2008), *Overkill: Sex and Violence in Contemporary Russian Popular Culture*, Ithaca, NY/London: Cornell University Press.
Borenstein, Eliot (2015), 'Dystopias and catastrophe tales after Chernobyl', in Evgeny Dobrenko and Mark Lipovetsky (eds), *Russian Literature since 1991*, Cambridge: Cambridge University Press, pp. 86–103.
Bourdieu, Pierre (1991), *Language and Symbolic Power*, ed. and intro. John B. Thompson, trans. Gino Raymond and Matthew Adamson, Cambridge: Polity Press.
Boym, Svetlana (2001), *The Future of Nostalgia*, New York: Basic Books.

Brinev, Konstantin (2009), *Teoreticheskaia lingvistika i sudebnaia lingvisticheskaia ekspertiza*, Barnaul: AltGPA.

Bukharkin, Petr (2004), 'Vmesto predisloviia', in Sergei Bogdanov, Petr Bukharkin, Natal'ia Rogozhina and Evgenii Iurkov (eds), *Besedy liubitelei russkogo slova: pisateli o iazyke*, St Petersburg: Politekhnika, pp. 3–6.

Burkhart, Dagmar (1999), 'Vorwort', *Poetik der Metadiskursivität: Zum postmodernen Prosa-, Film- und Dramenwerk von Vladimir Sorokin*, Munich: Otto Sagner, pp. 5–8.

Cameron, Deborah (2004), 'Out of the bottle: The social life of metalanguage', in Adam Jaworski, Nikolas Coupland and Dariusz Galasiński (eds), *Metalanguage: Social and Ideological Perspectives*, Berlin/New York: De Gruyter, pp. 311–21.

Cerquiglini, Bernard (1989), *Éloge de la variante: histoire critique de la philologie*, Paris: Seuil.

Chantsev, Aleksandr (2009), 'The antiutopia factory: The dystopian discourse in Russian literature of the mid-2000s', *Russian Social Science Review* 50 (4), pp. 61–96.

Chukovskii, Kornei [1962] (1990), *Zhivoi kak zhizn': o russkom iazyke*, Moscow: Molodaia gvardiia.

Clayton, J. Douglas and Natalia Vesselova (2012), 'Resexing literature: Tsar Nikita and his forty daughters', in Alyssa Dinega Gillespie (ed.), *Taboo Pushkin: Topics, Texts, Interpretations*, Madison, WI: University of Wisconsin Press, pp. 224–38.

Coupland, Nikolas (2014), 'Sociolinguistic change, vernacularization and broadcast British media', in Jannis Androutsopoulos (ed.), *Mediatization and Sociolinguistic Change*, Berlin/Boston: De Gruyter, pp. 67–96.

Coupland, Nikolas and Adam Jaworski (2004), 'Sociolinguistic perspectives on metalanguage: Reflexivity, evaluation and ideology', in Adam Jaworski, Nikolas Coupland and Dariusz Galasiński (eds), *Metalanguage: Social and Ideological Perspectives*, Berlin/New York: De Gruyter, pp. 15–51.

Dmitriev, Andrei, Vladimir Elistratov, Mariia Zakharova, Irina Levontina, Igor' Miloslavskii, Dmitrii Aleksandrovich Prigov, Natal'ia Rubanova, Mikhail Edel'shtein, Maksim Amelin, Il'ia Kukulin and Vladislav Otroshenko (2007), 'Iazyk kak glavnyi geroi', *Znamia* 7–8, <http://magazines.russ.ru/znamia/2007/7/ia12.html> and <http://magazines.russ.ru/znamia/2007/8/am11.html> (both last accessed 30 June 2016).

Dobrenko, Evgeny (2015a), 'Linguistic turn *à la Soviétique*: The power of grammar, and the grammar of power', in Petre Petrov and Lara Ryazanova-Clarke (eds), *The Vernaculars of Communism: Language, Ideology and Power in the Soviet Union and Eastern Europe*, London/New York: Routledge, pp. 19–39.

Dobrenko, Evgeny (2015b), 'Recycling of the Soviet', in Evgeny Dobrenko and Mark Lipovetsky (eds), *Russian Literature since 1991*, Cambridge: Cambridge University Press, pp. 20–44.

Dobrenko, Evgeny and Mark Lipovetsky (2015), 'The burden of freedom: Russian literature after communism', in Evgeny Dobrenko and Mark Lipovetsky (eds), *Russian Literature since 1991*, Cambridge: Cambridge University Press, pp. 1–19.

Dokusov, Aleksandr (1954), *Russkie pisateli o iazyke: khrestomatiia*, Leningrad: Uchpedgiz.

Dovlatov, Sergei (1989), *Ours: A Russian Family Album*, trans. Anne Frydman, New York: Weidenfeld & Nicolson.

Dovlatov, Sergei (1993), *Sobranie prozy v trekh tomakh*, vol. 2, Moscow: Limbus-Press.

Dulichenko, Aleksandr (1994), *Russkii iazyk kontsa XX stoletiia* (Slavistische Beiträge 317), Munich: Otto Sagner.

Efremov, Valerii and Marina Scharlaj (2016), 'Iazykovaia refleksiia kak platsdarm rechevoi agressii: internet-soobshchestvo grammar-natsi', *Zeitschrift für slavische Philologie* 72 (2), pp. 449–82.
Elistratov, Vladimir (1995), *Argo i kul'tura*, Moscow: Izdatel'stvo MGU.
Engel, Christine (1996), 'Tabubrüche in der Prosa von Evgenij Popov', in Jochen-Ulrich Peters and German Ritz (eds), *Enttabuisierung: Essays zur russischen und polnischen Gegenwartsliteratur*, Bern: Peter Lang, pp. 117–27.
Epshtein [Epstein], Mikhail and Aleksandr Genis (2007), 'Filosofiia rodnogo iazyka', *Radio Svoboda, Dar slova* 183, <http://old.russ.ru/antolog/intelnet/dar183.html> (last accessed 15 April 2015).
Epstein, Mikhail (2007), 'Slovo goda', *Dar slova* 262, <http://www.emory.edu/intel net/dar_sl1.html> (last accessed 18 September 2016).
Ermen, Ilse (1993), *Der obszöne Wortschatz im Russischen*, Munich: Otto Sagner.
Ermoshin, Fedor (2007), 'Rech' pro rech'', *Znamia* 10, <http://magazines.russ.ru/znamia/2007/10/er16.html> (last accessed 30 June 2016).
Erofeev, Viktor (1990), 'Pominki po sovetskoi literature', *Literaturnaia gazeta*, 4 June.
Erofeyev, Victor (2003), 'Dirty words: The unique power of Russia's underground language', *The New Yorker*, 15 September.
Eshelman, Raoul (1993), 'Von der Moderne zur Postmoderne in der sowjetischen Kurzprosa: Zoščenko – Paustovskij – Šukšin – Popov', *Wiener Slawistischer Almanach* 31, pp. 173–207.
Fleischmann, Eberhard (2007), *Postsowjetisches Russisch: Eine Studie unter translatorischem Aspekt* (Leipziger Studien zur angewandten Linguistik und Translatologie 3), Frankfurt am Main: Peter Lang.
Florida, Richard L. (2002), *The Rise of the Creative Class: And How It's Transforming Work, Leisure, Community and Everyday Life*, New York: Basic Books.
'Fond Russkii mir' (n.d.), 'Informatsionnyi portal fonda "Russkii mir"', <http://russ kiymir.ru/fund/> (last accessed 10 June 2016).
Franklin, Simon (2002), *Writing, Society and Culture in Early Rus, c. 950–1300*, Cambridge: Cambridge University Press.
Gabowitsch, Mischa (2013), *Putin kaputt!? Russlands neue Protestkultur*, Berlin: Suhrkamp.
Gasparov, Boris (1984), 'The language situation and the linguistic polemic in mid-nineteenth-century Russia', in Riccardo Picchio and Harvey Goldblatt (eds), *Aspects of the Slavic Language Question*, vol. 2: *East Slavic*, New Haven, CT: Yale Concilium on International and Area Studies, pp. 297–334.
Germanova, Nataliia (2011), *Teoriia i istoriia literaturnogo iazyka v otechestvennom i angloiazykchnom iazykoznanii*, Moscow: Librokom.
Gigolashvili, Mikhail (2012), *Zakhvat Moskovii: natsional-lingvisticheskii roman*, Moscow: Eksmo.
Gigolashvili, Mikhail and Platon Besedin (2013), 'Mikhail Gigolazhvili: "kazhdyi, kto pishet po-russki, dolzhen chuvstvovat' za spinoi dykhanie nashikh velikikh uchitelei ..."', *Blog Thankyou.ru*, 13 March, <http://blog.thankyou.ru/mihail-gigolashvili-kazhdyiy-kto-pishet-po-russki-dolzhen-chuvstvovat-za-spinoy-dyihanie-nashih-velikih-uchiteley> (last accessed 10 June 2016).
Glazunova, Ol'ga, Leonid Moskovkina and Evgenii Iurkov (eds) (2008), *Sovremennaia russkaia rech: sostoianie i funktsionirovanie: sbornik analiticheskich materialov*, vol. 3, St Petersburg: Izdatel'skii dom 'MIRS'.
Goldschmidt, Paul W. (1999), *Pornography and Democratization: Legislating Obscenity in Post-Communist Russia*, Boulder, CO: Westview Press.

Gölz, Christine (2004), 'Das ABC der russischen Katastrophen: Tat'jana Tolstajas Roman "Kys"', in Christine Gölz, Aage A. Hansen-Löve and Lazar Fleishman (eds), *Analysieren als Deuten: Wolf Schmid zum 60. Geburtstag*, Hamburg: Hamburg University Press, pp. 689–718.

Gorham, Michael S. (2006), 'Language culture and national identity in post-Soviet Russia', in Ingunn Lunde and Tine Roesen (eds), *Landslide of the Norm: Language Culture in Post-Soviet Russia* (Slavica Bergensia 6), Bergen: Department of Foreign Languages, pp. 18–30.

Gorham, Michael S. (2014), *After Newspeak: Language Culture and Politics in Russia from Gorbachev to Putin*, Ithaca, NY/London: Cornell University Press.

Gorham, Michael S., Ingunn Lunde and Martin Paulsen (eds) (2014), *Digital Russia: The Language, Culture and Politics of New Media Communication*, London/New York: Routledge.

Gorham, Michael S. and Daniel Weiss (eds) (2016/17), *The Culture and Politics of Verbal Prohibition in Putin's Russia*, special issue of *Zeitschrift für slavische Philologie* 72 (2)–73 (1).

Goriunova, Ol'ga (2009), '"Muzhskaia literatura" Udaffkoma i drugie khudozhestvennye praktiki kul'turnogo soprotivleniia', in Natal'ia Konradova, Henrike Schmidt and Katy Teubener (eds), *Control+Shift: publichnoe i lichnoe v russkom internete*, Moscow: Novoe literaturnoe obozrenie, pp. 235–59.

Goscilo, Helena (2004), 'Tatyana Tolstaya', in Malina Balina and Mark Lipovetsky (eds), *Russian Writers Since 1980*, Detroit: Gale, pp. 316–28.

Govorukhin, Stanislav (2015), 'Pozitsiia', *Obshcherossiiskii narodnyi front*, 21 January, <http://onf.ru/2015/01/21/govoruhin-avtoram-idei-vozvrashcheniya-necenzurnoy-leksiki-v-kino-sovetuyu-vspomnit-stihi/> (last accessed 30 June 2016).

Grachev, Mikhail (1997), *Russkoe argo: monografiia*, Nizhnii Novgorod: Izdatel'stvo NGLU.

Graham, Seth (2009), *Resonant Dissonance: The Russian Joke in Cultural Context*, Evanston, IL: Northwestern University Press.

Graham, Seth and Ol'ga Mesropova (eds) (2008), *Uncensored? Reinventing Humor and Satire in Post-Soviet Russia*, Bloomington, IN: Slavica Publishers.

'Grammaticheskii natsizm' (2009), LiveJournal blog *Sclon*, <http://sclon.livejournal.com/56972.html?thread=345484> (last accessed 30 June 2016).

Grigor'ev, Viktor (1987), 'Iazyk khudozhestvennoi literatury', in Vadim Kozhevnikov and Petr Nikolaev (eds), *Literaturnyi entsiklopedicheskii slovar'*, Moscow: Sovetskaia entsiklopediia.

Grois, Boris (1993), 'O novom', *Utopiia i obmen*, Moscow: Znak.

Gumperz, John J. (1982), *Discourse Strategies*, Cambridge: Cambridge University Press.

Guseinov, Gasan (2003), *D.S.P.: materialy k russkomu slovariu obshchestvenno-politicheskogo iazyka XX veka*, Moscow: Tri kvadrata.

Guseinov, Gasan (2004), *D.S.P.: sovetskie ideologemy v russkom diskurse 1990-kh*, Moscow: Tri kvadrata.

Guseinov, Gasan (2005), 'Berloga vebloga: vvedenie v erraticheskuiu semantiku', *Govorim po-russkii*, <http://www.speakrus.ru/gg/microprosa_erratica-1.htm> (last accessed 30 June 2016).

Haugen, Einar (1966), 'Dialect, language, nation', *American Anthropologist* 68, pp. 922–35.

Hristova, Daniela S. (2011), 'Velikii i moguchii olbanskii iazyk: The Russian internet and the Russian language', *Russian Language Journal* 61, pp. 143–62.

Iampol'skii, Mikhail (2014), 'Totalitarnaia rech',' *Gefter*, 26 March, <http://gefter.ru/archive/11809> (last accessed 30 June 2016).
Jaworski, Adam, Nikolas Coupland and Dariusz Galasiński (eds) (2004), *Metalanguage: Social and Ideological Perspectives*, Berlin/New York: De Gruyter.
Jonson, Lena (2015), *Art and Protest in Putin's Russia*, London/New York: Routledge.
Kalinin, Ilya (2013), 'The blue lard of language: Vladimir Sorokin's metalingual utopia', in Tine Roesen and Dirk Uffelmann (eds), *Vladimir Sorokin's Languages* (Slavica Bergensia 11), Bergen: Department of Foreign Languages, pp. 128–47.
Kalinin, Ilya (2015), 'Culture matters: Why the Kremlin wants to be the keeper of Russia's cultural heritage', *The Calvert Journal*, 28 January, <http://calvertjourn al.com/comment/show/3608/Culture-matters-Russia-cultural-policy-Ilya-Kalinin> (last accessed 30 June 2016).
Karaulov, Iurii (1989), 'Velikii . . . moguchii . . . mnogostradal'nyi . . .', *Nedelia* 40, pp. 14–15.
Karev, Igor' and Aleksei Krizhevskii (2015), 'Skazhi matu "da"', *Gazeta.ru*, 21 January, <http://www.gazeta.ru/culture/2015/01/21/a_6382465.shtml> (last accessed 30 June 2016).
Karev, Igor', Nataliia Mitiusheva, Iaroslav Zabaluev and Polina Ryzhova (2014), 'Pole bez brani', *Gazeta.ru*, 1 July, <http://www.gazeta.ru/culture/2014/07/01/a_6093465. shtml> (last accessed 30 June 2016).
Kenzheev, Bakhyt and Aleksandr Levin (2000), 'Iz perepiski Kanzheeva s Levinym', *Ogonek* 2, <http://kommersant.ru/doc/2287157> and <http://www.levin.rinet.ru/TEXTS/Kenjeev-Levin.html> (both last accessed 30 June 2016).
Kheveshi, Mariia (2002), *Tol'kovyi slovar' ideologicheskikh i politicheskikh terminov sovetskogo perioda*, Moskva: Mezhdunarodnye otnosheniia.
Khimik, Vasilii (2000), *Poetika nizkogo, ili Prostorechie kak kul'turnyi fenomen*, St Petersburg: Filologicheskii fakul'tet SPbGU.
Klemperer, Victor (1947), *L.T.D. Die unbewältigte Sprache: Aus dem Notizbuch eines Philologen*, Darmstadt: Joseph Melzer.
'Komitet Gosdumy' (2015), 'Komitet Gosdumy po kul'ture bydet protiv vozvrashcheniia mata v kino', *Gazeta.ru*, 21 January, <http://www.gazeta.ru/culture/news/2015/01/21/n_6845937.shtml> (last accessed 30 June 2016).
Koreneva, Marina (2011), 'Die Geschichte der russischen Übersetzungsliteratur und die Entwicklung der russischen Literatursprache', in Harald Kittel (ed.), *Ein internationales Handbuch zur Übersetzungsforschung*, vol. 3, Berlin/New York: De Gruyter, pp. 2023–41.
Koschmal, Walter (1995), 'Ende der Verantwortungsästhetik?', in Jochen-Ulrich Peters and German Ritz (eds), *Enttabuisierung: Essays zur russischen und polnischen Gegenwartsliteratur*, Bern: Peter Lang, pp. 19–44.
Kostomarov, Vitalii (1994), *Iazykovoi vkus epokhi: iz nabliudenii nad rechevoi praktikoi mass-media*, Moscow: Zlatoust.
Kovalev, Manuela (2014), 'From an unprintable to a printable language of literature? Russian obscene language in late and post-Soviet literary cultures', *Russian Journal of Communication* 6 (2), pp. 113–26.
Kovalev, Manuela (2016), 'Law and (verbal) order: The politics of Russian obscene language from Soviet Russia to the present day', *Zeitschrift für slavische Philologie* 72 (2), pp. 323–48.
Krongauz, Maksim (2005), 'Zametki rasserzhennogo obyvatelia', *Otechestvennye*

zapiski 2, <http://www.strana-oz.ru/2005/2/zametki-rasserzhennogo-obyvatelya> (last accessed 20 June 2016).
Krongauz, Maksim (2007), *Russkii iazyk na grani nervnogo sryva*, Moscow: Znak.
Krongauz, Maksim (2013), *Samouchitel' olbanskogo*, Moscow: Ast.
Krongauz, Maksim (2016a), 'Russian and newspeak: Between myth and reality', in Nikolai Vakhtin and Boris Firsov (eds), *Public Debate in Russia: Matters of (Dis)order*, Edinburgh: Edinburgh University Press, pp. 31–51.
Krongauz, Maksim (2016b), 'Zakon o gosudarstvennom iazyke Rossiiskoi Federatsii: istoriia obsuzhdeniia i popravok', *Zeitschrift für slavische Philologie* 72 (2), pp. 255–70.
Krysin, Leonid (ed.) (2000–12), *Russkii iazyk segodnia*, vols 1–5, Moscow: Azbukovnik.
Krysin, Leonid (2004), *Russkoe slovo, svoe i chuzhoe: issledovaniia po sovremennomu russkomu iazyku i sotsiolingvistike*, Moscow: Iazyki slavianskoi kul'tury.
Krysin, Leonid (2013), 'Russkaia literaturnaia norma v proektsii na sovremennuiu rechevuiu praktiku', in Daniel Müller and Monika Wingender (eds), *Typen slavischer Standardsprachen: Theoretische, methodische und empirische Zugänge*, Wiesbaden: Harrassowitz, pp. 145–60.
Kucherskaia, Maiia (2012), 'Roman "Zakhvat Moskovii": prikliucheniia nemetskogo slavista v Rossii', *Vedomosti*, 28 March, <http://www.vedomosti.ru/newspaper/articles/2012/03/28/ne_zhalejte_zavarki> (last accessed 20 June 2016).
Kukulin, Ilya (2015), ' "The golden age of Soviet Antiquity": Sovietisms in the discourse of left-wing political movements in post-Soviet Russia, 1991–2013', in Petre Petrov and Lara Ryazanova-Clarke (eds), *The Vernaculars of Communism: Language, Ideology and Power in the Soviet Union and Eastern Europe*, London/New York: Routledge, pp. 196–220.
Kukulin, Il'ia (2016), 'Iz "padonkov" – v "patrioty": voskhod i zakat odnoi internet-subkul'tury v "silovom pole" sovremennogo rossiiskogo politicheskogo rezhima', *Ab Imperio* 1, pp. 223–76.
Kupina, Nataliia (1995), *Totalitarnyi iazyk: slovar' i iazykovye reaktsii*, Ekaterinburg: ZUUNC.
Kupina, Nataliia (ed.) (1999a), *Kul'turno-rechevaia situatsiia v sovremennoi Rossii*, Ekatarinburg: Izdatel'stvo Ural'skogo universiteta.
Kupina, Nataliia (1999b), *Iazykovoe soprotivlenie v kontekste totalitarnoi kul'tury*, Ekaterinburg: Izdatel'stvo Ural'skogo universiteta.
Laletina, Alla (2014), 'Kak moskovskie teatry gotoviatsia k zapretu netsenzurnoi leksiki', *Interfaks*, 23 June, <http://www.interfax.ru/culture/382199> (last accessed 20 June 2016).
Levin, Iurii (1996), 'Ob obstsennykh vyrazheniiakh russkogo iazyka', in Nikolai Bogomolov (ed.), *Anti-mir russkoi kul'tury: iazyk, fol'klor, literatura*, Moscow: Ladomir, pp. 108–20.
Levin, Iurii and Boris Tomashevskii (1954), *Russkie pisateli o iazyke (XVIII–XX vv.)*, Leningrad: Sovetskii pisatel'.
Levinson, Aleksei (2012), 'Eto ne srednii klass – eto vse', *Vedomosti*, 21 February, <http://www.vedomosti.ru/opinion/articles/2012/02/21/eto_ne_srednij_klass_eto_vse> (last accessed 20 June 2016).
Levontina, Irina (2005), 'Bukva i zakon: sudebnaia lingvisticheskaia ekspertiza', *Otechestvennye zapiski* 2, <http://www.strana-oz.ru/2005/2/bukva-i-zakon-sudebnaya-lingvisticheskaya-ekspertiza> (last accessed 20 June 2016).
Levontina, Irina (2010), *Russkii so slovarem*, Moscow: Azbukovnik.

Levontina, Irina (2015), *O chem rech'*, with a preface by Liudmila Ulitskaia, Moscow: Ast.
Lipovetskii, Mark (2001), 'Sled Kysi', *Iskusstvo kino* 2, <http://kinoart.ru/archive/2001/02/n2-article21> (last accessed 7 September 2016).
Lipovetskii, Mark (2010), *Paralogii: transformatsii (post)modernistskogo diskursa v russkoi kul'ture 1920–2000-kh godov*, Moscow: Novoe literaturnoe obozrenie.
Lipovetsky, Mark (2011), 'Post-Soviet literature between realism and postmodernism', in Evgeny Dobrenko and Marina Balina (eds), *The Cambridge Companion to Twentieth-Century Russian Literature*, Cambridge: Cambridge University Press, pp. 175–94.
Lipovetsky, Mark (2015), 'Postmodernist novel', in Evgeny Dobrenko and Mark Lipovetsky (eds), *Russian Literature since 1991*, Cambridge: Cambridge University Press, pp. 145–66.
Loxley, James (2007), *Performativity*, London/New York: Routledge.
Lucy, John A. (ed.) (1993), *Reflexive Language: Reported Speech and Metapragmatics*, Cambridge: Cambridge University Press.
Lukin, Evgenii (2012), 'Manifest Partii Natsional-Lingvistov', *Zhurnal samizdat*, Biblioteka Maksima Moshkova, <http://samlib.ru/c/cenzor/rusyz.shtml> (last accessed 20 June 2016).
Lundby, Knut (2009), 'Introduction: "Mediatization" as key', in Knut Lundby (ed.), *Mediatization: Concept, Changes, Consequences*, New York: Peter Lang, pp. 1–18.
Lunde, Ingunn (2008), 'LIS (Lingua imperii sovietici): filologiens håndtering av den nære språklige fortid i Russland', in Ingunn Lunde and Susanna Witt (eds), *Terminal Øst: Totalitære og posttotalitære diskurser*, Oslo: Spartacus, pp. 169–83.
Lunde, Ingunn (2009), 'Performative metalanguage: Negotiating norms through verbal action', in Ingunn Lunde and Martin Paulsen (eds), *From Poets to Padonki: Linguistic Authority and Norm Negotiation in Modern Russian Culture* (Slavica Bergensia 9), Bergen: Department of Foreign Languages, pp. 110–28.
Lunde, Ingunn (2016), '"A revolution for Russia's words": Rhetoric and style in Mixail Šiškin's political essays', *Zeitschrift für Slawistik* 61 (2), pp. 249–61.
Lunde, Ingunn and Martin Paulsen (eds) (2009a), *From Poets to Padonki: Linguistic Authority and Norm Negotiation in Modern Russian Culture* (Slavica Bergensia 9), Bergen: Department of Foreign Languages.
Lunde, Ingunn and Martin Paulsen (2009b), 'Introduction', in Ingunn Lunde and Martin Paulsen (eds), *From Poets to Padonki: Linguistic Authority and Norm Negotiation in Modern Russian Culture* (Slavica Bergensia 9), Bergen: Department of Foreign Languages, pp. 7–17.
Lunde, Ingunn and Tine Roesen (eds) (2006), *Landslide of the Norm: Language Culture in Post-Soviet Russia* (Slavica Bergensia 6), Bergen: Department of Foreign Languages.
'Mad World' (2001), video of Gary Jules and Michael Andrews's cover version of *Mad World*, directed by Michel Gondry, <http://www.youtube.com/watch?v=4N3N1MlvVc4 htm> (last accessed 30 June 2016).
Makanin, Vladimir [1999] (2010), *Andegraund, ili Geroi nashego vremeni*, Moscow: Eksmo.
'Manifezd antigramatnasti' (1999), <http://www.guelman.ru/slava/manifest/istochniki/shelli.htm> (last accessed 30 June 2016).
Mechkovskaia, Nina (2005), 'Postsovetskii russkii iazyk: novye cherty v sotsiolingvisticheskom statuse', *Russian Linguistics* 29 (1), pp. 49–70.
Menzel, Birgit (2001), *Bürgerkrieg um Worte: Die russische Literaturkritik der Perestrojka*, Cologne: Boehlau Verlag.
Menzel, Birgit (2005), 'Writing, reading and selling literature in Russia 1986–2004', in

Stephen Lovell and Birgit Menzel (eds), *Reading for Entertainment in Contemporary Russia: Post-Soviet Popular Literature in Historical Perspective*, Munich: Otto Sagner, pp. 39–56.

Meyers, Walter E. (1980), *Aliens and Linguists: Language Study and Science Fiction*, Athens, GA: University of Georgia Press.

Mikhailova, Tatiana (2011), 'Glamour à la Oksana Robski', in Helena Goscilo and Vlad Strukov (eds), *Celebrity and Glamour in Contemporary Russia: Shocking Chic*, London: Routledge, pp. 90–104.

Milroy, James (2001), 'Language ideologies and the consequences of standardization', *Journal of Sociolinguistics* 5 (4), pp. 530–55.

Milroy, James and Lesley Milroy (1985), *Authority in Language*, London/New York: Routledge.

Mohr, Dunja M. (2009), '"The tower of babble": The role and function of fictive languages in utopian and dystopian fiction', in Ralph Pordzik (ed.), *Futurescapes: Space in Utopian and Science Fiction Discourses*, Amsterdam/New York: Rodopi, pp. 225–48.

Mokienko, Valerii and Tat'iana Nikitina (1998), *Tolkovyi slovar' iazyka Sovdepiia*, Moscow: Folio Press (2nd edition: Ast, 2005).

Morozova, Tat'iana (2013), 'Evgenii Vodolazkin: Lavr', *Znamia* 4, <http://magazines.russ.ru/znamia/2013/4/m18.html> (last accessed 7 September 2016).

Morris, Jeremy (2013), *Mastering Chaos: The Metafictional Worlds of Evgeny Popov*, Oxford/Bern: Peter Lang.

Müller, Daniel (2013), 'Das Russische als Standardsprachentyp: Empirische Untersuchungen zur Anglisierung und Substandardisierung', in Daniel Müller and Monika Wingender (eds), *Typen slavischer Standardsprachen: Theoretische, methodische und empirische Zugänge*, Wiesbaden: Harrassowitz, pp. 39–66.

Nabokov, Vladimir (1944), *Three Russian Poets*, New York: New Directions.

Naralenkova, Ol'ga (2014), 'Mikhalkov vystupil protiv total'nogo zapreta mata v kino', *Rossiiskaia gazeta*, 28 June, <http://www.rg.ru/2014/06/28/mmkf-site.html> (last accessed 30 June 2016).

Nikolina, Natal'ia (ed.) (2000), *Russkie pisateli XVIII–XIX vekov o iazyke: khrestomatiia*, 2 vols, Moscow: Russkoe slovo.

Nikolina, Natal'ia (ed.) (2012), *Russkie pisateli o iazyke: XIX–nachalo XX vv*, Moscow: Russkoe slovo.

Norman, Boris (2006), *Igra na graniakh iazyka*, Moscow: Flinta/Nauka.

Offord, Derek, Gensine Argent and Vladislav Rjéoutski (2015a), 'Foreign-language use in Russia during the long eighteenth century', *The Russian Review* 74 (1), pp. 1–68.

Offord, Derek, Lara Ryazanova-Clarke, Vladislav Rjeoutski and Gesine Argent (eds) (2015b), *French and Russian in Imperial Russia*, vols 1–2, Edinburgh: Edinburgh University Press.

'Organizatora kontserta' (2016), 'Organizatora kontserta gruppy "Leningrad" oshtrafovali za mat', *Russkaia sluzhba*, BBC, 5 August, <http://www.bbc.com/russian/news-36983589> (last accessed 5 August 2016)

'Osnovy' (2014), 'Osnovy gosudarstvennoi kul'turnoi politiki', <http://news.kremlin.ru/media/events/files/41d526a877638a8730eb.pdf> (last accessed 5 August 2016).

Oushakine, Serguei Alex. (2015), '(Post)Ideological novel', in Evgeny Dobrenko and Mark Lipovetsky (eds), *Russian Literature since 1991*, Cambridge: Cambridge University Press, pp. 45–65.

'Panikhida' (2014), 'Panikhida po matu: v Barnaule zavtra prostiatsia s krepkimi

vyrazheniiami', *Politsib.ru*, 29 June, <http://www.politsib.ru/news/72233> (last accessed 30 June 2016).
Panov, Mikhail (ed.) (1968), *Russkii iazyk i sovetskoe obshchestvo*, Moscow: Nauka.
Paulsen, Martin (2009), *Hegemonic Language and Literature: Russian Metadiscourse on Language in the 1990s*, PhD thesis, University of Bergen.
Paulsen, Martin and Vera Zvereva (2014), 'Testing and contesting Russian Twitter', in Michael S. Gorham, Ingunn Lunde and Martin Paulsen (eds), *Digital Russia: The Language, Culture and Politics of New Media Communication*, London/New York: Routledge, pp. 88–104.
Pavlenko, Aneta (2008), 'Russian in Post-Soviet countries', *Russian Linguistics* 32 (1), pp. 59–80.
'Pervoe chtenie' (2013), 'O proekte federal'nogo zakona "O vnesenii izmenenii v stat'iu 3 Federal'nogo zakona 'O gosudarstvennom iazyke Rossiiskoi Federatsii'" i otdel'nye zakonodatel'nye akty Rossiiskoi Federatsii v sviazi s sovershenstvovaniem pravovogo regulirovaniia v sfere ispol'zovaniia russkogo iazyka', transcript from the Duma hearings, 12 April, <http://api.duma.gov.ru/api/transcript/190238-6> (last accessed 30 June 2016).
Pikhurova, Anna (2006), *Sud'ba sovetizmov v russkom iazyke kontsa XX–XXI vekov (na materiale slovarei i tekstov)*, PhD thesis, University of Saratov.
'Pip-pip-pip' (2014), 'Pip-pip-pip', *Lenta.ru*, 1 July, <http://lenta.ru/video/2014/07/01/pip/> (last accessed 15 June 2015).
'Pisateli o iazyke' (2005), *Otechestvennye zapiski* 2, <http://www.strana-oz.ru/2005/2/pisateli-o-yazyke> (last accessed 30 June 2016).
Plutser-Sarno, Aleksei (2000), 'Russkii vorovskoi slovar' kak kul'turnyj fenomen', *Logos: filosofsko-literaturnyi zhurnal* 23 (2), pp. 209–17.
Plutser-Sarno, Aleksei (2001), *Bol'shoi slovar' mata: opyt postroeniia spravochno-bibliograficheskoi bazy dannykh leksicheskikh i frazeologicheskikh znachenii slova 'khui'*, St Petersburg: Limbus.
Plutser-Sarno, Aleksei (2005), *Bol'shoi slovar' mata: opyt postroeniia spravochno-bibliograficheskoi bazy dannykh leksicheskikh i frazeologicheskikh znachenij slova 'pizda'*, St Petersburg: Limbus.
Popov, Evgenii [1993] (2001), *Nakanune nakanune*, Moscow: Geleos.
Popov, Evgenii [1999] (2003), *Podlinnaia istoriia 'Zelenykh muzykantov'*, Moscow: Vagrius.
Popov, Yevgeny (1993), 'The silhouette of truth', trans. Michael Finke and Anatoly Vishevsky, *World Literature Today* 67 (1), pp. 37–9.
Porter, Robert (1994), *Russia's Alternative Prose*, Oxford: Berg.
'Poslanie Prezidenta' (2012), 'Poslanie Prezidenta Federal'nomu Sobraniiu', <http://www.kremlin.ru/transcripts/17118> (last accessed 30 June 2016).
'Pro iazyk "padonkov"' (2006–), *Liubov' i nenavist'*, <http://www.lovehate.ru/opinions/67727/1> (last accessed 30 June 2016).
Punsh, Eva (2014), 'Vse my vyrosli iz russkogo mata', *Novaia gazeta, Sankt-Peterburg*, 2 July, <http://novayagazeta.spb.ru/articles/8894/> (last accessed 30 June 2016).
'Rasstrel'nyi grammaticheskii spisok' (2013), *Lurkomor'e*, <http://lurkmore.to/Расстрельный_грамматический_список> (last accessed 30 June 2016).
Robski, Oksana (2005), *Casual*, Moscow: Rosmen.
Robski, Oksana (2006), *Casual*, trans. Antonina W. Bouis, New York: HarperCollins.
Rubinshtein, Lev (2009), 'Semechki glamurnye', *Grani.ru*, 9 February, <http://graniru.org/Politics/Russia/m.147372.html> (last accessed 16 June 2016).

Rudova, Larissa (2008a), 'Russland – in Glamour vereint', *kultura* 6, pp. 2–3, <http://www.kultura-rus.uni-bremen.de/kultura_dokumente/ausgaben/deutsch/kultura-2008-06.pdf> (last accessed 15 June 2016).

Rudova, Larissa (2008b), 'Die glamourösen Heldinnen der Oksana Robski', *kultura* 6, pp. 11–13, <http://www.kultura-rus.uni-bremen.de/kultura_dokumente/ausgaben/deutsch/kultura-2008-06.pdf> (last accessed 15 June 2016).

Rutten, Ellen, Julie Fedor and Vera Zvereva (eds) (2013), *Memory, Conflict and New Media: Web Wars in Post-Socialist States*, London/New York: Routledge.

Ryazanova-Clarke, Lara (2006a), '"The crystallization of structures": Linguistic culture in Putin's Russia', in Ingunn Lunde and Tine Roesen (eds), *Landslide of the Norm: Language Culture in Post-Soviet Russia* (Slavica Bergensia 6), Bergen: Department of Foreign Languages, pp. 31–63.

Ryazanova-Clarke, Lara (2006b), '"The state turning to language": Power and identity in Russian language policy today', *Russian Language Journal* 56, pp. 37–55, <http://rlj.americancouncils.org/issues/56/files/Ryazanova-Clarke_2006.pdf> (last accessed 30 June 2016).

Ryazanova-Clarke, Lara (2015), 'Linguistic mnemonics: The communist language variety in contemporary Russian public discourse', in Petre Petrov and Lara Ryazanova-Clarke (eds), *The Vernaculars of Communism: Language, Ideology and Power in the Soviet Union and Eastern Europe*, London/New York: Routledge, pp. 169–95.

Ryazanova-Clarke, Lara and Terence Wade (1999), *The Russian Language Today*, London/New York: Routledge.

Ryklin, Mikhail (1992), *Terrorologiki*, Tartu/Moscow: Eidos.

Samoilova, Dasha (2014), 'Proekt "Abanamat" v Kazani ili Proshchanie s russkim matom', *Sobaka.ru*, 1 July, <http://www.sobaka.ru/kzn/photo/photo/24855> (last accessed 30 June 2016).

Sandomirskaja, Irina (2015), 'Aesopian language: The politics and poetics of naming the unnameable', in Petre Petrov and Lara Ryazanova-Clarke (eds), *The Vernaculars of Communism: Language, Ideology and Power in the Soviet Union and Eastern Europe*, London/New York: Routledge, pp. 63–87.

Saprykin, Iurii, Igor' Mal'tsev, Arsenii Zhiliaev and Denis Boiarinov (2012), 'Kreativnyi klass v Rossii: kto vse eti liudi?', *Colta.ru*, 28 August, <http://archives.colta.ru/docs/4829> (last accessed 30 June 2016).

Sarnov, Benedikt (2002), *Nash sovetskii novoiaz: malen'kaia entsiklopediia real'nogo sotsializma*, Moscow: Materik (2nd edn: Eksmo, 2005).

Sauer, Christoph (1995), 'Sprachwissenschaft und NS-Faschismus: Lehren aus der sprachwissenschaftlichen Erforschung des Sprachgebrauchs deutscher Nationalsozialisten und Propagandisten für den mittel- und osteuropäischen Umbruch?', in Klaus Steinke (ed.), *Die Sprache der Diktaturen und Diktatoren*, Heidelberg: Winter, pp. 9–96.

Scharlaj, Marina (2014), '*Fuck.ru* und andere Szenen des Obszönen', in Hagen Pitsch (ed.), *Linguistische Beiträge zur Slavistik: XXI. JungslavistInnen-Treffen in Göttingen 13.–15. September 2012*, Munich: Otto Sagner, pp. 155–76.

Schieffelin, Bambi B., Kathryn A. Woolard and Paul V. Kroskrity (eds) (1998), *Language Ideologies: Practice and Theory*, New York/Oxford: Oxford University Press.

Schmid, Ulrich (2015), *Technologien der Seele: vom Verfertigen der Wahrheit in der russischen Gegenwartskultur*, Berlin: Suhrkamp.

Sebba, Mark (2007), *Spelling and Society: The Culture and Politics of Orthography around the World*, Cambridge: Cambridge University Press.

Selishchev, Afanasii (1928), *Iazyk revoliutsionnoi epokhi: iz nabliudenii nad russkim iazykom poslednikh let, 1917–1926*, Moscow: Rabotnik prosveshcheniia.

Shaposhnikov, Vladimir (1998), *Russkaia rech' 1990-kh: sovremennaia Rossiia v iazykovom otobrazhenii*, Moscow: MALP.

Shapovalova, Nadezhda (2008), 'ORFO-art kak primer karnaval'nogo obshcheniia v virtual'noi real'nosti', *Filologicheskie etiudy: sbornik nauchnykh statei molodykh uchenykh* 2 (2), pp. 292–5, <http://ec-dejavu.net/o/Orfo-art.html> (last accessed 30 June 2016).

Shargunov, Sergei (2013), *1993*, Moscow: Ast.

Shepelin, Il'ia (2013), 'Kak kuiutstia dukhovnye skrepy', *Slon.ru*, 14 November, <http://slon.ru/russia/kak_kuyutsya_dukhovnye_skrepy-1012408.xhtml> (last accessed 30 June 2016).

Shishkin, Mikhail (2005), *Venerin volos*, Moscow: Vagrius.

Shishkin, Mikhail (2012), *Maidenhair*, trans. Marian Schwartz, Rochester: Open Letter.

Shumarina, Marina (2011), *Iazyk v zerkale khudozhestvennogo teksta: metaiazykovaia refleksiia v proizvedeniiakh russkoi prozy*, Moscow: Flinta/Nauka.

Shvedova, Natal'ia (ed.) (1980), *Russkaia grammatika*, Moscow: Nauka.

Shyshkin, Ivan (2006), '"Preved, krosavchegi!" ili, Apologiia "padonkov"', *Zerkalo nedeli* 13, <http://gazeta.zn.ua/SOCIETY/preved,_krosavchegi,_ili_apologiya_padonkov.html> (last accessed 30 June 2016).

Silverstein, Michael (1998), 'The uses and utility of ideology', in Bambi B. Schieffelin, Kathryn A. Woolard and Paul V. Kroskrity (eds), *Language Ideologies: Practice and Theory*, New York/Oxford: Oxford University Press, pp. 123–45.

Sisk, David W. (1997), *Transformations of Language in Modern Dystopias*, Westport, CT: Greenwood.

'Snachala chitaem' (2013), 'Snachala chitaem tekst posta i varianty, zatem golosuem', *Grammar Nation*, group on VKontakte, <http://vk.com/wall-25451458?q=нецензурной%20брани&w=wall-25451458_205830> (last accessed 30 June 2016).

Sokolova, Lidiia (2014), 'Abanamat! V Barnaule poproshchaiutsia s netsenzurnoi leksikoi, zapreshchennoi zakonom RF', *Altapress.ru*, 29 June, <http://altapress.ru/story/136591?viewcomments=1#opinions> (last accessed 30 June 2016).

Sokolovskii, Dmitrii (2008), *Bibliia padonkov, ili Uchebneg albanskogo iazyka*, Moscow: Folio SP.

Solzhenitsyn, Aleksandr (1990), *Russkii slovar' iazykovogo rasshireniia*, Moscow: Nauka.

Sorokin, Vladimir (1992), 'Tekst kak narkotik', in Vladimir Sorokin, *Sbornik rasskazov*, Moscow: Russlit, pp. 119–26.

Sorokin, Vladimir (2010), 'Monoklon', in *Monoklon*, Moscow: Ast, pp. 7–19.

Sorokin, Vladimir and Nina Ivanova (2010), 'Dlia pisatelia zdes' – El'dorado', *TimeOut Moskva* 36, <http://www.timeout.ru/msk/feature/14452> (last accessed 15 April 2015).

'Sovetskii iazyk' (2005), BBC Russian Service forum, 11 October, <http://news.bbc.co.uk/hi/russian/talking_point/newsid_4291000/4291692.stm> (last accessed 6 June 2016).

Stalin, Iosif (1950), *Marksizm i voprosy iazykoznaniia*, Moscow: Gospolitizdat.

Stiazhkin, Denis (2014), 'Chtetsy v zashchitu mata v iskusstve – "Abanamat" (foto)', LiveJournal blog *Vestnik svobody*, 1 July, <http://styazshkin.livejournal.com/988578.html> (last accessed 6 June 2016).

Tchouboukov-Pianca, Florence (1995), *Die Konzeptualisierung der Graphomanie in der russischsprachigen postmodernen Literatur*, Munich: Otto Sagner.
Tolstaia, Tat'iana (2005), *Kys'*, Moscow: Eksmo.
Tolstaia, Tat'iana (2012a), 'Na lipovoi noge', in Tat'iana Tolstaia, *Den': lichnoe*, Moscow: Eksmo, pp. 301–98.
Tolstaia, Tat'iana (2012b), 'Russkii mir', in Tat'iana Tolstaia, *Den': lichnoe*, Moscow: Eksmo, pp. 445–59.
Tolstaia, Tat'iana and Andrei Zimin (2000), 'TT', *Afisha*, 4 September, <http://daily.afisha.ru/archive/vozduh/archive/tt_kis/> (last accessed 8 August 2016).
Tolstaya, Tatyana (2003), *The Slynx*, trans. Jamey Gambrell, New York: New York Review Books.
Tomashevskii, Boris (1951), 'Iazyk i literatura', in Aleksandr Egolin (ed.), *Voprosy literaturovedeniia v svete trudov I. V. Stalina po iazykoznaniiu*, Moscow: Izdatel'stvo akademii nauk SSSR, pp. 174–94.
Uffelmann, Dirk (2006), '*Led tronulsia*: The overlapping periods in Vladimir Sorokin's work from the materialization of metaphors to fantastic substantialism', in Ingunn Lunde and Tine Roesen (eds), *Landslide of the Norm: Language Culture in Post-Soviet Russia* (Slavica Bergensia 6), Bergen: Department of Foreign Languages, pp. 82–107.
Ushakov, Dmitrii (1935–40), *Tolkovyi slovar' russkogo iazyka*, Moscow: Gosudarstvennyi institut 'Sovetskaia entsiklopediia'.
Uspenskii, Boris (1994), 'Mifologicheskii aspekt russkoi ekspressivnoi frazeologii', in Boris Uspenskii, *Izbrannye trudy*, vol. 2, Moscow: Gnozis, pp. 53–128.
Uspenskij, Boris A. (1984), 'The language program of N. M. Karamzin and its historical antecedents', in Riccardo Picchio and Harvey Goldblatt (eds), *Aspects of the Slavic Language Question*, vol. 2: *East Slavic*, New Haven, CT: Yale Concilium on International and Area Studies, pp. 235–96.
Vepreva, Irina (2005), *Iazykovaia refleksiia v postsovetskuiu epokhu*, Moscow: Olma Press.
Verbitskaia, Liudmila and Vladimir Kuznechevskii (2005), 'Sokhranim russkii iazyk – sokhranim Rossiiu', *Gudok*, 21 September.
Vezhbitska [Wierzbicka], Anna (1993), 'Antitotalitarnyi iazyk v Pol'she: mekhanizmy iazykovoi samooborony', *Voprosy iazykoznaniia* 4, pp. 107–25.
'V Novosibirske' (2014), 'V Novosibirske proshel festival' netsenzurnogo iskusstva "Khu iz"', *Argumenty i fakty*, 1 July, <http://www.nsk.aif.ru/culture/1199067> (last accessed 30 June 2016).
Vodolazkin, Eugene (2016), *Laurus*, trans. Lisa C. Hayden, London: One World.
Vodolazkin, Evgenii (2012), *Lavr*, Moscow: Ast.
Vodolazkin, Evgenii and Kseniia Luchenko (2014), 'Evgenii Vodolazkin: chelovek v tsentre literatury', *Pravoslavie i mir*, 29 January, <http://www.pravmir.ru/chelovek-v-centre-literatury/#ixzz3alHy95Vu> (last accessed 7 September 2016).
von Staden, Heinrich (1967), *The Land and Government of Muscovy: A Sixteenth-Century Account*, ed. Thomas Esper, Stanford: Stanford University Press.
Votrin, Valerii (2012), *Logoped*, Moscow: Novoe literaturnoe obozrenie.
VTsIOM (2012), 'Sotsial'nyi portret protestnogo dvizheniia v Moskve', Press-vypusk no. 2056, <http://wciom.ru/index.php?id=236&uid=112859> (last accessed 30 June 2016).
Wachtel, Andrew (2006), *Remaining Relevant after Communism: The Role of the Writer in Eastern Europe*, Chicago: University of Chicago Press.
Weiss, Daniel (1986), 'Was ist neu am "newspeak"? Reflexionen zur Sprache der Politik

in der Sowjetunion', in Renate Rathmayr (ed.), *Slavistische Linguistik 1985: Referate des XI. Konstanzer Slavistischen Arbeitstreffens*, Munich: Otto Sagner, pp. 247–325.

Weiss, Daniel (2000), 'Der posttotalitäre politische Diskurs im heutigen Rußland', in Lew Zybatow (ed.), *Sprachwandel in der Slavia: Die slavischen Sprachen an der Schwelle zum 21. Jahrhundert: Ein internationales Handbuch*, vol. 1, Frankfurt am Main: Peter Lang, pp. 209–46.

Weiss, Daniel (2008) 'Umestno li nakazyvat' za publichnoe upotreblenie mata? Obshchestvennoe mnenie i zdravyi razum lingvistov', *Scando-Slavica* 54, pp. 198–222.

Weiss, Daniel (2009) 'Sudebnaia ekspertiza i vklad lingvista v interpretatsiiu zakona', in Ingunn Lunde and Martin Paulsen (eds), *From Poets to Padonki: Linguistic Authority and Norm Negotiation in Modern Russian Culture* (Slavica Bergensia 9), Bergen: Department of Foreign Languages, pp. 252–74.

Wingender, Monika (2003), 'Überlegungen zur Weiterentwicklung der Theorie der Standardsprache', in Wolfgang Gladrow (ed.), *Die slawischen Sprachen im aktuellen Funktionieren und historischen Kontakt: Beiträge zum XIII Internationalen Slavistenkongreß vom 15. bis 21. August 2003 in Ljubljana*, Frankfurt am Main: Peter Lang, pp. 133–52.

Wingender, Monika (2013), 'Modell zur Beschreibung von Standardsprachentypen', in Daniel Müller and Monika Wingender (eds), *Typen slavischer Standardsprachen: Theoretische, methodische und empirische Zugänge*, Wiesbaden: Harrassowitz, pp. 19–38.

Yurchak, Alexei (2006), *Everything Was Forever, until It Was No More: The Last Soviet Generation*, Princeton: Princeton University Press.

'Zakon 2005' (2005), 'Zakon o gosudarstvennom iazyke Rossiiskoi Federatsii', <http://www.gramota.ru/spravka/docs/16_3> (last accessed 30 June 2016).

'Zakon 2014' (2014), 'O gosudarstvennom iazyke Rossiiskoi Federatsii', <http://pravo.gov.ru/proxy/ips/?doc_itself=&&nd=102092715&&page=1&rdk=2#Io> (last accessed 30 June 2016).

Zemskaia, Elena (ed.) (1996), *Russkii iazyk kontsa XX stoletiia (1985–1995)*, Moscow: Iazyki russkoi kul'tury.

Zhelnina, Anna (2014), ' "Tusovka", kreativnost' i pravo na gorod: gorodskoe publichnoe prostranstvo v Rossii do i posle protestnoi volny 2011–2012 godov', *Stasis* 2 (1), pp. 260–95, <http://stasisjournal.net/images/zhelnina_rus.pdf> (last accessed 30 June 2016).

Zorin, Andrei (1996), 'Legalizatsiia obstsennoi leksiki i ee kul'turnye posledstviia', in Nikolai Bogomolov (ed.), *Anti-mir russkoi kul'tury: Iazyk, fol'klor, literatura*, Moscow: Ladomir, pp. 121–39.

Zubova, Liudmila (1998), 'Sovremennaia poeziia na pole brani mezhdu sintagmatikoi i paradigmatikoi', *Materialy XXVII mezhvuzovskoi nauchno-metodicheskoi konferentsii prepodavatelei i aspirantov* 12 (2), pp. 5–12.

Zubova, Liudmila (2000), *Sovremennaia russkaia poeziia v kontekste istorii iazyka*, Moscow: Novoe literaturnoe obozrenie.

Zubova, Liudmila (2010), *Iazyki sovremennoi poezii*, Moscow: Novoe literaturnoe obozrenie.

Zubova, Svetlana (2014), 'V Peterburge poety ustroili "pominki" netsenzurnoi leksiki', *Lenizdat.ru*, 1 July, <http://lenizdat.ru/articles/1121695/> (last accessed 30 June 2016).

Zvereva, Vera (2009), '*Iazyk padonkaf*: diskussii pol'zovatelei Runeta', in Ingunn Lunde and Martin Paulsen (eds), *From Poets to Padonki: Linguistic Authority and Norm*

Negotiation in Modern Russian Culture (Slavica Bergensia 9), Bergen: Department of Foreign Languages, pp. 49–79.

Zybatow, Lew (1995), *Russisch im Wandel: Die russische Sprache seit der Perestrojka* (Slavistische Veröffentlichungen 80), Wiesbaden: Harrassowitz.

Zybatow, Lew (ed.) (2000), *Sprachwandel in der Slavia: Die slavischen Sprachen an der Schwelle zum 21. Jahrhundert: Ein internationales Handbuch*, 2 vols, Frankfurt am Main: Peter Lang.

Zykov, Vladimir and Aleksandr Kondrat'ev (2013), 'Roskomnadzor nakazhet SMI tol'ko za chetyre maternykh slova', *Izvestiia*, 25 December, <http://izvestia.ru/news/563178> (last accessed 30 June 2016).

Social network groups

Abanamat, Barnaul, *VKontakte*, <http://vk.com/abanamatbarnaul>.
Abanamat, Kazan, *VKontakte*, <http://vk.com/abanamatrf>.
Abanamat FB, *Facebook*, <http://www.facebook.com/abanamatrf>.
Abanamat, Moscow, *VKontakte*, <http://vk.com/abanavrot>.
Abanamat, Moscow FB, *Facebook*, <http://www.facebook.com/events/656398377776398>.
Abanamat, Naberezhnye Chelny, *VKontakte*, <http://vk.com/abanamat_nch>.
Abanamat, Novosibirsk, *VKontakte*, <http://vk.com/overnah> and <http://vk.com/event73199051>.
Abanamat, St Petersburg, *VKontakte*, <http://vk.com/abaspb>.

Index

aggression *see* verbal aggression
Akhmatova, Anna, 46
Aksenov, Vasilii, 107
Aleshkovskii, Iuz, 49
alphabet, 32, 143, 145–6, 148, 151, 164n
Amelin, Maksim, 73, 79–80
Andersen, Henning, 8
Andreev, Aleksei, 41n
Andrews, Michael, 94
Androutsopoulos, Jannis, 2
anecdotes, 10, 19–20, 23, 27n, 109
anti-utopia *see* dystopia
archaism, 9, 119, 121, 140, 152, 157–8, 202
Austin, John, 200
authenticity, 52, 56, 116–17
Azbukovniki, 148, 151

Baitov, Nikolai, 108
Baranov, Anatolii, 77
Basinskii, Pavel, 159
Bauman, Zygmunt, 200
bespredel ('lawlessness'), 79, 88
bezdukhovnost' ('lack of spiritual culture'), 88, 95
birch-bark letters, 149, 151, 153, 156
Bitov, Andrei, 70, 75, 107
Blok, Aleksandr, 143
Borden, Richard, 118, 134n
Borenstein, Eliot, 138
Bourdieu, Pierre, 29–30, 93
Boym, Svetlana, 113
Brodsky, Joseph, 46, 89
Bulgakov, Mikhail, 46, 94
Burkhart, Dagmar, 120
Butler, Judith, 203

Cameron, Deborah, 6
Catherine the Great, 33
censorship, 4, 46, 74, 76, 87–90, 93–4, 100n, 168, 195
Chaadaev, Petr, 183, 193n
chastushki, 19–20, 111

chernukha, 56
Chukhontsev, Oleg, 70
Chukovskii, Kornei, 110
Church Slavonic, 32–3, 40n, 149–52, 154, 160, 163n, 164n; *see also* archaism
cliché, 12, 18, 48, 62, 88, 110–11, 118, 120–1, 128, 140
Coil, 94
colloquial language, 8, 50–2, 110, 118, 140, 168, 179, 181
Conceptualism, 46, 49, 107
Coupland, Nikolas, 2–4, 9
creativity *see* linguistic creativity
cultural policy, 53, 60, 88, 95
cultural reflexivity, 3, 9

Derrida, Jacques, 203n
dialect, 113–15, 93, 140, 159, 199
diminutives, 181–2
Dmitriev, Andrei, 78
Dobrenko, Evgenii, 47–8
Dovlatov, Sergei, 99n
dukhovnye skrepy ('spiritual ties'), 95–6
dystopia, 12, 137–48, 157–8, 161n

Ekho Moskvy, 7
Eppel', Asar, 78
Epstein, Mikhail, 71, 114–15
Ermakov, Oleg, 73
Ermoshin, Fedor, 80, 81n
Erofeev, Venedikt, 46, 94
Erofeev, Viktor, 46, 49, 53, 62, 83n, 107
errative, 35
Eshelman, Raoul, 136n
ethics, 5, 46–7, 62, 78, 87, 120–1, 131, 186, 188
ethnolinguistics, 183, 189–90
etymology, 181, 185
experimentation (linguistic and literary), 9, 47–8, 53, 60–1, 64, 76, 111, 120, 158, 172

Facebook, 38, 85, 90, 93, 100n
Fish, Stanley, 203n

INDEX

Florida, Richard, 103n
Florovskii, Pavel, 89
folk linguistics, 39, 181, 188, 197, 202
freedom of speech, 89–90, 97
French, 33, 81n

Gagarin, Iurii, 122–5, 127, 130
Galkovskii, Dmitrii, 108
Gandlevskii, Sergei, 75, 77
Germanika, Valeriia, 99n
Gigolashvili, Mikhail, 10–12, 167, 178–86, 188–90, 197–8, 202
glamour, literature of, 11, 52, 55–6
glasnost, 4, 195
Goethe, Johann Wolfgang von, 134n, 143
Gogol', Nikolai, 81
Gölz, Christine, 142, 144–5
Gorbachev, Mikhail, 4
Gorham, Michael S., 6, 35, 88
Gorlanova, Nina, 77
Goscilo, Helene, 139
Govorukhin, Stanislav, 84–5, 88, 90–1, 101n
grammar nazi movement, 11–12, 35, 38–9, 41n, 179, 182, 184–6, 188–90, 193n, 194n, 197, 202
Gramota.ru, 7, 64
Granin, Dmitrii, 70
graphomania, 117–19, 128–9
grazhdanskii shrift, 32
Grigor'ev, Viktor, 61, 64, 73
grotesque devices, 49, 54, 109, 121, 131, 172–3, 175, 177, 187, 190, 202
Groys, Boris, 61
Guseinov, Gasan, 17, 19, 35, 71, 119, 134n

hagiography, 32, 148–50
hate speech, 39
Haugen, Einar, 29
Heidegger, Martin, 51
historical novel, 50, 153, 156
humour, 12, 17–23, 39, 89, 94, 97, 99, 109, 112, 114–15, 117, 129, 145, 153, 157, 178, 190, 196

Iakemenko, Vasilii, 123
Iakovleva, Iana, 52
iazyk padonkov, 10–11, 35–9, 40n, 41n
identity *see* language: language and identity; national identity
ideological language, 23, 25–6, 48, 50, 128
Iduschie vmeste (Walking together), 123
intelligentsia, 47, 51, 56, 79, 81, 85, 93, 96–8, 141, 167, 148
irony, 18–23, 26, 37, 49, 74, 78, 81, 85, 93–4, 97–9, 108, 115, 117, 119, 128–9, 143–4, 152, 156, 158–60, 175, 178, 185, 199, 201
Iskander, Fasil, 107
iurodivyi, 148, 150–2, 156
Ivanov, Aleksei, 50

Jakobson, Roman, 60
jargon, 35, 50, 52, 62, 120–1, 180–1
Jules, Gary, 94

Karaulov, Iurii, 9
Karl Fuks, 85, 88, 94, 100n
Kenzheev, Bakhyta, 80–1
KGB, 112, 127
Kievan Caves Paterikon, 149
Klebanov, Sem, 90
Kochergin, Eduard, 52
Konchalovskii, Andrei, 99n
Konstantinov, Andrei, 98
Korobov, Vladimir, 108
Kovalev, Manuela, 99n
Krongauz, Maksim, 6, 26n, 40n, 56, 63, 65n, 78, 182
Krusanov, Pavel, 54
Krysin, Leonid, 6, 34
Kseniia of St Petersburg, 148–9
Kukulin, Il'ia, 40n
Kupina, Nataliia, 19–20
Kuznetsov, Il'ia, 92–3

language
  language and identity, 36, 62–3, 139, 142, 158, 178, 186–8, 197, 200, 202
  language and power, 29–31, 93, 98, 154, 167–9, 175–8, 186–90, 197–8
  language and time, 121–31, 137, 148–57, 159–61, 202
language change, 1–5, 10, 61, 71, 73–4, 78, 137, 169–70, 195; *see also* sociolinguistic change
language cultivation, 5, 7, 9, 13, 34, 37–8, 39, 64, 70–1, 74, 79–80, 100, 114, 167–70, 175–6, 186–8, 197
language culture, 1–2, 5–6, 9–10, 13, 17–27, 35, 45, 48, 71, 73, 80, 85, 107, 111, 113, 119, 127, 158, 172, 179, 201
language debates, 1–8, 10–12, 17, 31–2, 35, 37, 50, 57, 62–63, 65n, 69, 72, 74, 78, 81, 85, 88, 97, 107, 113–16, 128, 137, 157–8, 167, 169–70, 172, 178, 184–7, 189–90, 195, 197–8, 201–3
language ideologies, 3, 9–10, 39, 64, 167–94, 199–202
language legislation, 1, 5, 9, 13, 62–3, 70, 74, 81, 84–103, 167–9, 186–7, 195, 197–8, 202
language of literature *see* standard language *vs* language of literature
language planning *see* language policy
language policy, 3–4, 10–11, 37, 47, 62–3, 70–2, 74, 76, 79, 197; *see also* language legislation
Law on the Russian Language (2005), 63–4, 74, 81, 84, 86, 114, 167
Lenin, Vladimir, 33, 102n
Lermontov, Mikhail, 89, 143
Levin, Aleksandr, 80–1
Levin, Iurii, 77, 100n
Levinson, Aleksei, 103n
Levontina, Irina, 6, 83n
linguistic awareness, 38, 60, 93, 113, 121
linguistic creativity, 8, 36, 87, 114, 120, 161, 180–1, 189–90, 201; *see also* humour
linguistic diversity, 4–5, 35, 49, 76, 112–13, 149, 152–3, 157–8, 190, 197–8, 202
linguistic dystopia *see* dystopia

linguistic legacies, 9–10, 12, 17–18, 21–2, 25–6, 48, 62, 107–37, 197, 202
linguistic liberalisation, 1, 5, 172, 175, 186–7
linguistic memory, 10, 12, 17–28, 121, 125–7, 134n, 202
linguistic norms, 1, 11, 33, 37, 49, 61, 98, 114, 170
linguistic philosophy, 153–4
linguistic variation, 3, 10, 29–30, 32, 34, 50, 69, 85, 113, 115, 117, 120, 137, 140, 152–3, 158, 160, 176, 180–1, 187, 190, 197–8, 201–2; *see also* linguistic diversity; non-standard varieties
Lipovetsky, Mark, 50, 138, 145
literary criticism, 9, 47, 54, 62, 64
literature
  norm-maintaining role of, 1, 9, 59, 62, 64, 69
literary norm, 11, 50, 59–65; *see also* linguistic norms
literaturnyi iazyk see standard language
loanwords, 5, 33, 35, 45, 50, 62–3, 71, 80–1, 114–15, 157, 172, 183, 185
logocentrism, 52, 148, 153–4, 158, 175
Lomonosov, Mikhail, 32–3
Lucy, John, 6
Lukin, Evgenii, 194n
Lurkomor'e, 38

magical realism, 54
Makanin, Vladimir, 50–1, 70, 73
Mandel'shtam, Osip, 46, 143
Manifezd antigramatnasti ('Manifesto of antiliteracy'), 37, 41n
mass media, 4–5, 7, 9, 13n, 18, 36, 53, 72, 80, 87–9, 93–4, 97, 99n, 100, 170
mat see profanity
mediatisation, 3, 13n
Medinskii, Vladimir, 84
Medvedev, Dmitrii, 84, 90
Melikhov, Aleksandr, 75, 77
memory *see* linguistic memory
Menzel, Birgit, 62
metalanguage, 2–3, 6–9, 11, 13, 17–18, 32, 36, 38, 45, 48, 57, 108, 138, 140, 195–6, 198–203
  performative metalanguage, 8–9, 11, 13, 99, 195–6, 198–203
Mikhailova, Tat'iana, 55
Mikhalkov, Nikita, 84, 88
Milroy, Lesley and James, 30, 64, 74
Mokienko, Valerii, 19–20
Morozova, Tat'iana, 159
Morris, Jeremy, 129, 132n
Moshkov, Maksim, 194n
Müller, Daniel, 8
myth-making, 33, 48–9, 54, 119, 183

Narbikova, Valeriia, 49
Nashi (Ours), 123
national identity, 5, 32, 63, 156, 197
nationalist discourse, 53–4, 160
neologism, 119, 121, 140
new media, 3–4, 21, 47, 80
newspeak, 10, 12, 17–28, 62, 107, 110–12, 117, 119, 123–4, 129, 180

Nicholas I, 33
Nikitina, Tat'iana, 19–20
non-standard varieties, 4–6, 8–9, 11–12, 41n, 50, 62, 70–1, 85, 113–15, 117, 128, 157, 172, 197
norm-breaking, 11, 36–9, 48–9, 57, 61–2, 64, 198
norm negotiation, 2–3, 6–8, 10, 61, 129
norms *see* linguistic norms; orthoepic norms; social norms
nostalgia, 26, 53, 112–13, 117, 119, 137

orthoepic norms, 12, 168–71
orthography, 11–12, 33, 35–7, 39, 40, 152, 189
Osmolovskii, Anatolii, 102n
Otechestvennye zapiski, 70–1
Otroshenko, Vladislav, 72
Oushakine, Serguei, 53–4
Ozhegov, Sergei, 8

padonki see iazyk padonkov
Pakhomov, Sergei, 95
Panov, Mikhail, 34
parody, 108, 117
Pasternak, Boris, 46
patriotism, 18, 53, 63, 123, 160
Paul I, 33
Paulsen, Martin, 62
Pelevin, Viktor, 49–50, 53
perestroika, 1, 4–6, 9, 27, 46, 62, 71, 108, 128, 157, 169, 175, 186, 195
performative metalanguage *see* metalanguage
performativity, 200
Peter the Great, 32–3, 40n
Petrushevskaia, Liudmila, 49–50
P'etsukh, Viacheslav, 108
Platonov, Andrei, 20, 46
political discourse, 17–20, 22, 33, 54, 107, 119
Popov, Evgenii, 9–12, 49, 107–19, 128–9, 132n, 133n, 136n, 197, 202
postmodernism, 46, 48–50, 54, 57n, 111–12, 132n
Pravda, 21
Prigov, Dmitrii, 46, 107
Prilepin, Zakhar, 53
Primakov, Evgenii, 144
profanity (*mat*), 11, 36, 39, 49–50, 62, 76–8, 84–103, 113, 116, 140–1, 149, 158, 167, 179–80, 189, 196
Prokhanov, Aleksei, 53–4
prostorechie, 8, 113, 115, 133, 140, 143, 158, 202
public speaking, 4–5, 9, 45
purism, 5, 33, 62, 77–8, 114, 169–70, 172, 185, 188
Pushkin, Aleksandr, 33–4, 37, 88–9, 94–5, 98, 143, 146
Pussy Riot, 101n
Putin, Vladimir, 7, 53, 71, 88, 95–6, 100n, 123

Radio Svoboda, 19
Rakhmatullina, Zugura, 87
Robski, Oksana, 55–6
Roskomnadzor, 87, 94, 100n
Rubinshtein, Lev, 46, 56
Runet (Russian-language internet), 38–9, 189, 194n

Russian Academy of Sciences, 7, 39, 59, 77, 87, 96, 100, 148
'Russkii iazyk' federal target programme, 7, 64, 167
Russkii Mir Foundation, 71
Ryazanova-Clarke, Lara, 5, 63
Ryklin, Mikhail, 49

Saint-Exupéry, Antoine de, 153
samizdat, 107, 112
sarcasm, 23, 26, 96, 158
Sarnov, Benedikt, 19–20, 23, 26, 111
satire, 12, 17, 22, 25, 38, 112, 128, 141–3, 189–90
Searle, John, 203n
Sebba, Mark, 36
Sedgwick, Eve Kosofsky, 203n
Selishchev, Afanasii, 34
Shapovalova, Nadezhda, 37
Shargunov, Sergei, 53–4
Shishkin, Mikhail, 47, 50–2, 57n, 77
Shishkov, Aleksandr, 81
Shnurov, Sergei, 99n
Shumarina, Marina, 7
simultaneity of the non-simultaneous, 12, 128, 130–1, 202
slang, 4, 10, 18–19, 35–6, 38, 40n, 50–2, 62, 111, 113, 180–1, 201
Slapovskii, Aleksei, 50, 74, 78–9
slogans, 12, 17, 19, 22–3, 25–6, 36, 45, 48, 103, 121, 184, 188
Sobchak, Kseniia, 55
Socialist Realism, 51, 53, 111
social media, 7, 11, 47, 85, 89; *see also* Facebook; VKontakte
social norms, 3, 86, 91, 93, 98
sociolinguistic change, 1–4, 6, 9, 11, 31, 59, 195
sociolinguistics, 3, 6, 9, 29–30, 34, 99n, 181, 190, 198–9, 201
Solzhenitsyn, Aleksandr, 9, 46, 114–15
Sorokin, Vladimir, 9–12, 46, 48–9, 53, 62, 107, 119–28, 130–1, 187, 197, 202
Sots Art, 26, 48
Sovietism *see* newspeak
Sovietspeak *see* newspeak
Soviet Union of Writers, 71, 108
Staden, Heinrich von, 179, 193n
Stalin, Iosif, 33–4, 130
standard language, 4, 9–12, 29–41, 48–9, 59–65, 69–75, 77, 79, 85–6, 111, 113–15, 168, 170, 173, 175–6, 184, 196–8, 201–2
standard language ideology, 9, 39, 64
standard language model, 29–31, 197
standard language *vs* language of literature, 4, 9, 11, 33–4, 48, 50, 59–65, 70, 72–5, 79, 111, 157, 196
steb, 21
stereotypes, 128, 146, 182–4, 186

taboo, 45, 111
Tolstaia, Tat'iana, 9–12, 50, 137–48, 157–8, 162n, 164n, 169, 197–8, 202
Tsvetaeva, Marina, 46
Tsvetkov, Aleksei, 73, 75
Turgenev, Ivan, 37, 84–5, 101n, 112, 186

Uffelmann, Dirk, 187
Ulitskaia, Liudmila, 47, 50
Ushakov, Dmitrii, 20, 34
Uspenskii, Mikhail, 74, 77

Varlaam Keretskii, 148–9
Vas'ko, Ol'ga, 92
verbal aggression, 12, 38, 41n, 53, 118, 138, 141, 184, 188
verbal play, 6–7, 10, 18, 22, 87, 199; *see also* humour
Verbitskaia, Liudmila, 63, 70–1
Vergangenheitsbewältigung, 11, 47
vernacularisation, 4, 9
VKontakte, 38–9, 85, 92, 100n, 101n
Vodolazkin, Evgenii, 10–12, 137, 148–57, 159–61, 164n, 197, 202
Votrin, Valerii, 10–12, 167–78, 186–90, 197–8, 202
VTsIOM, 103n
Vysotskii, Vladimir, 25, 89

Wachtel, Andrew, 51
Wade, Terence, 5
Wierzbicka, Anna, 19
Wingender, Monika, 30–1, 197–8
word formation, 6, 9, 36, 87, 114–15, 140, 181, 185, 201
word play *see* humour; linguistic creativity; verbal play
writers
    role in language debates, 1–4, 6–12, 38, 45, 60–1, 64, 69–83, 88, 93, 117, 157, 167, 187, 195–8, 201
    social commitment, 1, 46–7, 51, 53, 62

Xenophon, 51

Year of the Russian Language, 7, 64
Yurchak, Alexei, 21

Zakharova, Mariia, 71
Zamiatin, Evgenii, 20
Zaudinova, Zarema, 91–2
Zhakipbekova, Aizhan, 91
Znamia, 70–2, 81n
Zoshchenko, Mikhail, 20
Zubova, Liudmila, 6–7, 60–1, 64, 73
Zvereva, Vera, 37–8
Zviagintsev, Andrei, 84

EU representative:
Easy Access System Europe
Mustamäe tee 50, 10621 Tallinn, Estonia
Gpsr.requests@easproject.com

www.ingramcontent.com/pod-product-compliance
Lightning Source LLC
Chambersburg PA
CBHW071839230426
43671CB00012B/2007